DECISION MAKING IN ORGANISATIONS

D0550703

David Lee, Philip Newman
and Robert Price

FT Prentice Hall
FINANCIAL TIMES

An imprint of **Pearson Education**
Harlow, England • London • New York • Boston • San Francisco • Toronto • Sydney • Singapore • Hong Kong
Tokyo • Seoul • Taipei • New Delhi • Cape Town • Madrid • Mexico City • Amsterdam • Munich • Paris • Milan

Pearson Education Limited
Edinburgh Gate
Harlow
Essex CM20 2JE
England

and Associated Companies throughout the world

Visit us on the World Wide Web at:
http://www.pearsoned.co.uk

First published in Great Britain in 1999

ISBN 0 273 63113 6

British Library Cataloguing in Publication Data
A CIP catalogue record for this book can be obtained from the British Library

10 9 8 7 6 5 4 3 2
07 06 05 04 03

Typeset by Pantek Arts, Maidstone, Kent.
Printed and bound in Great Britain by Bell & Bain Ltd, Glasgow

The Publishers' policy is to use paper manufactured from sustainable forests.

CONTENTS

PREFACE

There are currently some 600 degree courses, and more than a thousand post A-level non-degree courses in Business, Management and related subjects on offer at UK Universities and Colleges. A large proportion of these courses are modular in nature, and often require students to develop the requisite skills for a module in a relatively short period of time. It was with such students in mind, and particularly those following modules in Organisational Decision Making, that the writing of this book was undertaken. It is intended to be succinct but not superficial; to model the context of decision making; and to make practical recommendations that might enhance the effectiveness of decisions. Where organisational theory has been introduced, it has been our intention that it should inform the decision-making processes and enhance the reader's understanding of the decision-making environment.

Since decision making can be complex, and may be influenced by numerous factors both within an organisation and outside it, no attempt has been made to identify 'universal' techniques that will invariably bring us to the 'right' decision. Indeed, it is our preference to expose decision making as the contentious and imperfectible art it is. Nevertheless, it is our belief that, for many of us, appropriate solutions to complex problems might more readily be found by operating within broad and flexible frameworks that will guide us through the processes of decision making. Our approach, therefore, has been to try to create a loose structure for assessing the context of organisational decisions and for highlighting some key considerations for those responsible for decision making.

The 11 chapters of this book might readily be used as weekly topics for a module in Decision Making. It would be equally justifiable, however, to consider the book as having three broad sections. The first four chapters deal primarily with the environment in which decisions must be made, and the ways in which decision makers might respond to different contexts. Chapters 5–8 provide frameworks for analysing particular types of decision, including strategic decisions, financial decisions and decisions that might have a statistical dimension. The third section, covered in the final three chapters, is broadly concerned with issues surrounding the implementation of decisions, and here we have included a chapter on the social responsibilities of decision makers – an ethical dimension that, we believe, should figure prominently in an organisation's evaluation of the outcomes of the decisions it makes.

Each chapter of the book is concluded with one or two short case studies. The cases are primarily intended to illustrate points made within the particular chapter, but since the chapters are not mutually exclusive the cases may well prove useful in illustrating a range of issues relating to decision making. Sometimes an overlap between topics will be unavoidable; for example, the distinction between making and implementing a decision will sometimes be blurred within the setting of a case study. It is our hope, however, that this book will clarify many of the complexities surrounding the context and processes of decision making, and will inform and provoke discussion on this important aspect of organisational effectiveness.

A *Lecturer's Guide* with OHP masters is available from the publishers free of charge to lecturers adopting the book.

AN INTRODUCTION TO THE CASE STUDIES

It is in the nature of many decisions that they will be contentious, and that there will not be a 'correct' solution. This does not, of course, mean that there can be no *incorrect* solutions, because a decision that does not achieve its objectives is necessarily ineffective, and hence inappropriate. There will, however, be situations where all objectives cannot be met simultaneously, or where objectives conflict with each other. This is part of the complexity of decision making, and many such situations are illustrated in the case studies found in this book.

As an introduction to the intricate problems facing decision makers, it is worth examining the case of the budgetary problems facing the imaginary island nation of Belinsula. In this short case we begin to see how the objectives of the island's government may conflict with each other, and how the final decision may be influenced by attitudes towards risk. As with many of the cases presented in this book, issues can be addressed at various levels. For example, we could simply address the allocation of funds between the different governmental departments, or we could consider issues of implementation, and the likely reactions of citizens to particular decisions.

The case is followed by just one suggested task. However, it is likely that responses to this task may be expanded in due course as further relevant aspects of the decision are addressed later in the book.

Case Study 1: Budgetary problems in Belinsula

Belinsula is an imaginary sub-tropical island with a population of around 250 000. It is recognised as having tourist potential if sufficient funds can be found for investment in hotels, an airport and improvements to the island's roads.

The island's GNP is currently almost $1bn. The government of Belinsula expects to raise $440m in tax revenue this year, and is committed to a balanced budget policy. Last year's revenue amounted to $400m, and was allocated as follows:

Health	$80m
Social Security	$88m
Home Affairs	$52m
Industry and Energy	$40m
Defence	$80m
Education	$52m
Arts and Culture	$8m
Total	$400m

The island is currently faced with the following challenges:

- Improved health care on the island has led to a 10 per cent increase in life expectancy in Belinsula. This has created pressure on all services for the elderly, because there has been a dramatic rise in the number of retired people living on the island.

- Expenditure on benefits for the unemployed has increased steadily over the last eight years as unemployment has continued to rise. Although unemployment benefit for most recipients is slightly lower than it was a year ago, the Department of Social Security has now taken over from the Department of Defence as the country's biggest-spending department.

- The invasion of Belinsula ten years ago by neighbouring Malevola has long since been suppressed, but peace has not formally been restored. There are those amongst the population of Belinsula who feel that there is a very real chance that hostilities might be resumed within the next year or two.

- The schools of Belinsula are now in a very poor state of repair. They have very few resources: books are out of date, basic equipment is lacking, and there is a short-age of modern equipment such as computers. The proposed building of a College of Further Education on the island has continually been shelved over the past ten years. A number of able young Belinsulans have not returned after continuing their education abroad.

- The new hospital built 15 years ago has been of great benefit to the islanders, but the costs of running it have increased rapidly. Two years ago, one ward had to be closed for lack of funds. There is now talk of closing a second ward.

- Geologists believe there may be oil off the coast of Belinsula. Indeed, one team of experts has gone as far as to say there is a 60–70 per cent chance of a *major* oil strike; but a $170m survey would be required to establish conclusively whether or not there are substantial amounts of oil available for extraction. Even then, heavy investment would be needed to exploit this resource. Nevertheless, the potential rewards would be correspondingly great.

- The government subsidises The Belinsula Dance Company, The Island Players and The Belinsula National Gallery. None of them could continue without the subsidy.

- The Department of Home Affairs wants extra funding to extend the island's over-crowded prison.

Your task

Examine last year's allocation of public funds to the different departments and, justifying your decision, propose any changes for the coming year.

Part I

THE ENVIRONMENT FOR DECISION MAKING

Individuals make decisions every day in the course of their domestic and working lives. It is logical to assume that decisions are made in a rational and objective manner that require the decision maker to consider all relevant information, attendant options and outcomes. The reality however is that individuals because of their socialisation, life experiences and, in the context of the organisation, organisational influences will not make decisions in an entirely rational and objective manner.

In the organisational context a range of environmental forces influences individuals and the way in which they make decisions. The environmental forces, either internal or external to the organisation, may range from individual preferences, organisational culture and management style through to political and legal considerations. Such forces will therefore determine not only the way in which individuals approach and make decisions but also the boundaries that individuals create for themselves in order to frame and make decisions. The environment therefore influences the scope and nature of an individual's bounded rationality and hence the ways in which individuals make decisions.

This part of the book will discuss the environmental forces that influence and guide the way in which individuals make decisions, and the extent to which it is correct to assume that decision making is entirely rational.

CHAPTER 1

The decision-making context

Learning objectives

At the end of this chapter you should:

- be able to appreciate the wider context within which decisions are made;

- understand the impact of the external environment on organisational decision making;

- recognise why organisational structure affects the way in which organisations and individuals make decisions;

- understand and assess the ways in which organisational culture determines individual decision-making styles;

- be able to appreciate the differences between the implicit and explicit organisation and how such differences can affect individual decision making;

- recognise the importance and impact of organisational politics on decision making; and

- understand the ways in which the style of management determines the way in which subordinates make decisions.

Introduction

What is a decision? A decision involves choosing between alternatives. This process involves, or should involve, a systematic approach, which can be represented through five stages.

1 Identification of the problem.
2 The listing of alternatives.
3 Selection of the most beneficial outcome.
4 Implementation.
5 Feedback on the quality of the decision and its outcome.

The five stages in the process assume that decision makers are economic in orientation and have a desire to maximise outcomes and returns. It is also assumed that all alternatives and consequences are known and that the decision maker is able to rank in priority order the desirability of the outcomes. On the assumption that each of these criteria is met, the decision maker should be able to make the best decision for the organisation. This approach requires the decision maker to be entirely rational, which is to operate some kind of ideal decision-making world.

Assumptions are often made that individuals will behave in an economically rational manner, although quite how such rationality is to be interpreted is, perhaps, open to debate. Frequently it is equated with, for example, pursuing profit maximisation. Yet some decision makers may feel that the organisation could have broader obligations – to its employees or the wider community. These stakeholder groups may be less influential than the shareholders, but an organisation that at a philosophical level, embraces social or ethical objectives might adopt more of a 'satisficing' approach. Decisions are made therefore, not so much on the basis of maximising return for the shareholders but rather of providing sufficient return to keep the shareholders satisfied while seeking a balance between the interests of *all* stakeholders.

The notion of a rational decision may lead us to believe that there may be one best outcome from a decision-making process in a given circumstance. But since there are likely to be so many constraints or influences on a decision maker, outcomes will often represent a compromise, perhaps one in which the interests of none of the stakeholders are met in their entirety. Indeed, if the outcome of the decision may be seen to be imperfect in some way, so the process is likely to be too, for the result of the multiplicity of influences on the decision makers is likely to bring about a bounded-rationality approach to decision making (Simon, 1951).

Decisions in an ideal world would be entirely rational and enable individuals to maximise resources within clearly specified constraints. The classical approach to decision making assumed that individuals think and act with complete objectivity and that rational decisions are those where:

- the problem is clearly defined;
- the goals are clearly defined;
- all alternatives and outcomes are known;
- preferences are clear, constant and stable;
- there are no constraints; and
- the final choice will maximise results for the individual and the organisation.

In reality most decisions do not meet the above criteria and therefore bounded rationality informs the decision-making processes, bounded rationality (Simon 1951) being defined as rational behaviour within set parameters that contain the main features of a problem. Bounded rationality will therefore not only recognise parameters but will also be influenced by the decision maker's environment, both external and internal to the organisation.

Decision makers may also lack information and face a range of constraints; for example, there may be:

- imprecise definition of the problem;
- lack of alternatives;
- no clear criteria;
- time and cost constraints;
- an inability to calculate the optimal choice;
- imperfections of the decision makers' perceptions; or
- incompatibility between attitudes.

There are therefore a number of factors, related to not only bounded rationality but also external and internal organisational factors, that will determine the way in which organisations and individuals make decisions, as shown in Fig. 1.1. Although external forces will largely determine organisational strategic decision making, there are also internal organisational forces that will influence the way in which individuals make decisions, which in turn could have an impact on the performance of the organisation and hence the achievement of its strategic aims. Therefore the way in which individuals make decisions will have an impact upon organisational performance. It is the way in which an individual faces a problem, based on organisational culture, for example, that will determine how the problem

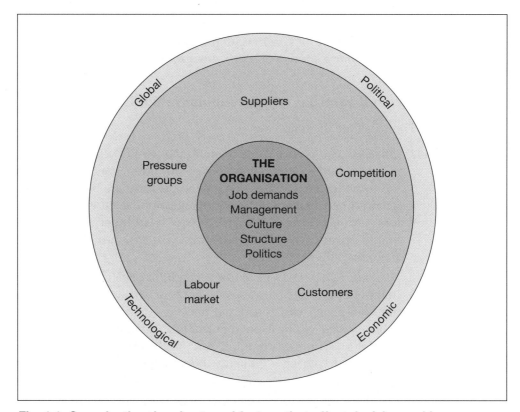

Fig. 1.1 Organisational and external factors that affect decision making

is treated and whether or not decisions are being made for the right reasons in order to maximise the outcomes.

The purpose of this chapter is therefore to discuss the ways in which the internal and external forces, which are mutually inclusive of one another, will have an impact upon organisational and individual decision making.

External decision-making constraints

Every organisation must interact with its external environment and must recognise that it will be constrained by external environmental forces. Decisions that are strategic in nature must therefore take account of these forces in order to achieve the best fit with the external environment. For example, it is obviously of no value deciding to produce goods that are not going to sell, because the market within which the organisation operates does not demand the goods. Understanding the nature and composition of the external environment is therefore crucial to effective decision making.

The term 'external environment' can be broken down into two distinct components, namely the general external environment and a specific external environment.

- *General external environment* includes those factors outside the organisation, such as economic conditions, political conditions, legal requirements, social influences, globalisation and technology;
- *Specific external environment* includes those factors that directly relate to the achievement of an organisation's goals, such as suppliers, customers, competitors, labour resources and pressure groups.

General external environmental factors

These include the following.

1 *Economic conditions.* These relate to the way in which resources are being used and distributed, which may include inflation, wage rates, corporation tax and the cost of raw materials. For instance, if taxes are high and wages are low, then would it be worthwhile for an organisation faced with such environmental factors to produce a range of goods that would, because of production costs, be highly priced? Organisational strategic decision making must therefore reflect such conditions if they exist.

2 *Political conditions.* These relate to conditions such as government policies, industrial policy and the nature of the government with regard to market controls or proposed legal changes that may affect organisations. Such changes not only relate to the national political environment but also to the international context. How, for example, should organisations react to the opening up of markets in China and how will such changes influence the strategic decisions that are made?

3 *Legal requirements.* These relate to legislation that is already in existence. Legislation that is in existence defines the rules by which society wishes to live and therefore, by definition, the rules by which organisations should operate.

4 *Social influences.* These are the factors that determine the make-up of the society in which the organisation operates. Social influences can be considered at two levels, namely the values that society holds at any one given time and demographic changes within the population. Changes in both of these, which are not mutually exclusive, must be identified and acted upon if such changes are relevant to the organisation and the way in which it operates. For example, changes in population distribution combined with a heightened ecological awareness on the part of an increasing number of the population may determine the reception of a new product that may be environmentally sensitive in some way.

5 *Globalisation.* This refers to the international dimension. If globalisation issues such as cultural, political, economic and differing legal requirements affect an organisation, then it is clear that such factors must be taken into account when considering entering foreign markets.

6 *Technology.* The advances made since the mid-eighties have an obvious relevance to organisations today. New computerised equipment and manufacturing procedures enable organisations to be more cost-efficient, competitive and profitable. For example, what should be done if competitors are managing to gain such advantages from using technology and are eroding an organisation's market share? Does the organisation go the technology route to make efficiency gains, or does it try to maximise what already exists in the way of personnel and equipment? The decision made may determine the success or otherwise of the organisation.

Specific external environmental factors

These include the following:

1 *Suppliers.* This component of the specific environment deals with such issues as the number of suppliers, the quality of their products or services, and the reliability of supplies. Having reliable and quality supplies as and when an organisation demands them can obviously aid an organisations stock control, changes in manufacturing volume and the speed of response to changes in the level of demand within a market.

2 *Customers.* Being able to understand what the customers – those people who buy from the organisation – want and expect from an organisation is crucial to their organisational success. Having such an understanding helps the organisation to decide what to produce and what to change in order to remain in line with customer expectations. This aspect is, it could be argued, of increasing importance, given the impact of globalisation on the degree of competition within some industries. Decision making must therefore take this factor into account.

3 *Competitors.* The degree to which other firms actively compete will determine the way in which an organisation responds through the decisions that are taken. Strategic decision making is concerned with understanding what competitors are doing and how best to respond effectively. Competitive analytical decision making should enable an organisation to identify those aspects of its own strategies, and those of existing and potential competitors, that are strengths or weaknesses.

4 *Labour resources*. These relate to labour wage rates, the supply of skilled labour, and the supply of labour generally. Such factors will determine the amount of people that can be employed at a given wage rate and whether the existing pool of labour has the skills required. Take, for example, the situation where an organisation is looking to recruit people with appropriate qualifications and skills but finds that such people are not available. What does the organisation do? Does it employ people and then train them to the desired level, or does it try to recruit from outside its locality? Once again an external factor will determine the decision made.

5 *Pressure groups*. These are generally special interest groups, and the way in which they may attempt to exert pressure on an organisation is important. These groups aim to raise public awareness about certain issues as a means of getting an organisation to change its policies. For example, the sale of arms to certain countries deemed to be operating repressive regimes or trying to get organisations to review their investment policies toward such countries. Organisations are mindful of such campaigns because of the potential damage they can do to sales and corporate image, an example being the Greenpeace campaign in the mid 1990s to halt Shell's Brent Spar oil rig from being dumped at sea. The campaign was highly successful from Greenpeace's point of view, in that Shell changed its mind because of the high level of media interest the campaign generated, which, it was perceived, was beginning to damage its image. This was a classic example of organisational decision making being determined by pressure from a particular grouping that appealed to changing ecological values within society.

Organisations therefore are, to a lesser or greater extent, limited by the environment within which they operate and must therefore make decisions accordingly. No organisation can ignore the external environment when making decisions, and in fact should actively aim to pre-empt any changes that may occur in order to maintain a competitive edge. As David (1993) points out,

> Organizations should take a proactive rather than a reactive approach in their industry, and should strive to influence, anticipate, and initiate rather than just respond to events. The strategic-management process embodies this approach to decision making.

Strategic management, which will be covered in more depth in Chapter 8, can be defined by three simple words: formulation implementation and evaluation. In reality, the process is of course not as straightforward as the three terms would suggest and is in fact a complex procedure that involves numerous decisions being taken in order for the organisation to arrive at an appropriate strategy. Drucker (1974) put forward that strategic management requires the organisation and managers to ask, '"What is our business?" This leads to the setting of objectives, the development of strategies, and the making of today's decisions for tomorrow's results.' This is, if organisations are being truthful, quite a tall order, especially given the complex nature of today's markets that are becoming increasingly global in nature.

No matter how much management theorists urge organisations to be proactive when formulating and deciding upon the future direction of an organisation, it is as well to be reminded at this stage that the extent to which an organisation can influence its environment is limited. Pettinger (1996) stated that the degree to which influence is possible is, 'In many cases … very limited. Organisations must therefore work within the constraints imposed. They must also be prepared for any new limitations or hazards that may arise under the legal, economic, social, ethical or political headings to which they would have to respond (again from a position of limited influence).' Such 'limited influence' will have an impact upon the way in which organisations make strategic decisions – for example, the available information will not be perfect, which immediately begins to work against the classical approach to decision making and moves the decision makers toward bounded rationality. The external environmental constraints have therefore had an immediate impact on the decision makers and the decisions they will eventually make.

<table>
<tr><td>Exhibit 1.1</td><td></td></tr>
</table>

Exhibit 1.1

Horizon Telecommunications

Horizon Telecommunications was in a precarious position. It operated in a very competitive market, which demanded continual technological improvements in products and quality of the services provided. Therefore, the external forces of technology and customer demand were dictating the firm's business strategy.

Horizon Telecommunications, because of the market pressures it was facing, tried to decide whether or not to formulate a strategy for diversification, as a means of spreading the risks involved with operating within such a competitive industry. To make such a move would require careful judgement and informed decision making based on a knowledge of the industry into which Horizon Telecommunications wished to diversify. They would need to decide upon, for example:

- how much capital investment would be required;

- the extent to which customer perception of the firm would be affected, and its impact on revenue; and

- how successfully it could convince customers in the new industry that the company has expertise in that field of product/service provision.

The example begins to illustrate the complex nature of strategic decision making, in that the extent of information required can be (and needs to be) quite extensive in order for relevant decisions to be made. Although there are only three information areas, each of them would represent substantial time and effort in order to generate the information required. Even with the appropriate information having been provided, analysis by management is thereafter required, which then begins to introduce the individual aspects to decision making such as judgement and even intuition. (The role of judgement and intuition will be discussed further in Chapter 4.)

Not only do organisations have the complex nature of the external environment to contend with but also the way in which individuals make decisions based on their perception and interpretation of a given situation. The question is then to what extent individuals can be rational and how will the decision making constraints on them affect the way in which not only the organisation makes decisions but also individuals. Individuals, for example, create, or have created for them either by other individuals, the organisation and/or the external environment, their own boundaries when making decisions. They also may wish to reduce what is known as cognitive dissonance (see Chapter 3 for a more detailed discussion of bounded rationality and cognitive dissonance) in order to arrive at a decision that they and the organisation can accept.

The external environmental aspects combined with individual decision making styles therefore together add to the overall complexity of making strategic decisions.

Internal decision-making constraints

An organisation's internal environment in relation to decision making covers organising, planning, controlling and influencing. Within the scope of these functions, managers will be concerned with making, communicating and implementing decisions. The way in which individuals make decisions will therefore reflect the way in which an organisation is structured, the prevailing culture, the management style and the organisational politics.

It is important, therefore, to consider each of these in turn in order to appreciate the ways in which each can and does influence decision making.

Organisational structure

Mintzberg (1979) defines organisational structure as, '... the sum total of the ways in which [an organisation] divides its labour into distinct tasks and then achieves co-ordination between them.' The 'sum total' can of course be represented by an organisation chart but that in itself does not show that in reality organisations are composed of complex interrelationships, between individuals, groups, departments, levels, functions and responsibilities. Organisation charts are used as a means of illustrating these relationships however, such charts fail to show that informal structures also exist, which do not conform to the formal structure.

One key aspect of organisational structure is the way in which it should outline and facilitate decision making. The structural form of an organisation as represented by the organisation chart will determine, through the levels of responsibility and authority, for example, the way in which individuals make decisions and/or even participate in the decision-making process. The nature of an organisation's structure will therefore determine the way in which decisions should be made, in that the structure creates boundaries within which individuals are expected to operate.

Burns and Stalker (1961) identified through their research that organisations could be categorised depending on the degree of structured formality that exists within the organisation. They defined organisations as either 'mechanistic' or 'organic' in nature. Fig. 1.2 shows a continuum of organisational forms and the associated degree of decision-making freedom. An organisation can lie anywhere between the two extremes, depending upon a number of factors.

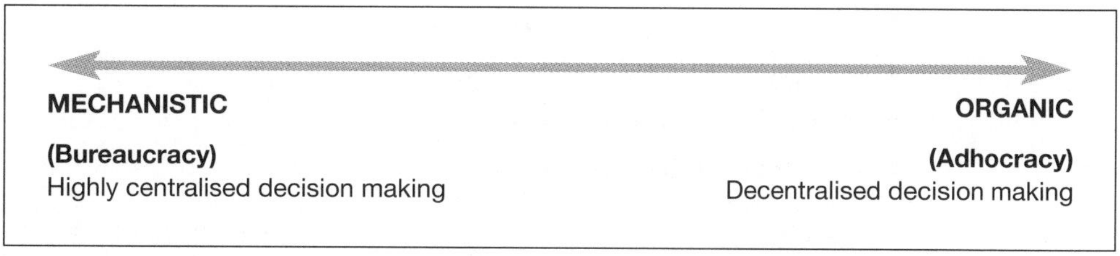

```
←─────────────────────────────────────────────────→

MECHANISTIC                                    ORGANIC

(Bureaucracy)                                  (Adhocracy)
Highly centralised decision making             Decentralised decision making
```

Fig. 1.2 Continuum of organisational forms

Mechanistic structure

Mechanistic organisations, reflected through their rigid structures, were identified as being suitable for conditions of stability and would tend to have the following characteristics:

- rigid hierarchical relationships, with insistence on obedience to superiors;
- very high levels of formalisation;
- rigid and formalised communication channels, with a preference for vertical communication;
- rigid job specifications and job functions, with very precise definitions of rights and obligations; and
- decision making that is highly centralised.

The above list actually describes the 'classical' or 'bureaucratic' approach (Weber, 1947). The dominant feature of such organisations is one of control in order to create efficiency and maximise the resources available. Control would be exercised over all aspects of organisational life, as the list clearly indicates, and especially decision making. Individuals would not be expected or encouraged to make decisions that would take them outside their job specification. Most employees would only be required to make routine decisions that would require very little thought or use of judgement and intuition. The emphasis would be on programmed decisions, those decisions that are routine and are to all intents and purposes repetitive in nature. (Chapter 4 discusses the difference between programmed and non-programmed decisions in more detail.)

Organic structure

An organic organisation would be suitable for fluid conditions that require flexibility on the part of the organisation and employees. Such organisations tend to have the following characteristics:

- senior management is not seen as being all-powerful and knowing;
- high levels of collaboration between and across levels;
- control and authority is exercised through networks;
- a belief in, and commitment to, organisational objectives are seen as more important than loyalty and obedience;

11

- non-rigid job specifications and job functions;
- low levels of formalisation;
- informal communication; and
- decentralised decision making.

Organic organisations aim to involve individuals to a greater extent than mechanistic ones, through the less rigid command and control systems that are used. That is not to say that such organisations do not have structure or systems in place. Every organisation needs structure and systems in order to give form and to create a whole; otherwise there would be anarchy, which would not be conducive to effective organisational performance. The key difference is the way in which individuals are treated and are respected for the contribution they can make. Not only through performing their specified jobs well but also through the way in which they contribute to the decision-making process. Individuals would be expected and encouraged to participate actively in the decision-making process and would tend to be involved in non-programmed decisions that are non-routine and not repetitive in nature.

The differences

The significance of the differences between mechanistic and organic organisations is the amount of freedom given to individuals, especially with regard to decision making. As a general rule it can be said that within mechanistic organisations individuals, at all but the highest levels, are not allowed to exercise decision making beyond their job remit. Conversely, within organic organisations there would tend to be much greater freedom and involvement in the decision-making process at all levels. When trying to determine the way in which organisational structure can influence decision making it is useful to consider, at least in the first instance, whether the organisation is mechanistic (a bureaucracy) or organic (an 'adhocracy').

Some organisations will, of course, not fit neatly into a clear category and may in fact reflect aspects of both. Burns and Stalker (1961) stated that:

> ...the two forms of system represent a polarity not a dichotomy; there are ... intermediate stages between the extremities ... the relation of one form to the other is elastic, so that a concern oscillating between relative stability and relative change may also oscillate between the two forms. A concern may (and frequently does) operate with a management system that includes both types.

It must be noted at this point, however, that there is no one correct organisational structure. As stated earlier, an organisation must achieve a best fit that is contingent upon a number of factors, namely strategy, size, technology and environment. All of these factors must be taken into account when designing an appropriate structure that best enables the organisation to achieve its stated aims. This approach is referred to as 'contingency theory' (Lawrence and Lorsch, 1967), which emphasises that there is no single best structure and organisational form. Furthermore, Scott (1987) defined the difference between contingency theory and the classical bureaucratic approach in the following way:

The previous [classical] definitions tend to view the organisation as a closed system, separate from its environment and comprising a set of stable and easily identified participants. However, organisations are not closed systems, sealed off from their environments but are open to and dependent on flows of personnel and resources from outside.

Morgan (1986) went a stage further than simply using the terms 'mechanistic' and 'organic'. He used metaphors as a way of trying to define the manner in which an organisation functions through its structure. Morgan saw organisations as fitting into one of the following metaphors, which can also be related to the way in which decisions would be made within such organisations:

- *Machines* (classical/mechanistic approach) – decisions would be programmed and individuals would not be permitted to become involved in non-programmed decisions.

- *Organisms* (organic) – individuals would be encouraged to participate in decision making, both programmed and non-programmed, and would not be confined to their area of responsibility as defined by their job specification.

- *Brains* (cybernetic, concerned with control systems) – systems are in place to facilitate decision making and to create order through connections between and across levels, although this does not mean that the systems are rigid but are in place to shape the connections that individuals make when making decisions.

- *Cultures* (dominant values determine the structure) – those individuals who are dominant within an organisation will shape it, whether they be senior managers or owner-managers. They will create an organisation in their own image, which if it is one of absolute control may preclude individuals within the decision-making processes, and vice versa.

- *Political systems* (power through political manoeuvring) – power is gained through the way in which individuals play political games in order to further their own careers. Such an approach will work against the desire to make decisions that are always going to be in the best interests of the organisation because individuals will be reflecting on the political consequences of their actions and decisions. The political dimension will form part of the bounded rationality.

- *Psychic prisons* (individuals can be stressed) – there would tend to be high workloads, oppressive management and high expectations of individuals to perform to very high standards, all of which can cause high levels of stress or other adverse conditions. If individuals are stressed, then that will begin to manifest itself through the way in which decisions are made and in the quality of those decisions. An individual who is working to very tight deadlines demanding high standards, while being pressurised to make a decision, may not necessarily take the time to make a rational decision. Some individuals are, of course, able to handle stress better than others and their decision making will not be affected.

- *Flux and transformation* (constant change) – although no organisation can stand still, constant change can create a state of flux whereby individuals do not understand what is really going on or what the rules of the game are. Under such conditions, can individuals be expected to make rational decisions in the interests of the organisation if they do not know what is actually expected of them?

- *Instruments of domination* (power exertion) – power is exercised by various means, which does not necessarily conform to hierarchical position, and it is used as a means of ensuring compliance and will also affect the level of individual involvement in the organisation (Etzioni, 1975). If power is exercised in an oppressive way, then it will alienate individuals, not only in terms of commitment to the organisation but also in the way in which they conduct themselves with regard to their tasks. Decision making will be no exception from this effect, even if individuals are only expected to make programmed decisions. Therefore the way in which power is gained and exercised will have an impact on the way in which decisions are made.

Morgan believed that organisations were not, as put forward by classical writers such as Taylor (1947), Fayol (1949) and Urwick (1952), rational because of their complex nature. The very mix of, for example, systems, tasks, communications and, of course, people precludes them from operating like machines no matter how tightly structured they may be. He believed that 'the whole thrust of classical management theory and its modern applications is to suggest that organisations can or should be rational systems that operate in as efficient manner as possible.' If organisations cannot be entirely rational, perhaps because of the human dimension, then to what extent can entirely rational decisions be made.

Having structure and systems in place does not of itself make decisions; it is people who make decisions. People are subject to a whole range of influences within an organisation, from the way in which the structure begins to dictate what is expected of them to the general culture of the organisation. It is important therefore, to consider the impact of organisational culture on the way in which individuals make decisions as structure and culture are invariably linked.

Organisational culture

Organisational culture has been defined by many writers, including Handy (1993), Mintzberg and Quinn (1991) and Schein (1992), and all agree that although it is easy to define it at the theoretical level it is very difficult at times to establish what the culture of an organisation actually is. However we do need to have a definition to act as a basis for discussing the link between organisational culture and decision making. Schein (1992) defined 'culture' as:

> A pattern of shared basic assumptions that the group learned as it solved its problems of external adaptation and internal integration, and that has worked well enough to be considered valid and, therefore, to be taught to new members as the correct way to perceive, think, and feel in relation to those problems.

The implication of this definition with regard to decision making is that if culture is about the 'correct way to perceive, think, and feel', then it will influence the way in which individuals do in fact perceive their role within the decision-making process.

Schein also argues that when analysing organisational culture there is a need to consider 'structural stability' and 'patterning'. Structural stability relates to the deep-rooted aspects of culture and goes beyond those values espoused by the organisation, possibly through a mission statement. Patterning involves bringing together all of the aspects of an organisation's culture in order to create a complete picture of the prevailing culture. Added to this there is a need also to consider what Schein refers to as:

- *Artefacts* – these are the visible signs of an organisation's culture that can be hard to define, such signs being the explicit aspects of culture, for example, the mission statement or other written definitions of what the organisation stands for. An organisation may claim to value its employees and has a culture that welcomes their involvement at all levels of, for example, the decision-making process.

- *Espoused values* – these represent the focal points for employees that are put forward by the organisation. However, the values espoused may not be the ones that are actually put into practice. It is one thing for an organisation to claim to welcome and support employee involvement in the decision-making process, but the truth, as determined through employee experience, may be somewhat different. If the learned reality is different from the espoused values, then it will have an impact on the way in which individuals respond and relate to the organisation.

- *Basic assumptions* – relate to those assumptions that are incorporated into the way in which individuals actually view an organisation and therefore determine actions. If the view of individuals is that the organisation does not really want employees to make, or become involved in, decisions other than mundane programmed ones, then that is the way in which they will react and perceive their role to be.

As a means of illustrating the above three points, let us consider a brief example. The culture of an organisation is such that management has faith in subordinates, there is delegation of responsibility and authority, including decision-making powers, and this is communicated by the artefacts and espoused values. Then what could the possible outcomes with regard to employee involvement be? If the prevailing culture and the basic assumptions did in fact reflect such an approach, the norm with regard to decision making would signal to employees that it is expected and genuinely welcomed that they become involved in the decision-making process. Employees in turn would respond by becoming involved because the basic assumptions held would reflect this.

Organisational culture defines the working norms, whether they are part of the explicit or implicit prevailing culture. Culture can therefore involve or exclude individuals, depending upon what has been created either deliberately or inadvertently through what has been learned, and are therefore part of the basic assumptions. In fact Fig. 1.2 (see p.11) can now be developed to show the relationship between structure type and culture, as shown in Fig. 1.3.

Autocratic cultures have highly centralised management. Decision making is not entrusted to employees, apart from programmed decisions that would anyway form part of their daily routine. In contrast, democratic cultures would entrust

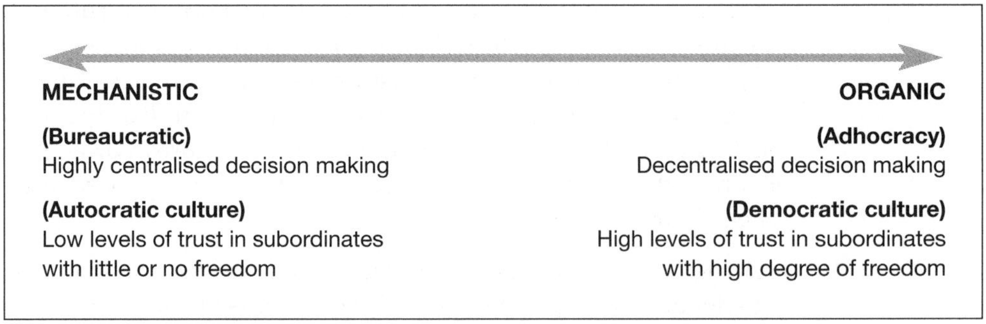

MECHANISTIC ⟷ ORGANIC

MECHANISTIC   **ORGANIC**

(Bureaucratic)   **(Adhocracy)**
Highly centralised decision making   Decentralised decision making

(Autocratic culture)   **(Democratic culture)**
Low levels of trust in subordinates   High levels of trust in subordinates
with little or no freedom   with high degree of freedom

Fig. 1.3 Continuum illustrating the link between organisational structure, culture and levels of trust and freedom

employees with decision-making powers. The point that needs to be remembered is that there is no 'correct' culture and that organisations do not necessarily neatly conform to one of the two extremes as represented on the continuum, just as organisations may not neatly conform to one organisational structure.

It is also necessary to remember that although organisations will have an espoused culture, it is possible to find that differing interpretations of the culture within different parts of an organisation. So not only is there a possibility of a covert (espoused) and overt (basic assumptions) culture but also different forms of the culture may exist within any one department or division. In essence, there could theoretically be many perceptions and practices to decision making, learned and incorporated into the basic assumptions, within the same organisation.

Egan (1993) put forward that organisations have an overt and a covert culture. He believed that although the overt culture may claim to stand for a set of beliefs, it was the covert culture that actually determined organisational behaviour in that:

> The covert set can be quite dysfunctional and costly. Culture – the assumptions, beliefs, values and norms that drive 'the way we do things here' – is the largest and most controlling of the systems because it affects not only overt organisational behaviour but also the shadow-side behaviour … Culture lays down norms for the social system.

The 'shadow-side behaviour' refers to the way in which the organisation is actually viewed by employees and becomes part of their basic assumptions, and it is this that will determine behaviour. The overt culture, which can be distinguished from what Egan refers to as the 'preferred culture', therefore determines not only behaviour, beliefs, values and norms but also decision making within an organisation.

Climate

Organisational climate is an aspect of organisational culture, and it will determine the extent to which individuals are motivated to work for an organisation and, for example, actively participate in decision making. Mullins (1996) defines organisational climate as '… the prevailing atmosphere surrounding the organisation, to the level of morale, and to the strength of feelings or belonging, care and goodwill among members.' The 'prevailing atmosphere', as defined, will have an impact on employees' attitudes that will be reflected through the quality of work, which includes decision making.

The extent to which the climate will positively or negatively affect behaviour will be determined by the employees' perception of the organisation in relation to the way in which it treats people. Two key areas of organisational climate that will affect the way in which individuals respond to decision making are:

- *Opportunities for participation* – this will, depending on the prevailing culture and style of management, either motivate individuals to participate more actively in decision making or alienate them from the process. Opportunities for participation would be more likely under the more democratic and participative based organisational cultures, which would tend to be reflected through the prevailing management style.

- *Feeling valued* – this will determine whether or not individuals will participate at all in decision making. For example, if an individual is expected to participate in decision making but holds a negative perception of the organisation, then it is likely that decisions would be made but they may not be of a high quality. This may be because the individual's motivation is low and so he/she does not therefore care or become overly involved in the decision-making process. If this is coupled with the expectation, on the individual's part, that any contribution made will not be fully appreciated, then the response is likely to be disinterested mechanistic decision making. Such an approach does not maximise the opportunity to participate in decision making and does not aim to achieve optimum outcomes either for the organisation or for the people involved in the decision-making process.

Organisations should aim to create a culture that fosters positive perceptions in order to maximise decision making at all levels. If individuals are motivated and feel valued, then they are likely to make greater efforts to participate in the process and also endeavour to maximise decision outcomes.

Exhibit 1.2 **Barnes Ltd**

Consider the following company and how the level of motivation could possibly affect the ways in which employees participate in decision making.

Barnes Ltd believes in superior customer service, and in order to achieve this provides intensive training for its staff and holds motivational seminars twice a month. The company's approach to employee relations can be described as paternalistic, and over the years there has been very good relations between management and the shop-floor employees.

However, over the last year or so there have been criticisms of the pressures placed upon employees at all levels because of the high standards expected in order to provide the high levels of service that Barnes' customers have come to take for granted. Employees are expected to take an active part in the company motivation seminars and their contributions are 'monitored', which is in direct contrast to the way in which the company used to run its briefing and discussion sessions. A strict dress code that has recently been introduced has also been perceived as being draconian in nature and not reflective of the way that the company used to be.

Prior to these changes, employees actively participated in decision making because they believed in the company and they welcomed the opportunity to participate and have an element of control not only over their work but also over the way in which it was done. In fact the company was renowned for its democratic approach to management and employee relations.

Since the introduction of the Customer First policy and the dress code, the perceptions of the employees have begun to change. Some individuals are already beginning to say that if the company expects them to work as hard as they are and reduces their 'freedom' even more, then they will withdraw their goodwill and simply work to contract. They would also consider withdrawing from participating in what some refer to as 'management functions', such as decision making (albeit low level). One employee is quoted as saying, 'If they want me to make decisions, then I want to be paid accordingly, especially if I'm also expected to work harder – and anyway I'm not paid to make decisions.'

It can be seen from this example how a perceived change in culture can have a detrimental effect on the way individuals begin to perceive their roles. If the perception of an organisation is positive, individuals tend to be more willing to take on roles that are not directly related to their job specifications and will also tend to be more committed to the organisation's goals. If, however, the perception is negative, the opposite occurs. A change in perception linked to basic assumptions, upon which the covert culture is based, will alter an organisation's climate and the way employees deal with decision making. If employees are inclined to be mechanistic in approach towards decision making, then no matter how much management otherwise exhorts them, the result will be that the organisation will fail to achieve the optimum outcomes even if a democratic and involvement-based culture is in place.

Management style

The style of management will tend to reflect the prevailing culture and have an effect on the way in which individuals participate, or are allowed to participate, in decision making. If a manager is autocratic or democratic in approach, it may be a reflection either of individual style or of the prevailing culture. Either way, it will influence the way in which decisions are made within a department or the organisation.

For example, Goldsmith and Clutterbuck (1985) identified the following aspects of good management that would influence not only organisational performance *per se* but also the way in which employees participated:

- *Leadership* – that should be based on a clear vision, commitment, respect of individuals, and the contributions they can make to the organisation.

- *Autonomy* – the extent to which there is a need for differing degrees of autonomy depending on the level of responsibility and the nature of the tasks undertaken.

- *Control* – the need to achieve a consensus within the organisation, becoming part of the basic assumptions on what aspects of organisational life requires control and what do not. Goldsmith and Clutterbuck state that control needs to be based on '… consensus that particular procedures are the right way of doing things.' The consensus is therefore essential in forming positive basic assumptions about the organisation, especially if the organisation is aiming to foster a participative approach to decision making.

- *Employee involvement* – this will create higher levels of commitment through extrinsic and intrinsic rewards. The involvement of employees in decision making may generate intrinsic rewards through greater job satisfaction and thus create higher levels of commitment; a virtuous cycle is created which benefits the organisation and the individual. It needs to be borne in mind, however, that not all individuals are motivated by the same rewards.

These concepts are interlinked. For example, in order to achieve more involvement on the part of employees, managers should give greater freedom to employees when making decisions that have an impact on their work routines. Empowerment of this kind helps to create a climate of employee control over work and any changes that are implemented. It may also foster a greater desire to take control through participating in decision making. One other benefit is that it places more reliance on the non-coercive forms of management, which can help to foster a climate that is conducive to participative decision making.

Etzioni (1975) suggested that there are three main types of power bases that relate to the way in which individuals can be either involved or alienated.

- *Coercive power with alienative involvement* – managers will exclude employees from decision making by using, for example, threats in order to compel employees to make or become involved in decision making. If the threats do in fact compel employees to participate, decisions will be made but the decision makers will not necessarily feel committed to the process or the outcomes.

- *Remunerative power with calculative involvement* – this may be used, for example, by a manager to achieve employee involvement through the use or prospect of payments offered in return for greater involvement in decision making. Such an approach assumes that most people are motivated by financial rewards, yet unfortunately, some would regard the offer of payment as a form of financial coercion and not in line with their motivational needs. If this is the prevailing view, the result will be the same as if there was overt coercion.

- *Normative power with involvement* – this is aimed at involving employees, treating them with respect and showing that their contributions through the decision-making process are genuinely valued. Such an approach may motivate individuals to become further involved in decision making and to maximise outcomes.

The type of power that is actually exercised by a manager will of course be dependent on the context, and on the manager's ability to identify and understand what motivates the people involved.

| Exhibit 1.3 | **Propjet Ltd** |

Some would argue that empowerment is fine for educated employees who have the knowledge and skill to deal with the extra decision-making responsibilities that carries. For employees who do not fit these criteria there is not a chance of it being successful because they require close supervision, guidance and a need to be directed at all times. Empowerment can, however, work for all sorts of different employees regardless of their educational background and could provide benefits for organisations and individuals.

Consider the case of Propjet Ltd, a company that employs over 500 people and produces components for the aerospace industry. The company faced competition and its market share was being eroded. Jacqueline Saunders, the owner, decided that the best way to react to the competition and shrinking market share was to create a more dynamic organisational culture by involving employees at all levels of the company. She believed that if the employees could be motivated through having a greater involvement in the way the company was run, then productivity gains would be made and overall efficiency would increase, thus helping to improve the company's market position. Employees were to be encouraged to become more involved in decision making, have greater freedoms to operate at their individual level of responsibility and organise and contribute to quality circles. The changes not only required the empowerment of employees through greater delegation but also required an intensive training programme for management in order for them to be able to adjust to the new culture.

The financial indicators since the changes took place over a year ago are positive in terms of the company's performance, and its previously decreasing market share has been halted and stabilised. However, the most telling result has been the extent to which employees now accept their redefined roles and Jacqueline has said that 'Up until a year ago I seemed to do all the thinking and the decision making. I led the way and everyone else followed. Today we work as a team but more importantly I am able to stand back more and let them come up with the ideas and make decisions. The changes seem to working.'

The case illustrates that a change in management style reflective of a change in culture can have positive results, at least in an ideal world. For such a change to work, the situational variables must be appropriate, that is, there must be an ability and willingness of the followers to take on responsibility and decision-making powers (Hersey and Blanchard, 1988).

The style of management can determine the basic assumptions through the way in which leadership, autonomy, control and employee involvement manifest themselves. The actions of managers will speak louder than the espoused values, and it is thus the actions of managers that will influence employee involvement generally and their commitment to participating in decision making.

Organisational politics

Since organisations are made up of people, often with diverse interests, it is perhaps inevitable that decision making can be both a political and psychological process. Certainly, numerous different needs and influences, both individual and organisational will affect major decisions. Take, for example, the restructuring of a company. The need for restructuring may arise from environmental change, perhaps technological advances, or a move into new international markets; but the new structure will not only affect the organisation's effectiveness but also have an impact on the position and interests of individuals. The restructuring will create individual, as well as organisational, opportunities and threats.

In such a situation it would be naïve to assume that those with power and influence would necessarily consider the interests of the organisation first. In other words, the process of change is political in that it may involve negotiation and persuasion, perhaps posturing and power struggles. It is also a psychological process in that those involved in, or affected by, the decision may perceive the potential benefits differently and their perceptions will, at least to some extent, dictate their actions and reactions.

One highly politicised view of organisations is that of players vying for position in games of self-interest (Crozier and Friedberg, 1980). Yet the politics of decision making need not be seen as a negative force but rather a process of accommodating the diversity of interests within an organisation. For instance, the introduction of a new product may alter power relationships between individuals, with the owners of the most successful ideas standing to advance their self-interests. In this way the organisation may be seen rather as a market for power and influence.

Hegarty (1976) succinctly defined organisational politics when he wrote that 'Company politics is the by-play that occurs when individuals (or groups, or groups of individuals) want to advance themselves or their ideas regardless of whether or not those ideas would help the company.' How do organisational politics therefore affect decision making, given this definition? The answer lies in the extent to which the individual is prepared to act against the best interests of the organisation and places more emphasis on the personal impact of decision outcomes. Consider the following case.

Exhibit 1.4

A new work-monitoring system

A section manager was asked by her line manager to investigate the possible use of a new work-monitoring system as part of the company's drive to improve efficiency by reducing unnecessary duplication of work. Both the line manager and the section manager did not really want the new system to be introduced, because it would reduce the power that they had, and enjoyed, over the way the department and section were run. The rest of the department did not want it either, as it would involve the identification of some loose practices, which had evolved over the years, with regard to the circumvention of some laid down procedures.

All parties were therefore looking for a less than favourable report because of the way in which the new system would, they perceived, change the whole nature

▶

of the way the department operated: it seemed it would fundamentally alter their working relationships within the department and with other deparments. It would also, they believed, reduce the amount of freedom that they presently had with regard to the way in which they could organise their individual work schedules.

The line manager made it clear that if the new system was introduced her 'freedom of action' would be much more limited in scope, which would actually reduce efficiency. She also pointed out that she was sure that the section manager, being a bright individual and ambitious, would be able to identify the obvious pitfalls of the proposed new system. The section manager also faced pressure from her colleagues. They made it abundantly clear that if the new system were to be introduced, she would be held responsible and seen as selling out completely to management in order to advance her own promotion prospects.

What should she do? She could, of course, look at the new system objectively and think of the benefits to the organisation regardless of the personal consequences, or she could consider the personal ramifications of recommending the new system. She chose to take into account her career prospects, based on the fact that her line manager could block her promotion, and she did not want to be alienated by her colleagues, some of whom were close friends outside work.

The report was written and it recommended that the proposed new system did not offer any advantages over the present set-up. The new system was therefore not implemented.

The idea of rational decision making in terms of individuals thinking about the best interests of the organisation has in this example been shown not to be the case. This example clearly illustrates that in reality individuals will make decisions that reflect their own primary interests and those of close colleagues. Rational decision making is therefore going to be framed within the context of organisational politics, depending upon the extent of course that the individual wishes to play the political game. Most people are political to a greater or lesser degree, and will either be active or passive in this respect. The active players, as the term suggests, actively play political games. The passive political individual will be political in the sense that it is recognised that some things can be done and said and others cannot, which is reflecting a political awareness of the way that the organisation operates.

Lawrence and Elliott (1985) put forward a number of points to consider when trying to analyse how individuals, when acting politically, make decisions:

1 *Subject of the decision* – with regard to its history and its importance to the organisation and individuals. This aspect of politicised decision making will influence the way in which the decision is viewed by the decision maker, and it will affect the outcome accordingly: the more important the decision, the greater the potential of political risk. Some politicised decision makers will actually begin to modify, and even deliberately omit, information in order to arrive at a decision that satisfies the decision maker's political considerations.

2 *Decision process* – relates to such issues as time, procedures and who actually makes the final decision. For example, if the decision is important in political

outcome terms, the person making the decision may create alliances and use available power bases to influence others involved in the process. Again, the outcomes in advantageous personal political terms are paramount and are not about striving to make decisions in an entirely objective way. Political manoeuvring is used to influence people, the very process by which the decision is made, and even the time frame, in order to achieve the desired outcomes.

3 *Decision Premises* – relate to decision objectives and constraints. If these can be influenced by the politicised decision maker, it will enable desirable political outcomes to be achieved. In order for this approach to work, there need to be clear regulations to which the decision maker can refer and preferences, in terms of the objectives, need to be stated. To influence the preferences and regulations, an individual must have the power to create the constraints that will determine the way in which the decision will be made and thus begin to predetermine the outcomes.

4 *Alternatives considered* – involves the elimination of politically unacceptable possible alternatives before the final options list is considered. If the decision maker can control this aspect of the process, the decision outcome is already being shaped to fit the desired outcome.

5 *Information about alternatives* – relates to the amount of information that is provided or withheld by the decision maker or someone involved in the decision making process. The provision or withholding of relevant information can obviously influence the final decision because the outcome will have been shaped by the information that is made available. The control of information is thus a means of exercising power.

6 *Parties to the decision* – involving the creation of power groupings and influencing individuals involved in the decision process. Politically oriented decision makers will identify allies and enemies and make great efforts to promote their involvement in the decision-making process, whilst endeavouring to get rid of or undermine those perceived as being enemies. A power base is therefore created, from which support is almost guaranteed when it comes to putting forward alternatives and when making the final decision.

Decision makers who are influenced by political considerations, regardless of the prevailing organisational culture, will make decisions that reflect their own ambitions and protection of their present position. They will not consider the best alternatives from the organisation's perspective but will almost always try to achieve outcomes that can be put forward as being in the best interests of the organisation whilst achieving benefits for themselves. This perhaps is the sign of a true political decision maker, someone who can seemingly represent the organisation while at the same time look after their own narrow interests.

In the final analysis, perhaps it is only realistic to expect individuals to think politically when it comes to their own interests. Who could blame someone, for example, for looking after his or her own interests if the possible outcome of a decision in which they were involved could possibly affect their promotion and future employment. It would take a very special kind of person to think entirely objectively under such circumstances and not use, if available to them, political influence to achieve an outcome that satisfied their own agenda of promotion and job security.

The decision-making context – final thoughts

A number of internal and external factors will influence decision making and all of the factors are mutually inclusive of one and other at any one given time. The decision-making context is therefore complex and as hard as an individual may try to be objective, the very nature of organisational decision making will preclude such an approach. Human beings are fallible and prone to succumbing to the pressures that exist. Organisational life will add to the pressures and the cumulative effect will have an impact upon the way in which individuals participate in and make decisions. The best that can realistically be hoped for is that individuals will try to be objective within the contextual framework that is either created for them or they create themselves.

Summary of the chapter

- Bounded rationality informs the decision-making process and will be influenced by the external and internal organisational environment.

- External forces will largely determine strategic decision making but will also influence individuals.

- The external decision-making environment is composed of the general external environment and the specific external environment.

- The general external environment is made up of economic, political, legal, social, global and technological influences.

- The specific external environment is made up of suppliers, customers, competitors, labour market conditions and pressure groups.

- Internal decision-making constraints include structure, culture, management style and politics.

- Based on the degree of centralisation or decentralisation of decision making, organisational structure will determine the way individuals respond to and participate in decision making.

- The overt and covert aspects of organisational culture will influence the behaviour of individuals generally and also the way in which they perceive the value and worth of participating in decision making.

- Management style, and the extent to which it incorporates leadership, delegation of responsibility and authority, trust and respect is involvement based, will affect individual participation in decision making because ownership of the decision process and its outcomes is democratic in nature.

- Organisational politics will influence decision making when politically desirable outcomes are paramount and when the decision is perceived to have personal consequences for such things as the decision maker's promotion, job security and maintenance of a power base.

Case Study 2: Aircom

Two brothers, Alun and John Richards, founded Aircom in 1969 to produce industrial air compressors for a range of industries. They had managed to build up the business through sheer hard work and determination to a point where they now employed over 200 people.

They had run the company very much along traditional lines, in that it was once described as being 'conservative, hierarchical and rigid' with regard to its management practices and its attitude towards changes in the external environment. In 1981 the company was, however, stung into action by an industry report that clearly emphasised the marketplace had changed, technology had changed, and the market was beginning to be dominated by large multinational corporations. Alun and John recognised that if the company was to survive, then they had to change which is exactly what they did.

They readily admitted that they had become out of touch with current management thinking and decided to call in a team of management consultants to offer advice as to the ways in which they needed to change. From this they decided to recreate their company and to move it away from being mechanistic towards a situation where the company would become far more flexible and open in nature.

After much thought they decided that if they were going to change, time was against them to do it incrementally, they had to do it quickly. The changes that took place involved the following:

- The company had to be restructured.
- Work activities became project led.
- Team working was introduced.
- Jobs were respecified and matched more closely to individual capabilities.
- Open plan offices were used to aid communication and to break down barriers.
- Communications were radically changed to move away from a top-to-bottom approach to one that was more informal and far less rigid.
- Regular team meetings and company-wide briefings were introduced.

At first there was some employee resistance because the changes that took place were so radical, and because the employees were sceptical as to whether the owners would really change themselves, in line with the way in which the company was changing. The resistance was overcome by the owners making great efforts to convince all the employees that in fact they were committed to the changes that were taking place. Alun and John went round the factory themselves to sell the changes and encouraged the involvement of as many employees as possible in the change process. Small groups were formed to discuss changes to working practices and to allow individuals to put forward their ideas, with a view to even taking ownership of their implementation. Over a relatively short period the employees began to believe in the changes – and that the changes were going to be permanent.

Were the changes successful in terms of the company's performance? Alun and John Richards believed that the changes had indeed been successful. They cited the way in which people were now more involved and talking to one another, and the way in which this had led to the seemingly rapid development of at least 18 product innovations to their range of compressors. The changes have enabled them to remain competitive and provide a basis for the company to be flexible in the future, and to take advantage of any opportunities that may emerge. The company is now, they feel, in a strong position and well placed to adapt within its environment.

Questions for discussion

1 *Why do you think that Aircom's original organisational structure and culture did not work?*

2 *How would you describe the way in which decisions were made under the original organisational structure?*

3 *Have Alun and John created a more flexible organisation?*

4 *What role will decision-making play in the new organisation and how is it helped by the new approach to management?*

Case Study 3: Belinsula Debt-Collecting Service

If you were to ask the inhabitants of Belinsula to describe the Belinsula Debt-Collecting Service (BDCS) they would most probably say that it is bureaucratic, slow to respond to debtors needs, does not understand people's financial problems, and takes far too long to process complaints of harassment.

In response to this criticism BDCS has decided to improve its performance and to become, in the words of its chief executive, 'more user friendly'. The biggest shake-up will be in the area of collecting unpaid debts and arrears from those people who, for one reason or another, are unable to pay. In the past the BDCS has chased such people without any regard as to whether or not they can pay, which has only resulted in the use of valuable resources in terms of time, money and people for very little or no return. The BDCS has consistently shown a very inflexible attitude towards this aspect of debt collection, but it has now realised that in order to maximise resources a more flexible and realistic approach is needed. The new approach is aimed at making the BDCS more understanding of customers' financial circumstances and even more willing to compromise in order to ensure that they receive regular, if small, payments from those customers who find themselves in severe financial difficulty.

The person tasked with bringing about this change has recognised that sending out demands for payment usually accompanied with the threat of legal action if payment is not forthcoming simply was not bringing in the money. If the money wasn't there in the first place, then no matter how much customers were chased they couldn't pay. BDCS therefore began to look toward long-term solutions as opposed to the immediate solution of trying to get customers to pay everything that was owed immediately. A Compromise Programme was created that allows those debtors who want to pay but have few assets to settle the debt by paying a part of what is owed if they can clearly prove that they are unable to pay. Such an approach has the distinct advantage of making economic sense, in that resources are not wasted chasing debtors who cannot pay, and by compromising they are at least receiving some money. BDCS has also decided to write off some debts in settlement for payment, which represents a proportion of the total debt.

The changes at BDCS have been slow in coming and the employees are the first to admit that this is the case. The bureaucratic systems are taking time to dismantle and some employees are slow to change their habits of a working lifetime and are not yet quite prepared to write off debts.

Questions for
discussion

1 *Do you think that the new structure is mechanistic or organic in nature? What evidence is there for your answer?*

2 *Discuss how the organisational culture of BDCS is affecting the successful implementation of the changes.*

3 *To what extent, and why, do you think the decision-making processes within BDCS would need to change?*

References

Burns, T. and Stalker, G. M. (1961) *The Management of Innovation*, Tavistock, London.

Crozier, M. and Friedberg, E. (1980) *Actors and Systems*, University of Chicago Press.

David, F. R. (1993) *Strategic Management*, Macmillan, Basingstoke.

Drucker, P. (1974) *Management: Tasks, Responsibilities, and Practices*, Harper & Row, New York.

Egan, G. (1993) 'The shadow side', *Management Today*, September, p. 37.

Etzioni, A. A. (1975) *Comparative Analysis of Complex Organizations: On Power, Involvement and their Correlates*, Revised edition, Free Press, New York.

Fayol, H. (1949) *General and Industrial Management*, Pitman, London.

Goldsmith, W. and Clutterbuck, D. (1985) *The Winning Streak*, Penguin Business, London.

Handy, C. (1993) *Understanding Organizations*, 4th edn, Penguin Business, London.

Hegarty, E. (1976) *How to Succeed in Company Politics*, McGraw-Hill, New York.

Hersey, P. and Blanchard, H., (1988) *Management of Organizational Behaviour: Utilizing Human Resources*, 5th edn, Prentice-Hall, Englewood Cliffs, New Jersey.

Lawrence, P. and Lorsch, J. (1967) *Organisation and Environment: Managing Differentiation and Integration*, Harvard Business School.

Lawrence, P. and Elliott, K. (1985) *Introducing Management*, Penguin Business, London.

Mintzberg, H. (1979) *The Structuring of Organisations*, Prentice-Hall, Englewood Cliffs, New Jersey.

Mintzberg, H. and Quinn, J. (1991) *The Strategy Process – Concepts, Contexts and Cases*, Prentice Hall International, Hemel Hempstead.

Morgan, G. (1986) *Images of Organization*, Sage Publications, California.

Mullins, L. J. (1998) *Management and Organisational Behaviour*, 5th edn, Financial Times Pitman Publishing, London.

Pettinger, R. (1996) *Introduction to Corporate Strategy*, Macmillan Business, Basingstoke.

Scott, W. R. (1987) *Organizations: Rational, Natural and Open Systems*, Prentice-Hall, Hemel Hempstead.

Schein, E. H. (1992) *Organizational Culture and Leadership*, Jossey-Bass, San Francisco.

Simon, H. (1951) *Administrative Behaviour*, Macmillan, Basingstoke.

Taylor, F. W. (1947) *Scientific Management*, Harper & Row, New York.

Urwick, L. (1952) *The Elements of Administration*, Pitman, London.

Weber, M. (1947) *The Theory of Social and Economic Organisation*, Free Press, New York.

CHAPTER 2

Group decision making

At the end of this chapter you should:

- understand the types of groups which are found in organisations and the roles they play;

- recognise how formal groups can be used in the decision-making process;

- appreciate the factors that will determine the effectiveness of groups as decision-making units, and understand why the potential benefits of group decision making are not always realised;

- distinguish between decisions that might be more appropriately made by groups, and those which might logically be made by individuals; and

- be able to evaluate the performance of the group leader.

Introduction

In this chapter we shall examine the circumstances in which decisions might be made by groups rather than by individual managers. This will involve consideration of the type of decision to be made and the context in which it is made. We shall then go on to examine the processes by which group decisions might be made, and consider some of the pitfalls that are sometimes associated with group decision making. Finally, we shall offer some basic guidelines for the use of groups in decision making.

Types of groups

There are many types of group within the workplace, fulfilling a range of organisational and individual purposes. Some of these groups develop formally through the nomination of individuals to serve on committees; others arise through the psychological bonding of individuals, and might be termed informal groups.

Formal groups, or work groups as they are sometimes called, are created for a productive purpose, transforming resource inputs (which may include ideas as well as materials) into outputs (including decisions and reports as well as saleable products). An organisation may be made up of a network of many interconnecting work groups, with individuals participating in several groups linked by common (usually managerial) personnel. These groups may be permanent (e.g. a department of a company) or temporary, and their size might vary from just two or three people to hundreds.

Formal work groups frequently have clear, hierarchical patterns of communication, and well defined roles for their personnel. Informal groups, by contrast, are less obviously hierarchical. They form spontaneously, often as subgroups within a formal work group. For example, an informal group may take breaks together or eat together. Their importance lies in the psychological bonding that can take place within the group, resulting in similar patterns of behaviour, sometimes with positive, and sometimes with negative outcomes for the organisation.

Whilst we are primarily concerned in this chapter with the circumstances and ways in which formal groups make decisions, the existence of informal groups adds a degree of complexity to the task of managing group behaviour and decision making.

The use of groups for decision making

The responsibility for a managerial decision often rests with one individual, but it would be rare for the decision to involve no input from others. Indeed, in any organisational endeavour, one person may appear to have made a decision, but in fact that person may have performed only one part of the process. President Harry Truman's famous sign on his desk, 'The buck stops here' did not suggest that the decisions of state were made unaided, but rather that he accepted responsibility for them.

In general, the larger the organisation and the more complex and important the decisions, the less likely that decisions will be made by a lone individual. Indeed, it was suggested in the previous section that an organisation may often be seen as an interrelationship of work groups acting as decision centres; often these centres will represent different functional areas of a business, and will frequently bring different perspectives to the decision-making process. In large organisations facing intricate problems, formal groups tend to be used as part of the decision-making process. These groupings may be called conferences, committees, boards, teams or merely staff meetings. The term used for the group is often suggestive of its size, and the level of seniority of its members.

Much has been written about the use of groups for decision making, and there has been a certain amount of disagreement as to whether or not groups are efficient

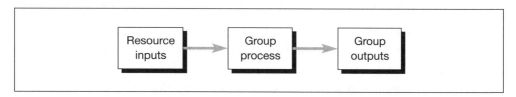

Fig. 2.1 The group decision-making process

and effective as decision makers. The effectiveness of group decision making will depend in part on group processes, that is to say, how well it transforms resource inputs into group outputs (see Fig. 2.1).

It must be recognised that the personnel within a work group represent a costly resource input. If a similar output could have been achieved without involving the group, efficiency gains could have been made. But efficiency cannot always be equated with effectiveness. For example, suppose the managing director of a manufacturing firm faces a difficult decision regarding the possible discontinuation of part of a company's product range. A consequence of dropping products will certainly be a reduction in the workforce, so that the move will doubtless be unpopular. The MD may be virtually certain that the products in question are no longer viable, and could make the decision to discontinue them himself. Alternatively, a committee could be established to examine the likely future profitability of these products. The committee may reach exactly the same conclusion as the MD, but the added legitimacy that the committee brings to the decision may mean that the group decision has been more effective.

It is worth noting from the outset, however, that the group's effectiveness will depend, at least in part, on the quality of the resource inputs. These will include:

- the organisational context – its physical resources as well as its size, structure, culture and reward systems;
- the competency of the group members;
- the social and psychological mix of the membership;
- the level of complexity in the task.

Some of the disagreement as to the effectiveness of group decision making is probably the result of a failure to fully recognise the purposes assigned to the group. Certainly, it is critically important for the success of group decision making that an explicit recognition is made as to what is expected of it.

The most obvious purposes of groups are *organisational*. These will include:

- the distribution of work;
- problem solving;
- increasing the involvement of individuals and, potentially, their commitment to the organisation;
- allowing appropriate individuals to take responsibility for a range of work.

However, there are also important psychological needs that can be satisfied by the use of groups. These *individual* purposes of groups might include:

- satisfying the individual's need for affiliation, as described by McClelland (1961), suggesting that groups fulfil a human imperative as much as a decision-making need;
- establishing the 'self' concept, whereby group membership may help the individual define his/her role within the organisation, potentially enhancing self-esteem.

Several psychological studies have linked this aspect of group membership to a reduction in work related stress; and

● providing intrinsic rewards from work through group participation.

While these may be generic purposes of groups, some of their more explicit purposes can be summarised in the eight following ways.

1 *To maximise creativity in the decision-making process.* Complex decisions will often benefit from the creative input of a group, generating a broad range of options.

2 *The collection of information.* A complex decision may require a considerable amount of information to be collected, some of which may require a degree of expertise on the part of the gatherer. A team approach may be appropriate in such circumstances.

3 *Making a decision.* Sufficient information may already be available, and the group may be required to evaluate various options to make a decision. Group participation would have certain advantages here, particularly if the members of the group are likely to be significantly affected by the outcome. Use of a group in such circumstances may also serve to legitimise the decision, and hence reduce resistance to it. It is often believed that the quality of the decision may be enhanced by the broad input of a group, though much may depend on the extent to which the expertise and skills of the group members complement each other.

4 *Gaining acceptability for a decision based on limited information.* When there is a high level of uncertainty surrounding the decision-making process, the inevitably difficult decision may be more acceptable to those affected by it if the decision is taken by a group.

5 *To provide representation for different elements of an organisation.* This may involve negotiation between conflicting positions taken by opposing interests, or it may be seen as a means of maximising the participation of the different organisational functions. Particularly in situations where the decision is unlikely to meet with unanimous approval from all the different stakeholders, a group decision can add legitimacy to the decision.

6 *Motivating members of the group.* Research has shown that individuals can be motivated by participating in groups. The organisational benefits resulting from individuals' sense of belonging to the group have been harnessed by a number of high-profile companies (e.g. Volvo and Hewlett-Packard) through the introduction of teamworking and autonomous work groups. Group membership can also confer status on an individual, resulting in a sense of personal worth. This status tends to be enhanced if the group either generates or controls information that is vital to the organisation as a whole, or if the group is seen to be performing a particularly important task for the organisation. These psychological benefits to the individual from group membership can act as a significant motivational force.

7 *To co-ordinate different parts or subgroups of an organisation.* In large organisations it is not uncommon for subgroups to diverge from overall corporate goals. Committees are a means of drawing together potentially disparate groups to ensure that there is consistency between functional aims and objectives.

8 *To train and develop personnel.* Less experienced members of a group can gain from the greater experience of their colleagues.

Types of problem that might be tackled by groups

Some problems are more suited to group decisions than others. Any decision requiring a range of knowledge (e.g. simultaneous input from engineers, accountants and marketers) will tend to encourage the committee approach. The conclusions of the committee are often taken to be 'advisory', with the final decision being made by a single line manager. In practice, however, the group's 'advisory' report often becomes the basis for action. This situation is, therefore, a further case of individual accountability for the process undertaken by the group.

Of course, there will be some circumstances where a decision needs to made by an individual; for example, when an immediate response to a situation is required, when the need for confidentiality is paramount, or where the decision requires a level of technical expertise available only from a particular individual. Even in these circumstances, it should be recognised that there is some potential for bias in the decision. Indeed, arguments advanced by senior executives that time is too short to involve others in the process, or that confidentiality must be maintained, can in reality be an excuse for retaining full control. Given sufficient resources, there will probably be many more situations that favour the broad input of a group rather than a decision made by an individual.

A decision that will have an impact on several departments may require some means by which the departments can become involved in the decision-making process. Group involvement will not only legitimise the decision but may provide an opportunity to develop a common understanding and a means for each department to obtain the benefit of comments from other departments. The group decision is then more likely to be a balanced decision that takes into account a range of viewpoints.

Planning decisions tend to lend themselves to committee work, where a range of scenarios may need to be explored. Decisions that require rapid forceful action tend to be made more effectively by an individual.

The advantages of group decision making

Clearly, there will be many circumstances in which a broad range of contributions can be beneficial in the process of making decisions. It would be useful at this stage to summarise some of the principal advantages groups have over individual decision makers.

Whether to use a committee or some other group method of decision making is a question that can be approached by looking at the following advantages of groups:

- Group work allows for a variety of specialists to be assembled, each contributing in his or her area of expertise. The composition of the group is, of course, critically important if its main purpose is to draw on such a range of expertise.

- Group decision making allows for the views of different interest groups to be aired. This is particularly important when the decisions made may have an adverse impact on certain stakeholders. Clearly, however, there is the potential for conflict within the group when the various participants have divergent interests. This conflict should not necessarily be seen as harmful, since one of the purposes of the group is to resolve differences and reach a suitable solution taking into account the interests of different factions. A decision made by a group including representatives of all the interested parties is likely to be more acceptable than one made by an individual executive. Nevertheless, decision making in such circumstances can be a slow process, however worthwhile.

- The activities of different departments can be co-ordinated through meetings. This can be particularly important in an organisation where there is a mechanistic structure (Burns and Stalker, 1961) or a role culture (Handy, 1985). In such organisations the horizontal flow of information is often limited, with the resultant risk that common goals are not adequately communicated or pursued.

- Group decision making can motivate members of a team or committee, and encourage a commitment to the organisation and its goals. Participation in the decision-making process is also likely to result in lower levels of resistance to changes arising from the decision.

- Committees provide a means by which executives can be trained in decision making. Whilst some decision making groups may be composed solely of senior executives, the practice of involving people of less seniority within the organisation can offer useful opportunities for staff development, and may form a part of an organisation's succession plans.

- Group discussion can stimulate creative thinking, creating synergies; the seed of an idea arising from one member of the group may spark off productive discussion amongst others present. The extent to which the group may gain from such synergistic interaction is likely to depend, once again, on the composition of the group and the effectiveness of intra-group communications. Belbin's (1981) work, based on the personality traits of the individual group members, and Tuckman's (1965) study of the design of work teams provide us with useful models as to how group effectiveness may be enhanced. These models will be explored later in this chapter.

Group conformity and cohesion

For a group to work effectively together there is clearly a need for its members to be bound together in some way. Moreover, a certain level of conformity is normally seen as a requirement of sustained group membership. From a managerial perspective, a complete absence of group conformity would make it impossible to channel the group's efforts towards the achievement of organisational goals.

There are various ways in which this conformity can be achieved, for example:

1 *Through group norms* – the standards that are shared by members of a group. Norms are only formed in respect of issues that are important to the group. For example, if completion of individual tasks on schedule is important to the group, then such a norm will develop. Naturally, group norms will be accepted more readily by some group members than by others. Some of the factors that are likely to influence conformity to group norms are:

   (a) the personalities and intelligence of the group members (research has shown that the more intelligent are less likely to conform than the less intelligent); and

   (b) contextual factors, such as the size and structure of the group, and the complexity of the group's overall task – in general, the more complex and ambiguous the task, the greater the extent of conformity to group norms.

   Group cohesion will be stronger in situations where norms are widely accepted.

2 *Through charismatic leadership*, where the group is bound together by the strength of one individual's personality.

3 *Where the group is small enough* for the contributions of all members to be seen as worthwhile or important. Small groups are less likely to contain 'outliers' who opt out of full participation within the group.

4 *Where the group has acquired a reputation for achieving its goals*, as a result of which its members can often be motivated by their collective success, causing the group to bond together.

5 *Cohesion* may be achieved through the mutual support offered by the members of the group in terms of personal growth and development. This support is most likely to be evident if the group is seen to be successful. If the group were to be criticised for failing to achieve its objectives, there is a greater likelihood of intra-group conflict.

The question of what is the optimal level of cohesion within a group is less obvious. In order to function effectively as a decision-making unit there has to be a certain level of trust and sustenance within a group. Nevertheless, too much cohesion can result in a deterioration of critical thinking, as group members tend to support each other's views without question. Janis (1972) referred to this as 'groupthink' (see below). Striking an appropriate balance between too much and too little group cohesion is an important consideration for managers, and one that will require monitoring and maintenance activities.

'Groupthink' and excessive conformity

'Groupthink' is the term Janis (1972) used to describe some groups' tendency towards excessive cohesion, revealing a deterioration of mental efficiency, reality testing and moral judgement, each resulting from pressures within the group. The symptoms of groupthink include:

- Excessive optimism and risk taking – the group collectively makes riskier decisions than its individual members might have done if operating outside the group environment. This is sometimes referred to as the 'risky shift' phenomenon.

- The group ignores the external environment or outside warnings. This can be partly because of an excessive confidence in the judgements of those within the group, and partly the result of the insularity of the bonded group.

- There is an unquestioned belief in the group's morality. As the group becomes more cohesive, its members often tend to think along similar lines, and their opinions become more convergent. They begin to believe that the group's values are 'right', and consequently, they reject opposing points of view.

- There is such confidence in the group's opinions, values, and decision-making capabilities that derogatory terms are used in relation to their opponents, e.g. 'weak', 'stupid', 'evil' or 'wet'.

- Deviation from the group norms is not tolerated – the more cohesive the group, the greater the demand for conformity.

- The group places pressure on any of its number who oppose the collective point of view. This pressure may start as reason, progressing to seduction, before the 'iron fist' is revealed, threatening ostracism or expulsion from the group if the 'outliers' fail to conform.

- There is an illusion of unanimity within the group, where silence is taken as consent. This may not be a conscious policy of the group, but rather an assumption that the group thinks as one.

- Some members protect the group, either from adverse criticism or from information that would be likely to sway the group from its chosen decision course.

Other studies have also demonstrated the tendency of members of cohesive groups towards excessive conformity, even when this conflicts with the individual's rational or moral judgement. Two such studies are the Asch experiments (1951) and Milgram's (1974) 'electric shock' experiments.

Asch used groups of seven subjects for his experiments, and asked members of the group to identify which of three lines drawn on a piece of paper was of exactly the same length as another line drawn on a separate sheet of paper. The task was simple, and the answer should have been obvious. However, only one of the seven members of each group was genuinely on trial; the other six had, unbeknown to the seventh, been primed beforehand as to the required response. On several occasions, some or all of Asch's confederates were asked to give a particular incorrect response. It was discovered that, in successive trials, the majority of the true subjects of the experiment were likely to accept the view of the group, in spite of their private recognition that the answer given was incorrect. This tendency to conform with the incorrect response was almost entirely eliminated as soon as one other member of the group agreed with the subject.

Milgram's controversial experiments involved subjects taking the role of a teacher in a learning situation in which learners (who were, in reality, Milgram's confederates) were asked to make word associations. If the 'learner' made a mistake, the teacher was required to administer an electric shock to the learner by pressing a button. No shock was actually delivered, but the 'teachers' were unaware of this. As more mistakes were made, the severity of the shock administered was to increase, resulting in apparent pain to the learners. It was discovered that, when pressured by other members of the group, two out of three individuals were prepared to administer shocks of an intensity that could prove fatal. However, when other members of the teaching group objected and refused to administer the shocks, the experimental subject tended to do likewise.

The conclusions drawn from both Asch's and Milgram's experiments demonstrate the power that groups of individuals can exert over another individual. Clearly, the effects can be positive, in terms of encouraging co-operation and commitment, but it is as well to be aware of the detrimental effects a group can have on an individual's judgement. It will not always be the case that a group decision will be of a higher quality.

Some further disadvantages of group decision making

Cost

The most obvious disadvantage of group decision making is the cost involved. It is, of course, not simply a question of the wages and salaries paid to the members of the group (including extra clerical support staff who may be required), nor the opportunity cost represented by the productive work that members of a committee might otherwise have done, committees deliberate for far longer than most individuals. Once a committee has been formed, its members have a right for their views to be heard. Options must be explored, and differences of opinion reconciled or accommodated. Moreover, these costs will increase if it is considered important that any decision should be fully accepted by the group, or if the decision must be unanimous.

If the organisation cannot afford this cost, either the direct financial cost or the opportunity cost, we have to question whether it was appropriate to form a committee in the first place. In circumstances where the decision is complex, or of particular importance to the organisation, the cost may by justified in terms of the quality of the decision that needs to be made. But there are many circumstances where the cost may not be so easily justified. The key issue for an organisation is whether the cost of using a group or committee matches the benefit gained from it.

The acceptance of responsibility

When a decision is taken by one individual the responsibility for it, and for the consequences of the decision, will normally rest with that individual. Subsequent actions may be delegated to others, but in most cases there is little doubt as to who 'carries the can'. This is not always true of a group or committee decision. Collective responsibility can be interpreted as meaning no individual blame; and actions agreed by the committee may not be followed through with the same rigour as if there were individual responsibility. While this may prove to be a problem for some decision-making groups, the solution really lies in the processes of group management.

It is important that any recommendations the group makes for future actions should be recorded, together with a clear indication as to who is to take responsibility for completion of these actions. The key issue here is that full records must be kept of individuals' responsibilities resulting from group decisions. Indeed, this raises the interesting and necessary distinction to be made between the decision and the resultant actions. Whereas it is appropriate in many circumstances for groups to be used in the decision-making process, the responsibility for subsequent actions is a managerial function – and one that cannot reasonably be performed by a committee.

Compromise decisions

The nature of group decision making is such that compromise will often be necessary. However, it is often a *radical* course of action that may permit a competitive organisation to establish a differential advantage. A group decision involving significant compromise would tend to preclude the acceptance of radical solutions, since agreement may prove impossible.

Failure to reach an agreement

Disagreement between the members of the group might prove so fundamental that there can be no realistic possibility of agreement or compromise. In this case the group has failed to meet its basic objective, and may even have to be disbanded.

Alternatively, with time pressing and no sign of agreement, the group leader may take responsibility for making a decision. This, of course, runs contrary to the whole principle of group decision making, undermining the value of the group. The group leader – or perhaps other managers outside the group – may possibly be deluded into believing that a group decision has been made, but many of the benefits of a team approach will have been lost. Alternatively, the group may react against the leader making an independent decision, with the result that a divisive split may appear within the group, with potentially damaging consequences for its future effectiveness.

If groups are to function effectively, it is important that no individual, however senior he or she may be within the organisation, is allowed to dominate or 'hijack' the decision-making processes. Indeed, it is not always the more senior members of the group who are guilty of exercising excessive individual influence over decision making. Another scenario that sometimes occurs in work groups is that one or two individuals vehemently oppose the collective view of their colleagues. While theirs is a minority view, it is expressed so forcefully that the majority is forced into backtracking and further compromise than might ordinarily be warranted.

Intra-group conflict

A degree of conflict within the group is probably inevitable. Indeed, if there is no conflict at all between the members of the group, it is highly likely that the group is excessively cohesive, and may suffer from groupthink. The traditional view is that conflict is bad for the group, or any other part of the organisation. However, an interactionist approach to group work (Wilson and Rosenfeld, 1990) suggests that the group can benefit from a certain level of conflict, and is likely to perform most effectively when individual views are challenged.

Intra-group conflict, therefore, only becomes a problem when it goes beyond purposeful argument. This is the point at which the leader's intervention may be necessary, initially through negotiation between the warring parties and then, if necessary, by means of mediation or arbitration. Intra-group conflict that requires that latter actions will almost certainly undermine the effectiveness of the group as a decision-making unit.

Role conflict

This can take a variety of forms, any of which can disturb the equilibrium of the group, impairing its effectiveness. Essentially, role conflict can exist because the expectations of the individual within the group may be at variance with his/her other roles outside the group. For example, a group recommendation that a product be discontinued may result in job losses. An individual may be in a position of helping to make such a decision, whilst also being a member of the production or sales team involved with this product. A more familiar case of role conflict for many working people is that of the conflicting demands of work and family life. If group membership places additional demands on its members' time, there will inevitably be less time available for other activities.

Excessive conformity

Conforming to group norms is sometimes erroneously seen as a case of group-think. However, conformity occurs when a group member avoids contradicting the majority view of the group, yet does not fundamentally alter his/her point of view. This contrasts with groupthink in that in the latter case, group cohesion results in opinions being changed in line with those of other group members.

The reason for conformity may be a perception on the part of the individual that the group is exercising pressure to conform. This pressure, whether real or imagined, is often felt most acutely either by new members of an established group, or by those at the lower end of the organisational hierarchy. Also, where there is a strong culture within the group (often reflecting the organisational culture) a tendency towards conformity is likely. The strong culture can impose a constraint on decision making by narrowing the boundaries within which an 'acceptable' decision can be made.

Compliance

A variation on conformity, compliance suggests that individuals might conform, either with the majority of the group or, more likely, with particular individuals because of ulterior motives. For example, a group's membership may include individuals at different levels of the organisational hierarchy. A junior member of the group may feel it is advantageous to be seen to agree with those who have influence within the organisation. When such considerations come into play, the decision-making processes can be biased, once again reducing the effectiveness of the group.

Intra-group communications

The way in which members of the group communicate with each other is of great importance to the effectiveness of group decision making. If, for example, it appears that there is a hierarchy within the group, and in particular if deference is shown to those of superior rank, communications, and hence individuals' contributions, can be stifled.

Effective communication involves a four-stage cycle (Fig. 2.2) wherein (1) the *sender* delivers (2) the *message* to (3) the *receiver*, who provides (4) *feedback*. While the cycle can be broken at any of the four stages, poor communication is perhaps most often due to inadequate feedback – a failure to 'close the loop'. In some cases this may represent a deliberate rejection of the message, for example, in complex political negotiations where compromise is sought. In other cases, it may be the result of poor relationships between members of the group, or a group whose members' roles fail to complement each other.

It should also be recognised that feedback can be non-verbal as well as verbal. Facial expressions, gestures and body language can suggest either approval or disapproval; can be dismissive or encouraging. Since non-verbal communications can be just as significant as words, a group that communicates well is likely to recognise the importance of this form of feedback.

The effectiveness of intra-group communications can often be judged on the basis of the level of mutual respect afforded by members to each other, and the group's ability to complete all four stages of the communications cycle. The latter is likely to involve both verbal and non-verbal communication.

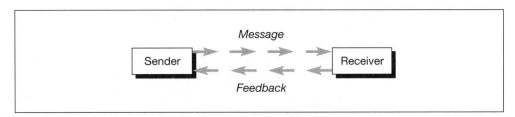

Fig. 2.2 The four-stage communication cycle

Group roles and performance

Groups are unlikely to be able to perform to their full potential from the instant that they are formed; they generally need to go through a process of socialisation first. The time that this socialisation process takes will usually depend on the extent to which the members are already acquainted with one another prior to the formation of the group. For example, a work group assembled for a particular task may draw upon people from various functions, some of whom have previously worked together and may even have met in other social situations. In this case there may already be informal subgroups within the formal working group.

The first task for a newly formed group will probably be to organise and orientate itself. This will involve finding a leader and allocating group roles. This may prove quite difficult for the group. There will be uncertainty about the purpose of the group, about authority, and how power will be distributed among its members. Individuals may be unsure about the extent of their commitment to the group. Conflicts may arise as power relationships are tested. Indeed, some groups remain ineffective as these early conflicts are never resolved; others do manage to overcome these difficulties and subsequently become more cohesive.

With cohesion may come the *false* impression that there are no more interpersonal conflicts or disagreements, and that the group is now a fully functioning unit. But cohesiveness can stifle the contributions of individuals and discourage original thought. It is therefore likely that the group will not really begin to function effectively until it reaches a stage of maturity, where there is mutual support, respect and confidence within the group, such that individuals might challenge and debate with each other, and decisions are made on the basis of rational discussion.

Influential work on the processes of group formation and development was carried out by Tuckman (1965), who suggested that, before a full working group begins to perform to its potential, it will need to pass through three other developmental stages first. These he referred to as 'forming', 'storming' and 'norming'. 'Performing' is the fourth phase – a stage that, according to Tuckman, is not reached by all groups; some get stuck in the earlier phases of group development and will remain ineffective as decision-making units.

The Tuckman model

Tuckman (1965) argued that groups progress through three phases of socialisation before they begin to perform fully effectively. It is suggested that the ineffectiveness of some groups as problem-solving or decision-making units relates directly to their failure to master one or other of these stages of development. The phases of group development, according to Tuckman, can be outlined thus:

- *Phase one – forming: the testing of acceptable behaviour* As the group is assembled, members are initially concerned with finding out about each other – exploring each other's attitudes and values. At this stage, the group will be seeking task direction as they try to establish what they are expected to achieve. Leadership is important here; if no formal leader is appointed, one is likely to emerge, as a broad plan of action is drawn up. The leadership role may, however, pass to another person as the group progresses through later phases of its development.

- *Phase two – storming: identifying a 'pecking order'* In this second phase, the group will have established its task and the members will have formed impressions of their colleagues. They must now establish roles, priorities and organise into a working unit. It may become apparent that some members of the group have personal objectives within the group, which have little to do with the organisational goals. Subgroups may form, consisting of like-minded individuals, or those with common personal objectives. This can, therefore, be an uncomfortable period for the group, as individuals 'jockey for position'. The task of organising the group against a background of conflict can be particularly difficult if the leader's position is not yet fully established or accepted by the group.

- *Phase three – norming: establishing the rules and parameters* In this phase, the inter-personal conflicts within the group will have been resolved. If the group reaches this phase, a consensus will have emerged with regard to the group's objectives, and the roles of individual members. Having gone through the tensions of 'storming', relationships between individuals are likely to be stronger, and trust and co-operation should now be possible. Information therefore tends to flow more freely between members of the group. The group's expectations will now be established, setting standards by which the group can measure its achievements.

- *Phase four – performing: collaboration and low levels of conflict* The group has now reached a phase of maturity, where individuals can work either separately on a part of their collective task or as a whole team. Gone are the conflicts and power struggles of the earlier stages of the group's development, and effective problem solving and decision making are possible through constructive collaboration.

What makes a 'performing' group

The characteristics of a mature, 'performing' group might be summarised as follows:

1 The group is able to accept without being judgemental that differences may exist between individuals.

2 Decisions are made through rational discussion, accommodating different points of view. No attempt is made to coerce members of the group into agreement or consent, or to force a decision.

3 Individuals fully understand their roles within the group and the group's processes.

4 Conflict may exist, but will be confined to the issues facing the group, rather than interpersonal conflicts based on the group's structure or power struggles between individuals.

One of the reasons for certain groups' failure to reach the final 'performing' stage can be the mix of personnel within the group and the roles adopted by each person. Each position within a group carries with it a role – that is, a pattern of expected behaviour. The expectations of the occupant of that role come not only from the occupant him/herself, but also from other members of the group and from external stakeholders. For example, we generally have a fair idea of how we expect a bank manager, a college tutor, or a dentist's receptionist to behave, and what their role entails. If, however, one of these people were to behave in a manner inconsistent with the norms of their role, there is the likelihood of conflict or frustration as there seems to be a poor fit between the person and the role – the *enacted* role diverges from the *expected* role.

The lesson here is that a more scientific approach may be necessary to group formation and the allocation of roles. Indeed, the issue of what makes a successful work group has been the subject of much research of the years.

The Belbin model

Important work by Belbin (1981) revealed a range of roles that need to be performed by members of a group if the group is to perform effectively. Different personalities will be suited to different roles, and Belbin's work demonstrated that individuals tend to adopt the same one or two roles fairly consistently. Indeed, this research has been developed to include psychometric tests to identify the roles most suited to particular individuals. Though Belbin identified nine roles, it is quite common, particularly in small groups, for individuals to take on more than one role. Nevertheless, there will be some roles that may not be suited to certain personality types.

The managerial significance of Belbin's work lies in the practical guidelines it can offer for the development of the group's effectiveness in decision making. Adherence to these roles, it is argued, should reduce conformity, compliance and role conflict. First of all, however, individuals will need to understand the roles to which they are most suited. Thereafter, the extent to which the effectiveness of group decision making can be enhanced should depend on individuals' willingness or ability to occupy the roles that exploit their personal strengths and minimise their weaknesses.

Belbin defined nine group roles, as follows:

1 *The Chairman* The main requirements for this role are discipline, focus on the task, and a balanced view of the arguments. The Chairman must ensure that time is used effectively and not wasted. This requires clarification of the group's objectives, recognition of matters that are not likely to be productive, and the ability to bring discussion back to the central issues. This will involve judgement and tact, since the chairman will certainly not wish to stifle creative thinking or alienate part of the group by appearing to take the side of others. It will also be the job of the chairman to delegate specific tasks to individuals.

2 *The Shaper* This is the role of the task leader, giving direction to the decision-making process. This person tends to be challenging, and sometimes provocative or abrasive, but his/her tenacity is invaluable in driving the group to explore and develop ideas.

3 *The Plant* This refers to the person who is often the source of original, creative ideas. The Plant is not usually concerned with operational detail, and may not be the most

effective communicator in the group. Nevertheless, he/she often contributes useful and sometimes unorthodox ideas that can help solve difficult problems.

4 *The Monitor–Evaluator* This member of the group is not a natural leader, and is unlikely to contribute many new ideas. He/she will scrutinise others' suggestions, and will tend to predict the likely flaws in them. The Monitor–Evaluator's critical approach tends to provide a sobering influence on the group – an ideal insurance against 'groupthink'.

5 *The Resource Investigator* This is likely to be the role of an enthusiastic extrovert. This person enjoys making contacts and maintaining them. However, the Resource Investigator is not necessarily someone who sees a project to its conclusion; his/her interest might wane once the initial contacts have been made and the necessary resources have been secured.

6 *The Company Worker* The group, of course, will normally be performing a task on behalf of an organisation. Whilst there can be many personal motives or benefits from group membership, it helps to have someone within the group whose attention to the organisational goals is unwavering. The Company Worker is, therefore, seen as a disciplined and reliable member of the team, whose main focus is on developing ideas into an action plan.

7 *The Team Worker* Whilst an element of conflict within the group might help to provide a challenge to individuals' ideas and a stimulus to debate, too much conflict can be damaging. The Team Worker's role is primarily that of managing relationships within the group, encouraging others by supporting their ideas, and building bridges between parties who cannot agree. The Team Worker tends to be diplomatic, and a good listener. He/she will seek points of agreement, rather than differences of opinion.

8 *The Completer* The group needs someone to ensure that their task is completed on time and to an appropriate standard. The Completer tends to focus on the end goal of the decision. He/she will ensure that there are no omissions from the group's recommendations, and that the fine detail is in order. The Completer will urge others towards a conclusion.

9 *The Specialist* In most circumstances, a group decision will require specialist knowledge, possibly in a variety of fields. Functional specialists of this kind may form a part of the group, or they may be co-opted to provide expertise where it is required for a specific part of the decision-making process.

The importance of leadership in group decision making

The group leader will probably be the key figure in determining the success of a decision-making group, particularly in the early stages of the group's development. 'Leadership' is the ability to influence the behaviour of others in a particular direction. Whilst this may suggest a degree of manipulation, the motives of the leader are not necessarily insidious. The organisational purpose of the group should, after all, be clear to all.

What is less obvious, however, is *how* the leader can be most effective. While a participative leadership style is often seen as attractive, it would not be true to say that it would be universally appropriate. Take, for example, the case of a military leader on the point of battle. A democratic, committee decision would not be expedient! But perhaps more interesting is why two leaders, adopting similar leadership styles in apparently similar circumstances can experience widely different rates of success. Why, for instance, might one schoolteacher find an autocratic style works when, for another teacher it fails to yield the desired result? The answer is that, for all the similarity of the physical environment (the same students in a similar classroom), the context is probably quite different.

First, it must be recognised that leadership behaviour is not determined by the leader alone; a number of contextual factors will be of influence. These will include the following.

- The personal characteristics of the rest of the group. The less the leader has in common with the members of the group, the more distant the leadership style is likely to be. On the other hand, if the leader is surrounded by friends who will offer support and reinforcement, the style may be more participative.

- The complexity and degree of structure in the task. Less structured tasks lend themselves to individual autonomy, since decisions have to be made as problems arise. By contrast, a structured task, such as the assembly of components, may give rise to a more authoritarian approach, as the leader simply instructs the group as to which tasks are to be completed.

- Conscious or unconscious imitation of the leadership style of others close to the leader, particularly those of higher rank within the same organisation.

- The organisational culture and 'atmosphere'. A confident and successful organisation may encourage a less autocratic style amongst its leaders. A climate of anxiety or crisis tends to have the reverse effect, promoting directive, autocratic leadership.

Leadership style: Fiedler, Vroom and Yetton

Recognising the different leadership styles that have proved successful (or otherwise) in different contexts, Fiedler (1967) devised what he called 'a contingency model of leadership effectiveness'. An interesting aspect of the Fiedler model is that it suggests that the leader has limited ability to adapt his/her leadership style to suit the group context. Therefore, different leaders will be needed for different circumstances.

Fiedler assessed the decision-making context in terms of three variables:

1 relations between the leader and the other members of the group (good/poor), reflecting the degree of support the leader is likely to receive from the group;

2 the complexity or degree of structure in the task (high/low);

3 the position power of the leader (strong/weak).

These three variables combine to give an impression of how favourable (or otherwise) the decision-making context might be. For example, a leader who is an experienced senior manager, who has the confidence and support of the rest of the group, and who faces a straightforward task, is in a favourable position. The same person, facing a less structured task, and working with a group of relatively unfamiliar people, will find the context more ambiguous. A new, relatively junior, and unproven manager, leading a team with which he/she is unfamiliar on a complex project is clearly facing an unfavourable context.

Fiedler went on to suggest that if the context is either very favourable or very unfavourable, an autocratic leadership style is likely to prove most suitable. If the context is more ambigous (which, more often than not will be the case), a more participative style will be appropriate (see Fig. 2.3).

Relating this to the earlier example of the two autocratic schoolteachers, it becomes clear that they will almost certainly not have faced similar contextual circumstances. One may command the confidence and respect of his/her students to a far greater extent than the other; moreover, the task itself may have been more structured for one of the teachers. The autocrat who was ineffective may well, according to Fiedler, have been facing more ambiguous contextual circumstances than his/her colleague.

Vroom and Yetton's (1973) contingency model of decision making also stresses that leadership style must be matched to the context if decision effectiveness is to be achieved. Unlike Fiedler, however, Vroom and Yetton assume that the group leader must be sufficiently flexible to change the leadership style to suit the situation.

Vroom and Yetton identify five decision styles, which can be grouped as follows:

Autocratic styles

1 The leader makes the decision him/herself, based on information available at the time.

2 The group is used purely as a means of gathering information for the leader, and may not even be made aware of the nature of the problem and the decision to be made. The group has no evaluative role to play.

Consultative styles

3 The leader shares the problem with individual members of the group, but without ever holding discussions with the group as a whole. The leader then makes a decision that may or may not reflect the influence of members of the group.

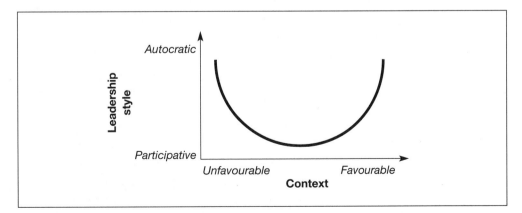

Fig. 2.3 Leadership style: the Fiedler model

4 The leader shares the problem with the group collectively, then makes a decision that may or may not reflect the influence of the group.

Group style

5 The problem is shared with the group collectively and discussion takes place. Consensus is sought without the leader attempting to direct the outcome. In this case, the leader's role is that of a chairman.

According to Vroom and Yetton, the first task of the group leader should be to assess the situation by applying a series of seven 'decision rules'. This assessment of the context of the decision is then related to the five decision styles. The seven decision rules are used for determining what procedures should *not* be used by a leader in a given situation. The first three rules are designed to protect decision quality; the remaining four rules are designed to protect decision acceptance.

R1 *The leader-information rule.* If the outcome of the decision is important to the organisation, and the group leader is short of information or expertise, then decision style 1 can be ruled out.

R2 *The goal congruence rule.* If the outcome of the decision is important to the organisation, but the group members are unlikely to place organisational goals ahead of their personal objectives, then decision style 5 can be ruled out.

R3 *Unstructured problem rule.* If the outcome of the decision is important to the organisation, and the leader lacks the necessary information or expertise to solve the problem alone, or the problem is complex, interaction among group members who are likely to possess relevant information is necessary. Thus, decision styles 1, 2 and 3 are eliminated.

R4 *The acceptance rule.* If the acceptance of the decision by subordinates is critical to effective implementation, and if it is not certain that an autocratic decision will be accepted, decision styles 1 and 2 are eliminated.

R5 *The conflict rule.* If the acceptance of the decision is critical, or an autocratic decision is not certain to be accepted, or group members are likely to disagree over the appropriate methods of attaining the organisational goal, efforts should be made to enable those in disagreement to resolve their differences with a full knowledge of the problem. Thus, decision styles 1, 2 and 3, which permit no interaction among subordinates and therefore provide no opportunity for those in conflict to resolve their differences, are eliminated as feasible styles.

R6 *The fairness rule.* If the outcome of the decision is relatively unimportant to the organisation, but the employees' acceptance is critical, and not certain to result from an autocratic decision, it is important that the decision process generates employee acceptance. Group members will need to interact with one another and resolve any differences. In these circumstances, decision styles 1, 2, 3 and 4 are eliminated from the feasible alternatives, leaving only style 5.

R7 *The acceptance priority rule.* If employee acceptance is critical, yet not likely to result from an autocratic decision, and if the group members are motivated to pursue organisational goals, then methods that provide equal partnership in the decision-making process can provide greater acceptance without decision quality. In these circumstances, styles 1, 2, 3 and 4 are eliminated.

Some guidelines for effective group decision making

Eight guidelines can be set down at this stage to help effective group decision making.

1 Groups must understand their purpose and the nature of the problem to be solved. The group must recognise whether they are expected to make a decision that involves an incremental step or whether they are to consider a fundamental change of direction.

2 Effective communication needs to be established, both within the group, and with external stakeholders.

3 It should be recognised that groups can serve organisational purposes (achieving the best possible decision), and individual purposes (satisfying psychological needs). A balance should be sought between these important generic purposes.

4 The group needs to be self-evaluative and flexible; if it is not, there is a risk that it will end up by simply 'rubber stamping' preconceived ideas.

5 A decision reached by the group must be acceptable to its members. If the decision is reached on the basis of a voting majority, there are likely to be 'outliers', who may begin to voice dissent against the group. Of there is no collective commitment to the decision, the functioning of the group will be undermined.

6 The composition of the group should be such that there is a range of complementary skills available. The roles adopted by individual group members will also be important; if possible, all nine of Belbin's group roles should be adopted by members of the team.

7 The group should avoid being dominated by one individual (usually the leader) and make use of the range of skills of its members.

8 The paramount importance of effective group leadership should be recognised, though it is unlikely that there will be one universally appropriate leadership style, or even that the same person will be the most suitable leader in all circumstances.

Summary of the chapter

- The chapter began by distinguishing between formal and informal groups, and identified some of the purposes and essential features of effective work groups, including their role as decision-making units.

- The individual and organisational purposes of formal groups were then explored in greater detail. Groups were seen to have psychological benefits for members of an organisation, which could motivate employees to superior performance.

- The relative merits of group and individual decision making were considered, and it was concluded that the nature of the decision and the context in which it is made are the principal determinants of which is preferable.

- We considered why many formal groups underperform as decision-making units; in particular, we examined situations in which excessive conformity, group cohesion or conflict reduced the effectiveness of the group.
- Research by Belbin, Tuckman and Janis was considered as we looked for ways of enhancing the group's decision-making performance.
- Finally, the importance of the group leader was explored, with particular reference to the contingency models of group leadership of Fiedler and Vroom and Yetton.

Case Study 4: JGH Advertising and Marketing Ltd

Graham Lock, Customised Services Manager of JGH Advertising and Marketing Ltd was contemplating the rapid growth of his department over the two years since he had been promoted to his present position. Eight new, young people had joined the department, all of them business graduates, and, unlike many of the older employees, very capable of producing and handling fairly complex marketing data on behalf of their clients. Indeed, Lock had managed to assemble a team that he felt was capable of taking JGH into new markets, namely generating and selling marketing data, rather than just producing tired old advertisements for regular customers. Above all, he valued their collective input in deciding how to meet the marketing requirements of their growing number of customers.

The team Lock had brought together was a fine group to work with. They were wonderfully self-motivated, and terrifically good company. In fact, they had got into a habit of lunching together fairly regularly at a local wine bar, and, since they often worked later than most of the other employees, they often revisited the wine bar in the evenings too. Lock was pleased to be included in these social gatherings, and had not felt so stimulated, in both his work and his social life, since he had left university. His social involvement with the newest recruits had caused a certain amount of resentment from the long-standing employees within the Customised Services Department, but Lock was always courteous towards the latter, and felt that his closeness to the new team was really in the long term interests of everyone working for JGH.

The brightest of Lock's young recruits was undoubtedly Abigail Inman. Lock was particularly pleased with her appointment because several of the senior managers had favoured a more experienced but less well qualified person, someone more in the traditional mould of the company. Lock had often felt that there had been a degree of resistance to the employment of women at JGH, particularly in key posts. He was pleased that this was a progressive and highly appropriate appointment. Abigail Inman had not only justified her employment, but had performed wonders for the department, developing information systems and complete marketing solutions for clients that had approached the company initially wanting an advertising product. The customers were delighted, and the 'elite team', as they had begun to see themselves, had followed Abigail's lead in finding new solutions for clients' needs. In fact, all eight of the team – nine including Lock – tended to work collectively on these projects, and there was a real buzz of excitement at the way the department was raising the profile of JGH.

There were, however, several of Lock's fellow middle managers who were less than enamoured with the developments that they saw taking place in the Customised Services Department. They felt that demands on their time had increased considerably as a result of having to support the production of Lock's new team and, at the request of these 'young upstarts', they were constantly having to change the way they worked. Some of the older workers felt quite threatened by the pace of change, and in Lock's opinion they deliberately attempted to slow things down. Indeed, Lock had twice found himself having to apologise to clients who had been kept waiting for several weeks for projects to be completed. The youngsters in his charge, however, took it all in their stride, and laughed off the friction with 'the old guard'. Lock always felt better when he was in the company of his talented team, and together they felt vindicated in the group's persistence in trying to transform the work of the Customised Services Department.

As time passed, however, the divisions caused by Lock's team's forging ahead with new ideas became more marked. A small number of (generally younger) members of other departments had begun to join the lunch time and evening gatherings in the wine bar, and an informal network began to develop amongst those who were keen to press ahead with modernising JGH's whole approach to their business. There was a sense of optimism amongst these people, and a growing conviction that the old-timers would eventually have to drag themselves into the twenty-first century or leave the company. The future was with the innovators, and with Graham Lock, who, it was rumoured, had applied to become Director of Marketing in succession to Harold McKenzie, would be retiring in less than a year.

Lock, meanwhile, was feeling pensive. He was sure that he had made the right decision in encouraging his elite team to press ahead with innovative new products; but he was troubled by something, Mr. Haywood, the Chairman, had said at a recent meeting. Mr. Haywood had stressed the importance of creating an organisational culture in which all employees felt involved and committed to their work and to the organisation. It had not occurred to him at the time that his department might be seen as anything less than an example to all the others.

Questions for discussion	
	1 *Comment on the group Lock has assembled in order to meet the needs of the Customised Services Department.*
	2 *How well did the group meet the needs of the organisation and its clients?*
	3 *Apply organisational theory to assess the effectiveness of Lock's new team.*

References

Asch, S. E. (1951) 'Effects of group pressure upon the modification and distortion of judgements,' in Guetzhow, H. (ed.), *Groups, Leadership and Men*, Carnegie Press, New York.

Belbin, R. M. (1981) *Management Teams: Why They Succeed or Fail*, Heinemann, London.

Burns, T., and Stalker, G. M. (1961) *The Management of Innovation*, Tavistock, London.

Fiedler, F. E. (1967) *A Theory of Leadership Effectiveness*, McGraw-Hill, New York.

Handy, C. B. (1985) *Understanding Organisations*, Penguin, London.

Janis, I. L. (1972) *Victims of Groupthink*, Houghton Mifflin, Boston.

McClelland, D. C. (1961) *The Achieving Society*, The Free Press, New York.

Milgram, S. (1974) *Obedience to Authority*, Tavistock, London.

Tuckman, B. (1965) 'Development sequences in small groups', *Psychological Journal*, Vol. 63, pp. 384–99.

Vroom, V. and Yetton, P. (1973) *Leadership and Decision Making*, University of Pittsburgh Press.

Wilson, D. C. and Rosenfeld, R. (1990) *Managing Organisations*, McGraw-Hill, London.

CHAPTER 3

Making decisions: factors that affect an individual's decision style

At the end of this chapter you should:

- be able to outline decision styles;

- understand the factors that can affect decision styles;

- be able to evaluate individual decision styles;

- understand the significance of 'perceptual set' on the decision making process;

- be able to outline the interdisciplinary aspects of decision making; and

- recognise and understand the importance of decision-making factors such as individual behaviour, group behaviour and context.

Introduction

A decision is a choice between alternatives, and hopefully choosing the best alternative to suit the needs of the individual and/or the organisation. It is clear that individuals must make many different kinds of decisions, either for themselves or the organisation they work for. For example, when to take holidays? Which project/task to complete first? What to do at the weekend? During each working day individuals within organisations will be concerned with making many decisions and implementing them. Not every decision will be important but those that are, and have significant consequences either for the individual or the organisation, will be treated differently from those decisions that are deemed of little or no significance. Why should this be the case?

When individuals make decisions they first clarify the nature and relative importance of a problem, and thus the nature of the decision will determine the way in which an individual attempts to deal with the problem, in that some decisions:

- are unique and are not regular in occurrence;
- have more than one possible outcome;
- are inclusive of factors external to the individual;
- are too complex for one person to deal with; or
- are important while others are not.

Making decisions whether as a private individual or as an employee requires consideration of the above points in order for an effective – that is, optimum – decision to be made.

In what ways would you deal with problems that come your way, that is, how would you make and then carry out decisions? The outcomes of the decisions taken will have consequences for not only yourself but also for the organisation. It becomes obvious that an effective decision taken is one that maximises the outcomes for all concerned, at least in theory!

Types of decisions

The way in which an individual approaches a decision may be determined by how much time there is, the extent to which others are or can be involved in the decision process, and the nature of the decision. In this connection, Simon (1960) put forward that decisions could be classified as either 'programmed' or 'non-programmed'.

- *Programmed decisions* are defined as routine and repetitive and can be dealt with through the use of specific handling methods. A programmed decision may, for example, involve the way in which items are to be stored in a warehouse. This can be classified as a routine decision and therefore dealt with in a routine and standard way determined by set guidelines.
- *Non-programmed decisions* can be defined as one-off occurrences and may also be less structured. When restructuring an entire organisation, for example, to what extent should there be redundancies? If such a situation has not occurred before, those faced with the decision would not have any guidelines to operate by. Therefore the decision is one that can be said to be non-programmed with regard to the organisation *per se* and the individual(s) making the decision. Such decisions are obviously more difficult to deal with and will be more problematical for those concerned with the decision.

Programmed and non-programmed decisions must, however, be regarded as being at the opposite ends of a continuum, in that a whole range of decisions may in fact be a combination of the two.

Factors affecting decision-making style

Generally, individuals can use some kind of framework for making decisions such as the one put forward by Stott and Walker (1992). They advocate that for 'deep decisions', namely non-programmed decisions, a six-stage system should be used, as follows.

1 Identify and understand the problem and its causes.

2 Isolate the details of the problem and further define your understanding and desired outcome criteria.

3 Involve those people whom it is advantageous or necessary to involve.

4 Investigate various possible solutions and then evaluate the alternatives for applicability to the decision.

5 Implement and communicate your decision.

6 Inquire into the effectiveness of your decision, review results and think how a similar decision can be improved next time.

The above approach should work when dealing with non-programmed decisions. It does, however, assume rationality in the decision-making process, which dictates that:

- objectives are perfectly clear to all concerned;
- there is perfect knowledge;
- all alternatives are known; and
- outcomes can be predicted.

Unfortunately neither organisations nor individuals operate within such an environment. The reality of any non-programmed decision-making situation is that there is certainly no such thing as perfect knowledge, all alternatives cannot be known, outcomes cannot be predicted with any degree of certainty, and objectives may not be perfectly clear to all concerned. What is then apparent is that decisions cannot be made along the lines of the classical decision-making approach, which assumes that decisions are made in a rational and objective manner. Once again the reality surrounding non-programmed decisions is that decision making can and will be affected by a range of factors that will impact upon the individual making the decision. The factors may range from organisational expectations, individual expectations, motivation, experience, and ability etc, through to organisational constraints and ideological beliefs.

In short, some decisions are straightforward and can be dealt with easily without much thought. Other decisions that are more complex, and by definition non-programmed, require greater consideration because of the range of factors that will influence the way in which an individual deals with such a problem.

Decision styles

Individuals generally could be said to have different decision-making styles.

Schermerhorn (1993) believes that individuals may adopt one of three approaches:

- *problem seeker* – someone who actively seeks out problems;
- *problem solver* – someone who solves problems as they arise;
- *problem avoider* – someone who avoids and/or ignores problem-relevant situations.

As can be seen the attitude of an individual toward involvement in decision making will very much depend on psychological orientation toward active problem solving. It is best perhaps to regard the three approaches as representing a continuum of attitude, where individuals may actually adopt a different mind set dependent on the situation and the other relevant factors as previously outlined. A problem seeker may therefore not always seek solutions to a problem if the process and/or the perceived outcomes may cause, for example, a high level of cognitive dissonance, that is psychological disruption within the individual caused by actions that are not in line with beliefs. The theory goes on to emphasise that individuals aim to reduce such disruption in order to minimise the level of dissonance (Festinger 1957), this will be discussed later in more detail. As well as the individual's attitude toward decision making, ambiguity tolerance will also affect the way in which the individual approaches and makes decisions.

Robbins (1995) believes that four decision styles can be identified that relate an individual's 'way of thinking' to 'tolerance for ambiguity':

- *directive* – low tolerance for ambiguity and a rational way of thinking;
- *analytical* – high tolerance for ambiguity and a rational way of thinking;
- *conceptual* – high tolerance for ambiguity and an intuitive way of thinking; and
- *behavioural* – low tolerance for ambiguity but an acceptance of intuition.

The four styles are based on decisions being related to the way in which an individual thinks – that is, rationality set against the use of intuition, and the desire for consistency and logical order set against inconsistency (ambiguity) of information and ideas. The greater an individual's desire to be rational, the more that individual will seek to be entirely logical in their approach to decision making. Such an approach precludes 'grey' issues that have no clear-cut answers and also assumes, as does the classical approach, that an individual can be entirely logical and ignore other influencing factors.

To what extent is this approach possible when all individuals are subject to a whole range of factors that will influence the way in which decisions are made? In reality such a rational approach, although understandable with regard to being entirely objective, does not, as previously stated, allow for ambiguity and the extent to which non-programmed decisions can be very complex and 'grey' in nature. Once again the very nature of the decision and the context within which the decision is made will determine the approach adopted.

To return to our earlier example, whereby the decision to store items within a warehouse could be deemed to be a programmed decision, such a decision may dictate a directive approach because there is little or no ambiguity and certainly no need to adopt a rational approach to a situation that has predetermined outcomes. Given that context, attitude, ambiguity tolerance and rationality all influence the decision-making process, it is clear that there is no one definitive way that an individual will approach non-programmed decisions.

Individuals therefore do not conform neatly to a particular style of decision making. In reality individuals have dominant tendencies that influence their style of decision making. It is the individual's perception of the context that may finally determine the decision style used – in other words, an individual's 'perceptual set'. Decision-making styles can therefore be said to build upon perception and values and other factors such as context are also relevant. The complex nature of decision making can be illustrated, as shown in Fig. 3.1, by outlining the relationship between tolerance for ambiguity, the need for structure, and logical/relational forces. This relationship will determine the way that an individual approaches decision making, whether it is programmed or non-programmed.

As the level of ambiguity becomes more of an issue, the tolerance level is reduced; the individual will become more directive as there is a desire for a rational and logical approach to be adopted. Conversely, if there is a high tolerance for ambiguity, then a more analytical approach may be adopted. Relational factors will also play a part, as Fig. 3.1 illustrates, in that the degree of ambiguity tolerated will either lead to a conceptual or behavioural bias. Once again the caveat must be that although the model provides a framework for analysing an individual's approach to decision making, it does not provide definitive answers. At best it can act as a model with which to begin to analyse the way that some individuals approach decision making.

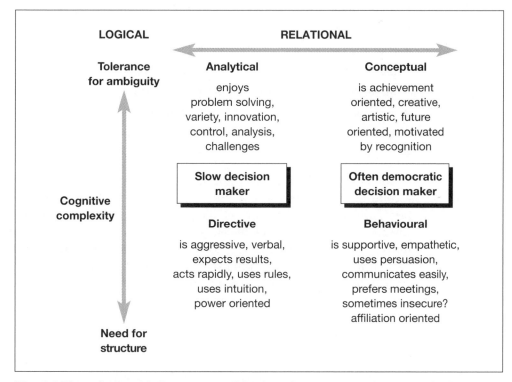

Fig. 3.1 The relationship between ambiguity tolerance, structure, and logical relational forces

The 'perceptual set'

Perception is the way in which individuals interpret information (stimuli) whether written, spoken, or even communicated through body language. Individuals may therefore interpret messages, even the same message, in completely different ways. The process itself can be illustrated by means of a flow diagram, as shown in Fig. 3.2.

Further, Mullins (1996) defines perception very succinctly as

> The process . . . in which information (stimuli) from the environment around us is selected and organised to provide meaning for the individual. Perception is the mental function of giving significance to stimuli such as shapes, colours, movement, taste, sounds, touch, smells, pain, pressures and feelings. Perception gives rise to individual behavioural responses to particular situations.

It is the response to the stimuli that will influence the individual's view as to the importance or otherwise of a decision, which in turn influences the way that the decision will be tackled.

The range of perceptual forces can be summarised as:

- context
- motivation
- personality
- learning
- intelligence
- interests
- emotion
- individual differences
- cultural factors

- reward
- punishment
- goals
- assumptions
- motivation
- instructions
- training
- expectations
- experience

The perceptual forces will determine the way in which an individual perceives incoming information so that stereotypical beliefs, that is, preconceived expectations, are either reinforced or challenged. Information can therefore be difficult to filter so as to reduce bias based on the selection of favoured information that reflects the individual's belief system. It must be remembered that perception is very much concerned with the subjective selection of information. The impact of such subjectivity can have a major impact on the way in which decisions are made in relation to an individual's view of the world.

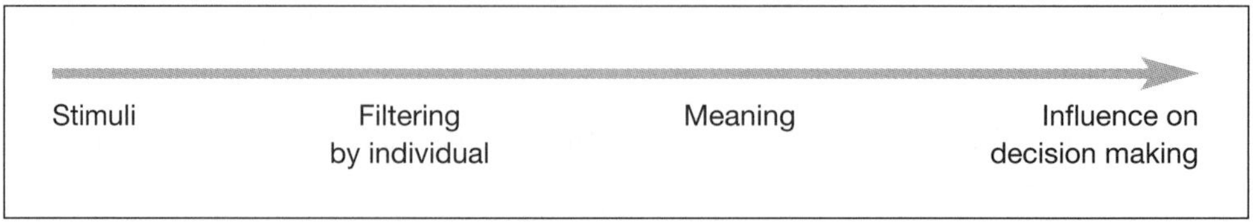

| Stimuli | Filtering by individual | Meaning | Influence on decision making |

Fig. 3.2 The stimulation filtration process

Exhibit 3.1	**Perceptual forces at work**

Imagine that you are faced with making a decision that requires you to decide whether or not to proceed with a project that, although beneficial to your company, could possibly endanger a rare species of spider. How and which perceptual forces would influence your decision? For example, you may decide that one species of spider would not be missed, and then the decision becomes somewhat easier. However, based on your interest in entomology and what you have learned from a recent scientific study, which clearly emphasises the need for ecological balance (especially the preservation of the spider under threat) your decision becomes more informed and therefore possibly more difficult. Your view, based on your interests and learning, is now influenced by your perception, and therefore your perceptual set would be different from that of a colleague unaware of ecological concerns.

This is obviously a somewhat simplistic example but it illustrates the way in which an individual's view of the world, and hence decision making, can be influenced by extra information and individual interests. In this example the individual's 'new' perceptual set would have an influence on the decision-making process and thus even possibly affect the decision that is finally made. The decision-making process has been influenced by external stimuli and does not therefore allow a truly objective and rational decision to be made.

Cognitive dissonance

The previous example also helps to highlight the extent to which an individual can experience cognitive dissonance, namely the state of mind of an individual whose perceptions of related objects, events or circumstances are out of balance. The individual's perceptions are inconsistent in that they do not fit together and the individual feels uncomfortable with the imbalance and is thus anguished (Festinger, 1957).

Usually cognition is constant in that one cognition follows on logically from another. For example, the knowledge that if an individual takes a bath then this is consonant with becoming wet. If, however, the individual takes a bath and does not get wet then he or she would certainly experience cognitive dissonance. Logic dictates that if someone takes a bath they become wet, and not to do so would be very psychologically unsettling: It follows therefore that cognitive dissonance has a number of implications for an individual, these being:

- seeking to change the environment within which they operate in order to eliminate dissonant elements;

- seeking collateral evidence to support initial views;

- changing perceptions and or behaviour to achieve dissonance;

- avoiding views and information that conflicts with the individual's views, thus achieving consonance.

Festinger's (1957) theory of cognitive dissonance deals with the perceptions that people have of themselves in the context of their environment, that is, there is a tendency for individuals to seek consistency among their cognitions (beliefs, opinions and behaviour). When there is inconsistency between attitudes or behaviours, something must change to eliminate the dissonance.

In the case of a discrepancy between attitudes and behaviour, it is most likely that attitude will change to accommodate the behaviour. The conflict that can develop between perception and environment can lead to irrational coping behaviour, which stems from the blocking of motives and unsuccessful rational coping behaviour. The individual moves from a rational search for an informed and objective decision to one that provides consonance equilibrium, albeit based on an irrational approach. The individual adopts a coping behaviour to suit the perceptions held of the context within which the decision has to be made, thus reducing the level of psychological tension.

The number of beliefs and their importance will affect the strength of the dissonance. Individuals can eliminate dissonance by reducing the importance of the dissonant beliefs and/or by changing the dissonant beliefs so that they are no longer inconsistent with what is required of the individual.

Festinger, based on his research of heavy smokers, found that inconsistency is uncomfortable, and that individuals will seek to reduce dissonance, and thus, achieve stable minimum dissonance. He put forward that if smokers, who are aware of the associated health risks, cannot give up smoking, they tend instead to remain sceptical about the harmful effects. In other words, the decision to try and give up will cause psychological tension and cognitive dissonance based on the desire to smoke and the obvious health benefits of giving up. To reduce such tension it is 'easier' for smokers to ignore the health risks and continue smoking. They have not made a rational decision based on clear evidence, but one that is irrational and provides 'safe' consonance equilibrium based on irrational processes. A good decision has been made for the confirmed smoker but a bad decision for those who would accept the evidence of the health risks.

Another example would be someone who buys an expensive boat but discovers that it is not comfortable on long sailing trips. Dissonance exists between their beliefs that they have bough a good boat and that a good boat should be comfortable. Dissonance could be eliminated by deciding that it does not matter since the boat is mainly used for short trips (reducing the importance of the dissonant belief) or focusing on the boat's strengths such as safety, appearance, handling (thereby adding more consonant beliefs). Getting rid of the boat could also eliminate the dissonance, but this behaviour is a great deal harder to achieve than changing beliefs.

The principles of dissonance can thus be summarised as follows:

- Dissonance results when an individual must choose between attitudes and behaviours that are contradictory.
- Reducing the importance of conflicting beliefs, acquiring new beliefs that change the balance, or removing the conflicting attitude or behaviour can eliminate dissonance.

The need for individuals to reduce dissonance and thus 'cope' becomes increasingly important as the factors that are creating the dissonance become more important. Individuals, when determining the degree of importance of the contributing factors, also consider the influence they have over the factors and the rewards that may be forthcoming.

The influence that people believe they have over the contributing factors will influence the degree and relevance of dissonance. For example, if dissonance is brought about by an order from a line manager then the relevance of the dissonance tends to be less than when compared with a persons sole responsibility for making a decision at work. Individuals in this situation rationalise and then justify, internally and externally to themselves, their decision based on lack of control, which therefore reduces the level of dissonance. Quite literally, a case of 'following orders' makes the decision and the resultant outcomes easier to live with.

The level of rewards also has an influence on the level of dissonance, in that high rewards can reduce the tension from high levels of dissonance. The potential for greater rewards creates consistency through the reward justifying the decision; that is, the level of the reward increases the individual's belief that there is consistency between attitudes and behaviour. Therefore, high rewards will not motivate an individual to reduce the level of dissonance, whereas low rewards will.

The impact of these factors will tend to influence the desire to control or alleviate the level of dissonance. If, for example, the decision is believed to be important, the decision maker has control over the decision, and potential rewards are minimal, then the individual will seek to reduce dissonance. This may arise because the individual has control or responsibility over the decision and therefore needs to 'think things through', which in itself creates tension and dissonance.

Perceptual defence

For any more hardheaded manager in the previous example involving the spider, but one who has entomological interests, there is a way out that enables the company's interests to be put first through the use of 'perceptual defence'. Mullins (1996) states that perceptual defence involves the avoidance of uncomfortable stimuli. Individuals will select information that will enable them to make a decision that minimises the degree of cognitive dissonance.

In the example given, the individual could ignore information based on personal interests, and what has been recently learned about the spider, in order to create a perceptual set that favours the interests of the organisation at the expense of ecological concerns. In order for such a decision to be made by the individual in our example, only that information supporting the interests of the company would be selected. Other information such as that dealing with ecological concerns would be ignored, thus allowing the individual to make a decision that fits the organisation's needs. The individual's needs with regard to possible advancement within the company may also be met, assuming that this was a factor in the decision-making process.

In reality, of course, the process of perceptional formation is not as straightforward as the example would have us believe. It does, however, provide a framework for understanding the way in which perception, the filtering process and perceptual defence can influence decision making.

The process of perceptional formation can be refined so as to differentiate between internal and external organisational stimuli. These stimuli extend the range of factors that can influence an individual's perceptual set and once again complicate the decision-making process. The individual then has not only perception of stimuli to contend with, but also internal and external organisational expectations. There are as follows:

Internal

- personal
- organisational goals and objectives

External

- customer expectations
- competition from competitors
- social pressures
- economic pressures
- political pressures
- technological changes

Decision making is, as already stated, a complex process that can create high levels of cognitive dissonance. The very complex and interdisciplinary nature of decision making will therefore influence the way in which an individual makes a decision, that is, the decision style. But before decision styles are discussed, there is a need to consider the interdisciplinary aspects of decision making.

Interdisciplinary aspects of decision making

The interdisciplinary aspects of decision making can be described through the use of four decision-making models.

1 *Rational model.* This has its foundations in the quantitative disciplines of economics, statistics and mathematics. It is a normative model that represents the classical approach to decision making. It is also based on the assumption that the situation can be quantified to some degree. It is a model that operates within an artificial and closed environment.

2 *Organisational model.* This is based on behavioural and quantitative disciplines in order to fit the external environmental constraints. This model aims to exclude uncertainty and create patterns of decision making for future use.

3 *Political model.* This model is behavioural in its orientation. Decision making is aimed at producing outcomes acceptable to external constituencies. Its approach is based on compromise and/or bargaining, and thus moves the decision maker from following an objective-oriented approach.

4 *Process model.* Here we have an objective-oriented approach. This model recognises the interdisciplinary aspects of decision making and does not have a rigid approach to the way in which a decision should be made.

The four models are not 'free' from other factors acting upon them. All decisions will be subject, to a lesser or greater extent, to a range of forces. These forces can include individual behaviour, group behaviour, values, ethics and environmental forces. These forces are cognate to perceptual set and thus decision styles.

Evaluating decision styles

It is perhaps appropriate at this point to consider the ways in which decision styles can be evaluated, and these can be categorised into four possible ways, namely: wrong decision/right approach; wrong decision/wrong approach; right decision/wrong approach; right decision/right approach. In more detail:

- *Wrong decision/right approach.* This means that the decision is one that uses a computational strategy and aims to maximise choice. Computational strategy means choosing among alternatives when there is a high degree of certainty and a strong preference associated with an outcome. Maximising choice involves an approach that is oriented toward obtaining an outcome of the highest quantity or value. In this case the decision will likely be taken that primarily benefits the individual in terms of profile within the organisation. Therefore, the right decision has been taken for the individual but not necessarily the right one for the organisation – hence the wrong decision using the right approach.

- *Wrong decision/wrong approach.* This means that the decision again uses a computational strategy and aims to maximise choice. The approach, however, involves the setting of unattainable objectives and uses a closed decision-making model. A closed decision model is based on a conceptual framework for maximising the outcome of the decision. In this example a decision will be made that solely concentrates on maximising outcomes. The individual excludes other more realistic alternatives that may provide better solutions to the problem. Such an approach can be equated with a 'tunnel vision' approach, where the unattainable objectives set will determine the way that the problem is viewed and it will therefore be tackled so that outcomes can be maximised.

- *Right decision/wrong approach.* This uses a judgemental strategy and is concerned with a satisficing choices' approach. Unobtainable objectives are set and a closed decision model is used. A judgemental strategy is one that involves choosing among alternatives when there is a great deal of uncertainty and a strong preference associated with an outcome. Satisficing choices mean obtaining an outcome that meets the objectives. In this case a decision would be made that reflects the individuals' preferred outcome that enables maximum benefit (satisficing) to be derived even though the objectives have not been met. The right decision has been made in terms of satisficing, but the closed decision approach is wrong in that it excludes the consideration of possible viable alternatives.

- *Right decision/right approach.* Again, this uses judgemental strategy and a satisficing approach to choices. However, attainable objectives are set and an open decision model is used. An open decision model uses a conceptual framework for decision making based on obtaining a satisficing outcome from a given choice. With this approach the individual clearly aims to make a decision that considers all the alternatives because of the degree of uncertainty. The final decision will be one that is realistic and meets the obtainable objectives set, i.e. the final outcome is acceptable to the organisation and the individual and hence it satisfices.

It is once again necessary at this stage to point out that although the four approaches are recognisable in terms of the way that some individuals will make decisions, there can be no absolutes. The context, along with the other factors discussed so far, will determine the approach taken.

Individual behaviour

The basis of behaviour

Behaviour is inherited and learned, and it is thus action resulting from conscious and unconscious processes. Behaviour can therefore be formed, and linked to personality. Individuals are by definition unique and are different in many ways based on personality, attitude and learning. Perhaps it is the behavioural factors that play a dominant role in the decision style adopted by individuals. There is a need, therefore, to examine the influence of individual behaviour on decision making. Firstly, however, there is a need to consider what makes one individual different from another, which can be summarised as follows:

- cultural/social background;
- attitudes;
- motivation;
- perception;
- developmental aspects;
- types/traits;
- abilities;
- gender;
- physique.

The way in which these differences interact make us unique and will therefore play a major part in the way that individuals approach decisions. It can be argued that because of these individual differences no two human beings will approach a given decision situation in the same way. Individuals can therefore be said to have decision style tendencies within which the actual decision-making approach will be different and hence unique.

Constancy of behaviour is another factor that needs to be considered when evaluating the impact of individual behaviour on the decision-making process. Constancy of behaviour may be linked to an individual's experiences and therefore behaviour can be expected to change. And if behaviour can be expected to change then so can an individual's approach to decision making. Figure 3.3 shows the link between experience, individual behaviour and decision style.

Life experiences will have an effect on the individual's attitude toward decision making. Individual differences will determine the way in which decisions are tackled, i.e. the way in which an individual perceives the problem and even the extent to which there is interaction with other individuals involved in the decision-making process. It must be recognised, therefore, that it is not only the behavioural factors that determine an individual's approach to decision making but also the extent of interaction with others. It should not be surprising that the added complexities of behaviour make the decision-making process that much more difficult to define accurately on an individual basis.

Attitude

As mentioned earlier, attitude also plays a part in determining decision styles. The first thing to appreciate is that people hold limitless attitudes and those attitudes are learned throughout life and the socialisation process. Attitudes can be described as either core or peripheral. *Core attitudes* tend to be very resistant to change; *peripheral attitudes* can and will change based on new experiences and information.

Gross (1987) defines attitude as a readiness to respond in a particular way and is equatable with tendencies. Alongside attitude, beliefs and values must also be considered. Beliefs can be defined as those that are known, and values are normative in the sense that they deal with what is desirable or what should, ideally, be the outcome. In the example of the manager who faced making a decision whether or not to benefit an organisation at the expense of a rare species of spider, the ideal outcome would have been value-based. The ideal would have been an outcome where the spider was saved and the organisation was able to maximise the opportunity. In this example, however, the manager had beliefs (because ecological information was readily available), which helped determine the way in which the problem was to be tackled; the manager's attitude was affected.

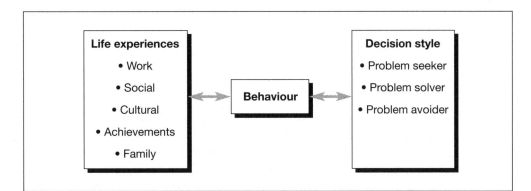

Fig. 3.3 The link between experience, individual behaviour and decision styles

As attitudes become affected by the interaction of beliefs and values, so must an individual's motivation. For example, a very problematical situation bringing on a high level of cognitive dissonance, as may exist in the spider case, may, if we are dealing with a problem avoider, reduce the motivation to tackle the problem. Conversely a problem solver may actually be motivated to seek a novel solution to the problem in order for the spider to be saved and the organisation to benefit.

Katz (1960) put forward that motivation is influenced by attitude, and that attitudes can be either knowledge, expressive, instrumental, or ego-defensive, as described as follows:

- *Knowledge.* This provides a base for the assimilation of new information so that comparisons can be made, as was the case with the manager faced with the spider problem. The manager faced with new information, assuming that he was environmentally aware, would change his decision style and be motivated to do so.

- *Expressive.* This allows the individual to inform others about his or her values. This can be done not only through simple expression but also through the way in which decisions are made, that is, the decision style adopted.

- *Instrumental.* This deals with rewards and sanctions. Such attitudes may be based upon experience, either good or bad, and thus will determine an individual's attitude toward the way in which a decision is made, reflective of the chosen decision style.

- *Ego-defensive.* This allows the individual to hold attitudes that protect her or him from undesirable truths. In the case of making any decision that would involve a high degree of dissonance, it would bring about an attitude that allowed a decision to be made, even though that decision may go against what the individual believed. The spider-problem manager may, faced with the prospect of losing out on promotion, take a decision that would enhance promotion prospects at the expense of the spider. An appropriate promotion-oriented attitude would have been adopted so as to allow the decision to be made.

The way in which a decision is made is going to be reflective of attitude. Attitudes can change and therefore decision style will change in order, depending on the individual, to accommodate the context. Heider (1946) puts forward the view that individuals, when faced with cognitive dissonance, will change attitudes in order to reduce the level of dissonance.

Learning from experience

Finally in this section it is necessary to consider the influence of learning on the decision-making process. Learning is linked to the internal processes of perception, ability, motivation, and attitude. It is also linked to such external factors as environment, relationships, rewards, and punishment. Learning is therefore very much an individual and social process, in that no two individual experiences will be the same or perceived to be the same.

If experiences are linked to the learning process, then an individual's experience of a decision-making situation must have an influence on the way in which future decisions would be made. A good experience of making a decision in a certain way may, assuming that the context was very similar, dictate that the same approach be used in the future, that is, a positive outcome with commensurate rewards would reinforce the decision style used. There is therefore a link between learning, attitude and motivation, all of which will combine through behaviour to determine the decision style adopted by an individual.

The other behavioural forces affecting an individual throughout the decision-making process can be summarised as follows:

- desire and need for achievement, which is important in objective setting;
- perceptual processes, which are important for searching and evaluation of potential alternatives;
- attitude to risk;
- rationalisation of mistakes;
- perceptual bias, which relates to outcomes and the way they are viewed; and
- personality, which may influence the tendency to overreact when the decision is going wrong.

Individuals cannot ignore the psychological forces that act on them and their decision styles. The most that can be done is to be aware of the forces and to adopt strategies for limiting the effects such forces may have on a decision-making process.

Values and ethics

Individuals acquire and alter their values throughout their lives. Values can be said to act as a guide when faced with choices and making decisions. Values are not rigid, and individuals will adjust and compromise their beliefs given different circumstances. Decisions can therefore create moral and ethical dilemmas for an individual if a decision involves conflicting pressures, as faced by the manager in our earlier example concerning the spider.

Values and ethics are intrinsic to making decisions and are constantly reflected both in the decision maker's behaviour and throughout the decision-making process. The role of ethics therefore involves making value judgements in relation to the following range of actions:

- setting objectives;
- developing alternatives;
- implementing the decision;
- taking corrective action.

The socially responsible decision maker aims to be effective in terms of beliefs held and the efficient use of organisational resources. An assessment would be made as to the positive and negative outcomes for society, the organisation and the individual making the decision. The desire on the part of an individual to be ethical in the socially responsible sense can perhaps create the greatest difficulties with regard to cognitive dissonance. Returning once again to the spider problem, it can be seen how a socially responsible manager would be faced with quite a dilemma, especially if promotion was dependent on the project going ahead at the expense of the spider. If the organisation were itself socially responsive, then the decision would obviously reflect that; if, however, the organisation did not have any such policy, there would be a problem in that the manager would either have to sacrifice promotion or sacrifice the spider. What then should the manager do?

The answer perhaps lies in the strategy that the individual uses to minimise dissonance that such a situation may cause. The individual may change attitudes held in order to accommodate the context (Heider, 1946) or simply stick to the socially responsible values held.

Group behaviour

An individual's personal values will merge into a broad range of social values. The social values of groups are based on sociology and social psychology. These two disciplines are important to the decision-making process in that they:

- reflect the individual's personal and social goals and the way in which they are modified in order to avoid conflict and thus reach consensus;
- reflect the individual's values and bear direct relation to the group's objectives.

Individuals' are subject to group psychological forces when making decisions. Such forces create complex patterns that arise from the necessity to add personal psychological factors to the sociological factors, thus affecting the way in which decisions are made. The values held by the group will therefore be picked up by individuals and incorporated into their decision style so as to reflect the group's decision style and norms. Experience and learning will be part of the socialisation process and thus shape individual attitudes within the group, which in turn will have an effect on behaviour and decision styles.

Decision scope

The organisational decision-making environment influences the selection of objectives, constrains the scope of search and the development of alternatives, and will therefore directly affect the acceptance of a decision style. The scope of the decision is perhaps the main deciding factor that influences the way that decisions are made and by whom. Decision scope can be defined as the extent to which a management system will be affected by a decision, that is; a broad decision scope will tend to affect higher-level management, whereas a narrow decision scope will tend to affect lower-level management.

The level at which a manager operates, combined with the preferred decision style, may therefore determine the way in which a problem is dealt with. Some middle managers who have a problem seeker/expressive approach to decision making may be inclined to adopt a problem-solving approach to reflect this, if this in turn reflects the decision-making style prevalent within the organisation. The prevalence of a particular decision-making style will be linked to the organisation's culture (which is discussed in Chapter 1).

Broad external decision-making factors

The forces that operate on a broader scale, and external to the organisation, within the decision-makers environment will include anthropology, political forces and law. These forces will be incorporated into the decision-making process and therefore influence the decision style adopted. The decision maker may find it very difficult, if not illegal with regard to the dimension of law, to ignore these forces – forces that can have a strong influence on the individual.

In slightly more detail, the three forces are as follows:

- *Anthropology*. This includes customs, folkways, the traditions and mores of society, and religious and cultural backgrounds. These forces tend to act externally on the acceptance of the outcome of a decision.

- *Political*. This covers groupings that have political power, such as political parties, unions, professionals, educators, the civil service, etc. Such groupings must be borne in mind by decision makers to ensure that decision outcomes are successful in that they do not go against any changes in political sentiment (for example, environmental issues or changes in social values generally).

- *Law*. Decision makers must consider relevant legislation that may influence their decision.

Internal organisational decision-making factors

The internal organisational forces an individual faces when making a decision also have to be incorporated within the decision-making process. These factors cover:

- significance to the organisation;
- significance to the individual;
- effect on the organisation's employees;
- cost;
- long-term effects on the organisation;
- risk;
- certainty conditions;
- uncertainty conditions, and
- level of responsibility.

As well as these factors, the degree to which the decision is denoted as programmed and non-programmed will be important. It could be argued that senior managers tend to face non-programmed decisions, which therefore require a custom-made solution; managers at lower levels and with less responsibility tend to face programmed decisions that can be dealt with in a routine way.

The range of factors and styles in decision making

Thus so far there are a range of factors affecting an individual's chosen decision style, as summarised as follows:

- programmed/non-programmed decision split;
- decision-making attitude;
- ambiguity tolerance;
- rationality;
- perceptual set, forces, and defence;
- behaviour;
- attitude;
- learning from experience;
- values and ethics;
- group influence;
- external environmental factors, and
- internal organisational factors.

These factors are not necessarily mutually exclusive and will come into play at different times and to differing extents. It is, however, an inescapable fact that these factors will influence the way in which individuals make decisions, depending on the way in which the decision context is perceived.

Generally there is no absolute decision style for most individuals. Aroba (1978) identified six decision-making styles.

1 *No thought*

2 *Compliant* with expectations from outside

3 *Logical,* careful and objective evaluation of alternatives

4 *Emotional* decision made on basis of wants or likes

5 *Intuitive,* the decision simply seemed right and/or inevitable

6 *Hesitant,* slow and difficult to feel committed.

Within the six styles, four were used frequently by individuals and could be ranked in the following way:

- *Logical* – used most often and for work-related decisions rather than personal ones.
- *No thought* – more often used for unimportant decisions.

- *Emotional* – used for quite important decisions.
- *Intuitive* – used for very important decisions.

The degree to which an individual uses any or all of the four main styles identified by Aroba can be linked to the degree to which the decisions are programmed and/or non-programmed. Figure 3.4 shows the relationships between problem type, individual level of responsibility in the organisation and the decision style used.

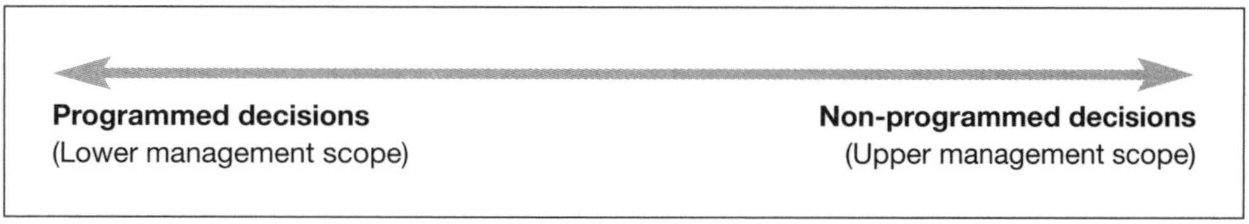

Programmed decisions
(Lower management scope)

Non-programmed decisions
(Upper management scope)

Fig. 3.4 The relationship between problem type and level of responsibility

As an alternative viewpoint to Aroba's, Janis and Mann (1977) identified five styles that are related to decision making. This analysis emphasises the role that psychological conflict plays in determining an individual's decision style. Janis and Mann believe that the conflict can range from unconflicted adherence to vigilance, as shown in Fig 3.5.

The five styles can be described further as follows:

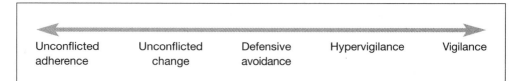

| Unconflicted adherence | Unconflicted change | Defensive avoidance | Hypervigilance | Vigilance |

Fig. 3.5 Continuum of psychological conflict inherent in decision-making styles

- *Unconflicted adherence* – the decision maker continues with the existing course of action, ignoring potential risks.
- *Unconflicted change* – the decision maker embarks on whatever new course of action is in their mind at the time, without evaluating it.
- *Defensive avoidance* – the decision maker avoids the decision by delaying it or denying responsibility.
- *Hypervigilance* – the decision maker desperately reaches for a solution, and seizes on the first one that seems to offer quick relief.
- *Vigilance* – the decision maker searches carefully for relevant information and weighs it up in an unbiased fashion.

Underlying these 'coping' strategies are three factors:

- awareness or unawareness of risks associated with an alternative;
- optimism or pessimism about finding an acceptable alternative; and
- belief that there is, or is not, enough time in which to make the decision.

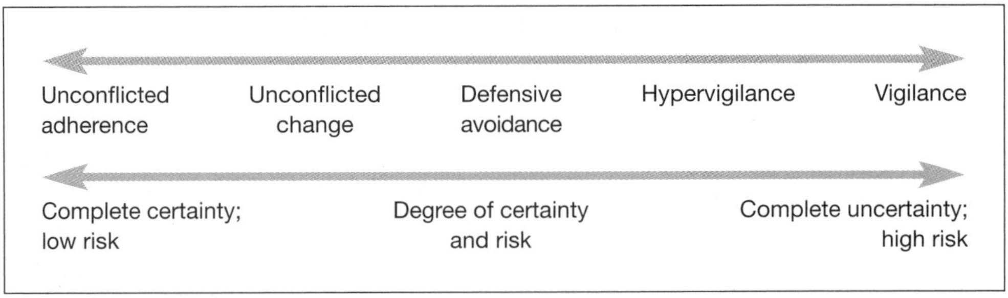

Fig. 3.6 The relationship between the degree of certainty and associated risks

A Continuum of Psychological Conflict could therefore be designed to incorporate awareness of risk and degree of certainty, as shown in Fig. 3.6. This diagram illustrates the possible relationship between the degree of certainty and associated risks that may, through the individual's perception of a problem, dictate an appropriate decision style. The individual therefore, through the perception of the degree of risk certainty, time available and the general context, will adopt a decision style that allows the individual to make a choice that provides a solution, while at the same time reducing the level of cognitive dissonance.

For example, a programmed low-risk/low-level decision may dictate an approach that reflects unconflicted adherence because of the perceived degree of complete certainty. Conversely a non-programmed, high-risk, high-level decision would dictate a vigilant approach due to the overall level of uncertainty.

An individual's decision style is therefore subject to a range of psychological and social forces that determine the approach to be adopted. The way an individual actually solves a problem, beyond taking account of the forces discussed, is then determined by the extent to which the individual's management style is autocratic or democratic.

Vroom (1973) put forward that managers may adopt the following decision styles as represented by Fig. 3.7.

An autocratic individual solves a problem or makes a decision using information available at the time. The necessary information is obtained from subordinates and a solution to the problem is individual. In obtaining the information from subordinates, those individuals may or may not be told what the problem is; the role of subordinates is therefore simply one of providing necessary information rather than generating or evaluating alternative solutions. The consultative approach

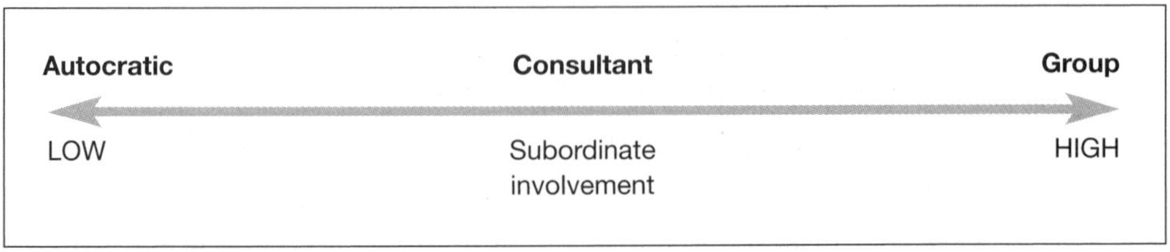

Fig. 3.7 Decision style continuum

involves sharing the problem with relevant subordinates individually, but getting their ideas and suggestions separately without bringing them together as a group. The decision made may or may not reflect the subordinates' influence. However, the problem may be shared with subordinates as a group, collectively obtaining their ideas and suggestions. Again, the decision may or may not reflect the subordinates' influence. The third aspect, group decision making, involves openly sharing the problem with subordinates as a group. Alternatives are generated and evaluated collectively in an attempt to achieve consensual agreement.

The style of leadership adopted by an individual can therefore act alongside the other decision forces in determining the way in which an individual makes and implements decisions. An autocratic individual, for example, faced with a non-programmed high-risk decision would use subordinates as a source of information only while displaying a vigilant approach.

At this point it is perhaps timely to remember that there are no absolutes in the way individuals make decisions, only, perhaps at best, tendencies.

Summary of the chapter

- Decision-making styles may be determined by the individual's approach to problems, namely as a problem seeker, problem solver, problem avoider.

- An individual's tolerance for ambiguity will be a decision-style factor alongside rational thinking.

- An individual's 'perceptual set' in relation to the decision context will affect the perception of the decision's importance.

- There are broader interdisciplinary factors that affect the decision maker, namely, individual behaviour, group behaviour, values and ethics, and environment.

- The decision style adopted by an individual will not be absolute but show a tendency towards a style. The style chosen may reflect the context.

Case Study 5: Simplex

Simplex, a leading manufacturer of components for the aerospace industry, is attempting to change the way its employees make decisions. A rapidly changing technological environment demands that Simplex employees must take a proactive approach to the adoption and incorporation of technology if the company is to remain competitive.

During its first 14 years, Simplex produced major breakthroughs in aeronautical engineering technology. Simplex, however, faced one major problem in that it was not wholly effective in quickly transferring its research and design efforts into production.

William Davies, chairman of the company, has recently stated that although Simplex has gained a well earned reputation for developing new approaches, it has recently let itself down in not turning ideas into tangible results quickly enough and has therefore begun to lag behind competitors. Something was wrong with the way Simplex approached turning research into viable products quickly enough. Davies believed that if an improvement in the aspect of the company's performance were to be achieved, employees would need to overcome their own decision-making biases. Simplex employees seemed, at least to Davies, to ignore any ideas that did not fit their decision-making perceptions.

Davies therefore has decided to instigate a programme that aims to identify the decision-making problems that he believed are evident within Simplex. He has discovered thereby that many employees defined technology in a rather limited way and that a large number of employees framed research and development decisions only in terms of the physical sciences. Davies has also discovered that the way employees interact with technology has effects on productivity. Davies believes that there is a clear need, based on his findings, to create an environment where employees move beyond the usual view of technology as simply hardware and software. There is a clear need for assessing the use of technology in creating new and more efficient ways of working, and to see technology as incorporating social-science factors.

Davies' new attitude towards a broader definition of technology has led him to believe that the defined role of research and development at Simplex is too narrow, and that more research should be undertaken at shop-floor level. Findings have shown a greater need to involve shop floor staff in the research process. This clearly means undertaking research at shop-floor level as opposed to the present system of basing it solely within the Research and Development Department. All employees therefore are to be encouraged to think of themselves as integral to the research and development process.

If Simplex employees can overcome their old decision-making biases, they should be able to better integrate new research into effective product development. Davies has moved quickly to change the way in which decisions are made, by improving and updating the company's decision-making processes. He has put forward a new approach, which incorporates a greater understanding of how people interact with technology. The challenge now is how to get employees to frame decisions about how technology could be better used in the development of new products.

Questions for discussion	1 *Simplex is aiming to provide the company's employees with new tools for decision making based around the involvement of individual workers. Is this approach best used for programmed or non-programmed decisions?*
	2 *What barriers to individual decision making do you find in this case? Are any of these barriers reduced by the new decision-making strategy being offered by Davies' new approach?*

Case Study 6: Samantha's dilemma

Samantha Richards had been in her present position for six months. She is now facing her first important decision; what production targets to set for next year? She knows that this decision presents her with the opportunity to be noticed and increase her profile within the company. She has one week to submit her figures and feels pressured for time.

Samantha is convinced that consensual decision making is the best way to make decisions and that her staff should be involved in all decisions. She has therefore called a meeting with all nine of her staff and presented them with the production target problem that needs to be made, what should the target figures be for next year?

Samantha has her own ideas but believes the figures could be more realistic. She announces at the meeting that she wants their involvement in the decision for setting the targets. She is surprised at the comments that are made: 'They're too high now. They should stay the same.' 'Our output can be doubled if you follow my suggestions.' 'We're already overworked and understaffed.' 'We need new equipment.' 'Do we get any extra money?' 'We could produce more if everyone did their fair share of the work.'

The meeting goes on in this vein and breaks up without any decision being made. Samantha then meets her staff once more. She has to have her targets submitted by Thursday, only three days away. She can see that her preferred consensual approach to decision making is not going to work and she therefore decides to get the staff to vote on the targets.

On Tuesday she asks for the vote and insists that the target be higher than this year. She says she will go along with the majority. The staff vote, six of the nine employees vote for a four per cent increase over last year's targets; the rest leave the meeting feeling that the targets are too high.

Samantha is staggered, as the other units have all set targets of at least nine per cent over this year's figures. She had hoped for at least the same increase in her unit, and is unsure as to what to do. She is now faced with another major decision in that she can either impose the targets, which involves disregarding the involvement of her staff which she had previously encouraged, or simply tell the boss that she is proposing only a four per cent increase. Either way, it is a no win situation for her.

Questions for discussion	1 *Which decision method do you think Samantha should have used?*
	2 *Could she have used a different approach?*
	3 *Did Samantha make any mistakes when trying to involve her staff? If so, what were they?*

References

Aroba, T. Y. (1978) 'Decision making style as a function of occupational group, decision content and perceived importance', *Journal of Occupational Psychology*, Vol. 51, pp. 219–26.

Festinger, L. A. (1957) *A Theory of Cognitive Dissonance*, Row, Peterson and Co. Reissued by Stanford University Press and Tavistock Publications (1962).

Gross, R. D. (1987) *Psychology: The Science of Mind and Behaviour*, Edward Arnold, London.

Heider, F. (1946) 'Attitudes and cognitive organization', *Journal of Psychology*, 21, pp. 102–7.

Janis, I. L. and Mann, L. (1977) *Decision Making: A Psychological Analysis of Conflict, Choice and Commitment*, Free Press, New York.

Katz, D. (1960) 'The functional approach to the study of attitudes', *Public Opinion Quarterly*, 21, pp. 163–204.

Mullins, L. J. (1998) *Management of Organisational Behaviour*, Financial Times Pitman Publishing, London.

Robbins, S. P. (1995) *Supervision Today*, Prentice-Hall, Englewood Cliffs, New Jersey.

Schermerhorn, J. R. (1993) *Management for Productivity*, Wiley, New York.

Simon, H. A. (1960) *The New Science of Management Decision*, Harper & Row, New York.

Stott, K. and Walker, A. (1992) *Making Management Work. A Practical Approach*, Prentice-Hall, Singapore.

Vroom, V. (1973) 'A new look at managerial decision making', *Organisational Dynamics*, Spring, p. 67.

CHAPTER 4

The role of judgement and intuition in decision making

At the end of this chapter you should:

- be able to define judgement;

- appreciate the forms that judgement can take;

- understand the need to de-bias judgement;

- understand the link between professionalism and judgement;

- appreciate the influence of experience and expertise on the use of intuition and judgement;

- be able to define intuition; and

- understand how managers use intuition.

Introduction

This chapter will discuss the role and appropriateness of judgement and intuition alongside rational decision making, and its influence on the way in which individuals make decisions.

Classical decision-making approaches regard decision making as a rational process. The assumption is that decision makers think and act objectively and are assumed to have perfect knowledge, at least in theory, with regard to alternatives and possible consequences. Such writers as Simon (1951), who put forward the concept of bounded rationality, and Lindblom (1959), who argued in favour of incrementalism, have since the 1950s challenged the classical approach.

Since this original questioning of the classical approach, a more critical stance has shown that decision making can be affected by a range of factors, as discussed elsewhere in the book, including judgement and intuition. It can be accepted that although rationality does play an obvious part in the decision-making process and is important in providing a logical framework by which the decision maker can begin to make a decision, it is not necessarily the sole factor. For example, Porter (1985) argues that decisions are based on analysis, which again one can readily accept as being logical. Critics of this view argue, however, that decisions are not necessarily rational in that they have limited information and that direction toward a decision emerges based on experience and experimentation (Quinn 1989). It is the experiential aspect of the decision-making process that perhaps provides the decision maker with different insights that enables the individual to go beyond the logical framework demanded by the rational approach.

In relation to the perceived benefits to using the rational approach to decision making, Morgan (1996) maintains that, 'Decisions, it seems, often become rational only as we use hindsight to rationalise and explain them.' If this view is accepted in its entirety, then rational decision making becomes valid only as a means of supporting and justifying a decision that has achieved a 'good' result. The implication of such a view is that the rational decision-making approach is not perhaps truly rational, as defined by theory, and thus the use of judgement and intuition is as valid as any other form of rational decision making.

Judgement: some definitions

Lawrence and Elliott (1985) refer to management as including

> the more intuitive processes of judgement involved in making decisions without 'perfect' information, where there are uncertainties involved, where effects of action have to be estimated, and where plans for an unknown future have to be drawn up.

The degree of uncertainty will therefore determine the extent to which judgement is used as part of the decision-making process.

Judgement and intuition can be very useful, therefore, when an individual is faced with conditions of uncertainty or if the situation is new. Agor (1986) for example discussed the value of judgement in relation to a situation that is complex and pressurised and where there are several alternatives available. The non-routine decision, for example, at the strategic level may well incorporate a whole range of variables that do not lend themselves to the use of rational and mechanistic decision making. The use of judgement and/or intuition based on experience may therefore prove to be more useful as a means of making a decision.

Mescon, Albert and Khedouri (1988) believe judgement is useful when decisions tend to recur frequently: if the context is the same, then what has worked once will work equally well again. It was also argued by them (1988) that because a judgemental decision is made within the manager's mind it has the added advantage of being quicker. They went on to state that judgement was not relevant in a situation that was truly new because judgement is almost always based on experience; a lack of experience precludes the use of judgement.

Stoner (1982), when discussing the link between judgement and experience, suggested that when judgement is used when the context is the same or similar, it is nothing more than 'relying on tradition.' If it is 'tradition' then it is not, as the authors are suggesting, judgement but merely a repetition of past experiences that allow the same decision to be made – in other words, a case of history, and therefore the decision, repeating itself.

Drucker (1982) put forward that

> A decision is a judgement. It is a choice between alternatives. It is rarely a choice between right and wrong. It is at best a choice between 'almost right' and 'probably wrong'… more often a choice between two courses of action, neither of which is probably more nearly right than the other.'

What is interesting about this view is that it again recognises the degree of uncertainty inherent in almost all decisions, which therefore calls for the use of judgement to some degree or other. The degree of uncertainty is therefore identified as the determinant of whether or not judgement is to be used, which supports Agor's view. This is obviously still only justifying the use of judgement, but it does clearly recognise the need to incorporate it into the decision-making process.

Stoner (1982), in countering Drucker's view, argued that the rational approach, which by definition would or should preclude the use of judgement is '… more likely … to come up with high-quality solutions…'. Such a view places great reliance on the logical and rational use of information, which supposedly lends itself to the selection of the most satisfactory solution. The problem with this view is that it does not readily recognise that in order to be rational there must be a high degree of certainty with regard to, for example, the information available, correct identification of the problem, and objective analysis of the facts. To what extent is this possible, given that decision-making situations are different and human beings are involved?

Peters and Waterman (1982) were quite strong in their condemnation of the emphasis placed on the use of rationality within decision making. They stated that

> … we deplore the unfortunate abuse of the term 'rational'. Rational means sensible, logical, reasonable, a conclusion flowing from a correct statement of the problem … it's missing all that messy human stuff, such as good strategies that do not allow for persistent old habits, implementation barriers and simple human inconsistencies.

Although Peters and Waterman were not directly arguing in favour of the use of judgement, they were recognising that decision making could not be entirely rational because of the human dimension. It is the human dimension that limits the extent, as discussed in previous chapters, to which such things as personal experience can be ignored.

How then can 'judgement' be defined? Bazerman (1990) defines judgement as 'the cognitive aspects of the decision-making process'. It is also perhaps the complexity of a problem that dictates the use of judgement based on experience, which is supported by Bazerman's view that it is part of the cognitive process within decision making. Contrary to this view, however, Dale and Michelon (1966) put forward that 'management is not an exact science like physics or chemistry. Although many things have been discovered about it, it is essential that the manager use judgement, based on good sense and experience.' What is interesting about this view is the relationship made between 'good sense' and 'experience', which ties in with the use of judgemental experience. Although Dale and Michelon are not advocating intuitive management *per se* they do recognise the role of experience, and perhaps the part it has to play in the exercising of judgement.

It also needs to be borne in mind that, as Mintzberg, Quinn and Ghoshal (1998) point out, there are organisations that almost *demand* that individuals use their judgement. They state that 'Professional organisations are distinguished by the fact that the determination of the basic mission – the specific services to be offered and to whom – is in good part left to the judgement of professionals as individuals.' They go on to state, 'That, however, does not quite constitute full autonomy, because there is a subtle but not insignificant constraint on that power. Professionals are left to decide on their own because years of training have ensured that they will decide in ways generally accepted in their profession.' Professionals develop their judgementally skills, therefore, through training and experience, whether it is organisationally or socially based. The point being made is that they have acquired years of experience, which enables them to use their judgement, and it is accepted as one way in which they can legitimately make decisions.

Not only has management over the years aimed to become more professional with the desire to exercise autonomy and judgement but also, through 'downsizing', decision making has been devolved to lower levels within organisations. This process of devolvement has, at least for some, brought with it greater autonomy and responsibility. The consequence of this for employees is that they are now required to exercise judgement either as individuals or as part of a group, in that they are expected to know 'the right thing to do' – to act in a 'professional' manner without necessarily having had the training or experience to do so!

Forms of judgement

The complexity of organisational life means that judgement is now possibly exercised on more matters with greater consequences, and a greater extent to which individuals are required to take and implement important decisions is now more commonly the case. Although objective mathematical decision-making tools (some quite sophisticated, such as linear programming, queuing theory, network analysis, probability theory and decision trees) do exist to aid the decision-making process, such tools only help in the accumulation and selection of information and its analysis. Such tools are clearly useful when dealing with quantitatively based decisions; however, they have limited use when decisions involve qualitative issues. Other nonmathematical methods could include game theory, simulation, 'jury of opinion', inventory models, economic analysis, causal modelling and the Delphi technique.

Many approaches to decision making therefore place great emphasis on the application of quantifiable data. In this way the decision is based on a calculation of what is likely to be the best outcome, based on probabilities, cash-flow forecasts or other numerical data. Although there is a superficial attraction in such a scientific (or perhaps pseudo-scientific) approach, it tends to ignore the philosophical aspects of decision making. A local authority, for example, might calculate that it would be economically efficient to close a particular primary school and bus the children to another school nearby; but such a decision is in all probability affected by the values of both those making the decision and broader stakeholder groups. Values act as a guidance system when faced with choices and serve as a yardstick for determining desirable or acceptable ends, and means to those ends.

The source of values may come from an individual's religious, moral or political beliefs. Sometimes individuals may find their values conflict with those of the organisation and therefore sometimes a difficult compromise has to be reached. Value judgements, therefore, are an important part of the decision-making process. If value judgements are equated with subjectivity, it must be realised that decision making can be a very subjective process. In short, facts are frequently open to interpretation.

It does, however, need to be recognised that even though judgement can be an important part of the decision-making process, most managers do perhaps place greater emphasis on the logical approaches, either mathematical or non-mathematical, to decision making. This may be because they can be more easily defended, that is, they are deemed to be tangible and facts are more difficult to argue with, as opposed to 'gut reaction', which is sometimes indefinable.

Experience can be used in order to move away from solely using a hard scientific approach to decision making. The uses of such an approach will, perhaps, be dependent on the conditions of certainty, or uncertainty, evident in the decision-making process. Hofstede (1981), when discussing the relationship between control, certainty and decision making, defined six forms of control (see below), each of which can be linked to the way in which individuals exercise judgement, in that the degree of control will determine the extent of freedom and whether there is a need to exercise judgement.

Hofstede put forward that control could be exerted in a number of ways, namely through:

- the degree of ambiguity in the objectives to be achieved;
- the measurability of the performance to be controlled;
- the extent to which the outcomes of activities are known; and
- the degree to which the activity is repetitive.

Hofstede defined his six identified forms of control as follows:

- *Routine control.* There is no ambiguity in objectives, the consequences of performance are accurately measurable, causal links are clear-cut so that actions are known, and the activity being controlled is repetitive. Control is automatic negative feedback, therefore: information concerning deviation between desired and actual outcome is fed back into the decision-making process to remove the deviation. An automated system to control inventory levels is a good example. Such control therefore does not require much thought and hence does not call for the exercising of judgement to any great degree, if at all.

- *Expert control.* This relates to the planning/monitoring approach in which actual outcomes are reported against projections. Individuals then discuss the differences and identify what to do to remove them. This situation begins to require the manager to exercise some judgement, depending of course on the degree of difference between the actual outcomes and the projections.

- *Trial and error.* This approach, as the term suggests, involves discovering the effects of interventions through trial and error, which is possible because actions are repetitive. Consequences and an analysis of actions are deemed to be part of the learning process. Judgement can therefore be exercised in relation to what has been learned from the experience and incorporated into the decision-making process.

- *Intuitive control.* With this form of control, objectives are unambiguous, performance is measurable, actions are not repetitive, and outcomes are not known. The individual is faced with a situation that, although it has clear objectives, the very fact that outcomes are unknown and there is no opportunity for repetition in order to learn makes it difficult to call upon past certainties. Control may therefore only be intuitive, art as opposed to science as, here are few rules to guide the decision maker.

- *Judgemental control.* With this approach activity is not repetitive, outcomes are unknown and not measurable, but objectives are clear. Under such conditions control has to take a subjective judgemental form. The individual is required, because of the high degree of uncertainty, to exercise judgement based on what has been learned through experience and relate it to the present situation requiring a decision.

- *Political control.* This relates to unique situations where objectives are unclear and outcomes and actions are not measurable or known. The only control possible is political, which uses power, negotiation, persuasion and manipulation through rituals and symbols. Under such circumstances the decision maker is unable to exercise rational judgement and in its place has to play political games as a means of getting people to accept or make a decision. A decision, based on the judgement of the individual, has been taken to use political means because the situation will not allow for any other decision-making approach to be used.

It is worth noting that, as Hogarth (1980) put forward, individuals exercise two forms of judgement which can be deemed to be common to most, if not all, decision situations:

- People make value judgements by which they express preferences – for example, one kind of car in preference to another.

- People make predictions that reflect what they expect to happen – for example, the way people may react to what is said or done.

Individuals exercise judgement on a daily basis. Such decisions can either be routine or non-routine, and the same can be said with regard to decision making within organisations. It is perhaps the non-routine decisions that lend themselves more to the use of judgement based on intuition, especially if the problem requires innovative solutions. The following example aims to illustrate the complexity involved when exercising judgement.

Exhibit 4.1

Weston Engineering

On Friday afternoon Mr Richards, the personnel director of Weston Engineering, decided that the purchasing manager, Mrs Wilson, was not up to the job and that she should be removed and replaced by Mrs Graham. How should this situation be handled?

The five options open to Mr Richards were:

1 move Wilson to another department, with the consequence that she would be worse elsewhere;

2 early retirement in accordance with the early-retirement pension scheme, but she is two years below the minimum age;

3 give her notice and let her go, but over the years she has served the company well even if she has not changed as the company has changed;

4 send her on another training course, but this has been tried before and failed and she does have a wealth of experience gained through 18 years of service with the company; or

5 move her sideways to act in an advisory role only and thus support Mrs Graham during the changeover period without having executive power.

Richards decided that the last option was the most positive in terms of outcomes and consequences for the individuals involved and the company. In reaching this decision Richards has exercised three forms of judgement (Vickers 1983):

● Reality judgement – that is, revision of the current state of reality in relation to the first three options;

● Action judgement – which involves moving from reality to action, that is, when judgements are made concerning what to do about the reality, as in the fourth option;

● Value judgement – that is, the judgement of which results are the most desired as, in the final option.

As can be seen from this example, judgement is integral to the decision-making process and can be regarded as essential when dealing with complex situations, especially if they involve consequences with regard to the human dimension. Of the three forms of judgement, it is value and reality judgements that are the most important; action judgement is only used through the relationship and interaction of value and reality judgement. The person doing the judging of course determines the value attached to each phase of the process!

Bias in judgement

Any individual exercising judgement should, of course, aim to eliminate any bias in order to reach as rational a decision as possible. Individuals therefore need to learn either to avoid or to control their own biases. It can be argued that judgement and decision making are fundamental to effective managerial practice, and therefore understanding the decision-making process and its potential for bias will help to improve managerial judgement.

The three main causes of bias can be attributed to:

- probability estimation;
- outcome evaluation;
- communication process.

These causes are not mutually exclusive and can impact upon the way in which an individual may exercise judgement.

Probability estimation can lead to bias when assumptions are false and when they lead to neglect of base information in estimating probability. For example, information X may be characteristic of problem Y and less characteristic of problem Z leading a manager to make diagnosis Y, but if the prevalence of Z is higher than that of Y a diagnosis of Z may be more appropriate. In this example the wrong decision, based on judgement, has been made because appropriate base-rate information has been ignored or not used.

Estimating the probability of the occurrence of X on the basis of how readily instances of X can be recalled can also lead to bias when certain events are more readily remembered. For example, individuals tend to overestimate their chances of dying from causes that can be easily envisaged, such as car accidents. Individuals may also adjust their point of view by relating to an anchor or comparison point. This can therefore lead to bias because the adjustment is inappropriate. For example, if a manager is asked to estimate how many employees are taking too many tea breaks per 100 workers, he will probably arrive at a figure that is higher in absolute terms than if he were asked to rate the incidences per 1000 employees.

Outcome evaluation bias can occur, for example, when the context has an effect on the evaluation of potential outcomes, in that different decisions can be made in response to similar problems when the decision is seen in a different light. A given outcome could be expressed either as a major gain or a major loss, and if this is then also influenced by the degree of certainty the decision maker's judgement could be influenced. The effect of certainty relates to the decision maker being prepared to accept sure gains, as opposed to taking a risk in order to achieve even higher gains or possibly taking a risk that may involve loss in order to avoid a guaranteed loss. The point being made is that the decision maker's perception of the possible outcomes will have an effect on the way in which judgement is exercised.

Communication process bias relates to the way that messages, verbal, written or visual, are perceived by the recipient. An effective message needs to be accurately perceived by the recipient, which involves encoding. Encoding can be defined as the process by which the sender effectively translates information so that the recipient can easily and clearly receive and understand the message. If the message is not encoded correctly, problems can occur because the recipient either does not receive the full message, the message is poorly communicated, or the message is in fact biased.

Campbell (1958) identified three distinct ways in which messages can become poorly encoded, namely condensation, accentuation and assimilation, defined as follows:

- *Condensation* is the process whereby successive encoders inadvertently or deliberately shorten the message.
- *Accentuation* is the process of exaggerating differences and even possibly, again either inadvertently or deliberately, omitting information.
- *Assimilation* involves the distortion of information so that it reflects the sender's or receiver's attitudes, beliefs or knowledge.

If encoding is important with regard to trying to eliminate the poor receipt of a message, in order to avoid bias, then the role of decoding is equally, if not more, important. Decoding can be defined as the process by which the message is perceived and interpreted by the recipient. The accurate interpretation of the message is therefore fundamental to the recipient clearly understanding the information received, which in turn helps in the decision-making process, especially if judgement is to be exercised. By recognising the potential for bias in information, however communicated, it should enable the decision maker to begin to be aware of its existence and then to develop a strategy to eliminate or at least reduce it.

A strategy for reducing bias can be defined as including the following:

- Be aware of the possibility of bias.
- Identify the source and the direction of the bias.
- Feedback and training are valuable tools for discussing and eliminating future bias.

The three strategies are mutually inclusive and are meant to be part of a reflective cycle suitable for individual or group use. The aim is to get individuals to think about their biases and thus, as part of their development, to de-bias the decision-making process as best they can. Such a bias-avoiding strategy can be developed to produce a multistage approach for de-biasing and improving decision making, as shown in Fig. 4.1.

Focus and judgement

The exercising of judgement based on experience, expertise and or professionalism, regardless of the context, can be useful and beneficial to organisations. Conversely the exercising of poor judgement because of poor focus can have dire consequences either for individuals or an organisation. The following example is used to illustrate the effect of poorly focused judgement and its potential consequences.

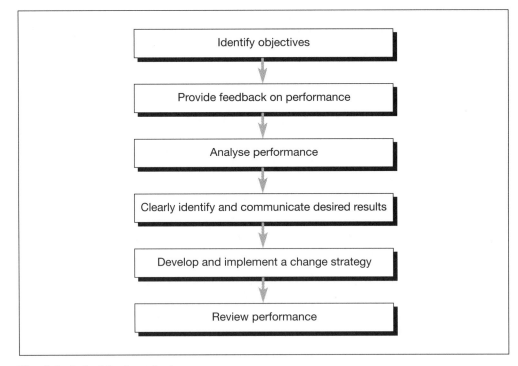

Fig. 4.1. A de-biasing strategy

| Exhibit 4.2 | **Newlee Wine Importers** |

The growth of Newlee, importers of Californian wine, rested on the ambitions of one man – Eric Newlee the owner. His ambition was to become the largest importer of Californian wines in the UK within three years. By 1998 he was part-way to realising his ambition, as Newlee became the second largest importer of Californian wines in the UK.

Eric Newlee was able to achieve this position through the receipt of heavy discounting on the amount of wine imported. Discounts could be as high as £100 000 in any one year. Although discounts could be high and an obvious benefit financially to the company, their attractions could cloud judgement. Towards the end of each period in which discounts could be claimed, there was a great temptation to receive the discount rather than consider either stock levels or whether there was a need to rationalise stock. This approach created excess stocks, which then led to storage and handling problems.

Eric Newlee's focus on the discount did not allow for the consideration of other alternatives, which may have been cheaper and of the same quality, such as South African wines. For example, turnover by 1998 had increased fivefold since 1993, to £2.25 m, bringing about a profit of £150 000. However where the profit margin had been 11 per cent in 1993 it was now only six per cent.

Eric had possibly made an error of judgement, but the question is why? Although over the years he had built up a wealth of knowledge, through experience of the wine importing business, he had become overfocused on the discounts as opposed to the firm's profit margins and profit. Such a situation could not be allowed to continue if the business was to survive.

Would such a situation have arisen if a more rational approach been used? The answer is that we don't know. However, those who would favour the rational approach, such as Eyre (1984), would argue that, '... formal systems ... provide ... management with all the relevant information they need with which to make appropriate decisions for the total control of an organisation.' Even with 'total control' the human element – that is, the unavoidable exercising of judgement by individuals – would not necessarily preclude the same decision being made. Human nature being what it is, it almost demands that we exercise some form of judgement as a means of maintaining our individuality and control over and through the decision-making process.

Intuition

Judgement is related to training and experience. Experience helps to inform the ways in which individuals exercise their judgement; that is, *informed* judgement is used and it can also be linked to the use of intuition. Intuition therefore also has a role to play within decision making. Given the right experience and context, the use of intuition may well prove to be entirely appropriate within the decision-making process.

Writers such as Braybrooke and Lindblom (1963) and Cyert and March (1963) tended to focus on the rational aspects of decision making and tended not to place much emphasis on the intuitive, and some would say, more creative aspects. Simon (1987), began to consider the intuitive and non-logical aspects of decision making by linking the ability of individuals subconsciously to recognise patterns from which decisions could be made. The concept of the logical mind has dominated the way in which cognitive capacities are perceived. Decision making and the way in which it is understood should therefore include the concept of the non-logical intuitive aspects, so as to move away from the idea that all decisions are framed within bounded rationality.

Not all management theorists are in agreement with such a view. Drucker (1982) argued that the 'manager works with a specific resource: people ... the days of the intuitive manager are numbered.' Drucker is arguing that the formalisation of management and its functions precludes the use of intuitive management, which is something that one either has or does not have. Although he is discussing 'management' as a whole, it could be argued that if management itself cannot be intuitive, there may be no room for the use of intuition within decision making.

Intuition in the philosophical sense is a form of knowledge or cognition independent of experience or reason; intuition, and intuitive knowledge, are generally regarded as inherent qualities of the mind. Intuition as a concept is derived from two sources: the idea of a self-evident proposition that does not require proof, and the belief that truth surpasses the power of the intellect. Intuition is, in relation to the two sources, the ability within all of us to identify what is right without requiring either proof or much information.

Henri Bergson (1859–1941), the famous French philosopher and Nobel laureate who explained the importance of intuition over intellect, regarded intuition as the purest form of instinct. He actually defined intuition as 'instinct that has become disinterested, self-conscious, capable of reflecting upon its object and of enlarging it indefinitely'. The instinct of the individual can, in essence, become finely tuned to recognising what is self-evident and right. Intuition and its use do not require the individual to rely on masses of information or empirical evidence.

Intuition can therefore be defined as that part of an individual's subconscious thinking process – what some people would refer to as their 'gut feeling' or 'hunch'. Choices are made on the basis of what the person 'feels' is correct. The decision maker does not consciously weigh the pros and cons of each alternative, and does not even need to understand the situation. Nevertheless, intuition as part of the subconscious does not mean that intuitive decisions are random or irrational. Agor (1986) for example suggests that intuitive processes are based on experience, which are then subsumed within (or as part of) the decision-making process.

Isenburg (1984) claimed that the majority of decisions made by senior managers were based on intuition, as opposed to the use of rational analysis. His research showed that 80 per cent of the managers interviewed used intuition when making important decisions. Such a high percentage is somewhat surprising given the pressures that may exist to utilise a rational decision-making approach. Perhaps the context, seniority of the managers interviewed, and their experience allowed them the freedom to use such an approach. Decision making should not, of course, be solely based on intuition. Perhaps the best approach should be the achievement of a balance between 'gut feeling' and logic.

Organisations tend to be afraid of this approach because they believe the quality of such 'soft' non-rational decisions is suspect, and therefore it is rarely accepted as an appropriate decision-making style. Albert Einstein, by way of an example, valued intuition and actually related it to inspiration. He is quoted as saying, 'I believe in intuition and inspiration. At times I feel certain that I am right while not knowing the reason.' (Raudsepp, 1960) It is the not-knowing-the-reason aspect to the use of judgement that perhaps concerns people when someone else makes decisions based on intuition. It is this intangible aspect of the process that seems to fly in the face of reason and logic, and hence goes against rational thought and decision making.

However, Einstein would have argued that the use of intuition and judgement could be more creative in that it, by its very nature, does not conform to neatly defined rational boundaries. Einstein goes on to say, in relation to intuition and inspiration that, 'Imagination is more important than knowledge, because knowledge is limited whereas imagination embraces the entire world.' (Raudsepp, 1960) Einstein also believed that, 'The intellect has little to do on the road to discovery. There comes a leap in consciousness – call it intuition or what you will – the solution comes to you and you don't know how or why.'

The use of such an approach does seem, based on Einstein beliefs, to have some merit, in that it may be more creative. Creativity does, however, have its price, namely risk! How many individuals would be prepared to make a decision based entirely on their judgement and intuition, especially if the stakes were high? When individuals use their judgement, it is in all probability based on experience, which is fed subconsciously into their decision making.

Drucker believes that intuition must be disciplined. He states that, 'I believe in intuition only if you discipline it. "Hunch" artists, who make diagnosis but don't check it out with the facts, are the ones in medicine who kill people and in management kill businesses.' (Nelson, 1985). Drucker is obviously emphasising the need to be sensible when using intuition, in that no individual should simply make a decision because it is a hunch or because they feel it is the right thing to do based on gut reaction; there is a need to control such reactions by at least checking the process through the use of a rational element to the process.

Harper (1988) states that making decisions based on the avoidance of facts is simply ignorance. He believes that a, 'don't bother me with the facts' approach is decision making based on ignorance and not intuition. What is needed therefore is a balance between judgement/intuition and an analytical approach. Most individuals develop intuition based on years of industrial and organisational experience that provides them with insights that enables them to utilise judgement as part of their chosen decision-making style.

The use of intuition

Isenburg (1984) characterised five different ways in which managers and, by definition, individuals use intuitive decision making:

- Managers intuitively sense when a problem exists.
- Managers rely on intuition to perform actions that have become frequent, and thus performance becomes automatic based on practice and hands-on experience.
- Intuition is used to synthesise pieces of information and experience to create an integrated picture.
- Managers sometimes use intuition to check results against quantifiable data.
- Individuals can use intuition to arrive rapidly at a workable and acceptable solution; in this case it is instantaneous and possibly based on experience and thus allowing a manager to recognise familiar patterns

Experience and knowledge

Some writers emphasise quite clearly the need to use intuitive and analytical decision making in tandem. David (1991) points out that:

> most organizations can benefit from strategic management, which is based upon integrating intuition and analysis in decision making. Choosing an intuitive or analytical approach to decision making is not an either or proposition. Managers at all levels in an organisation should inject their intuition and judgement into strategic management analyses. Analytical thinking and intuitive thinking complement each other.

| Exhibit 4.3 | **Profitability problems** |

Alison and Roy owned a small business that specialised in the production and marketing of computer systems tailored to the specific needs of businesses and individuals. They had three outlets, with a manager and four staff in each. Their relatively small factory was managed by one of their friends and employed 28 people. After a good first two years of trading they began to experience a downturn in their profits, which required them to take positive and immediate action.

After some thought on the problem they decided on their own that the recent poor performance figures must be due to inefficient staff. Both had noticed that at two of the outlets the staff seemed disinterested in their work, and that rival outlets nearby seemed to be doing quite well. Alison and Roy decided to cut staff from all three sites and at the factory in the hope that this would restore profitability.

In making the decision they had not examined the situation closely, neither of them had attempted to identify the cause of the problem, and they did not refer to any of the managers. Was this a case of them following their gut feeling, that is, their intuition, or was it simply poor decision making *per se*?

The answer to such a question obviously requires more information with regard to the outcome. For the purpose of this example their decision to cut staff did not halt the decline in profits. Therefore with this information we can say that their decision was a poor one because it was not based on any firm base of knowledge. Neither could it be said to be a truly intuitive decision because it was based on ignorance (Harper, 1988) and was not related to any previous experience. Alison and Roy have not conformed in any way to Isenburg's (1984) definitions of the five ways in which managers use intuition. This example is obviously intended to show that intuition is not simply about feelings based on shallow observations, but is more involved, in that it needs to be disciplined and facts need to be checked.

As a counter to this view Pettinger (1996) put forward that

Great play is made of intuitive and inspirational elements of the strategy process. It is nearly all myth and legend. It is possible to identify and define a professional or rational intuition that comes from knowing one's organisation, department, division or expertise to the level of being a true expert. All true expert 'intuition' is based on this.

These two approaches to the role of intuition in decision making can complement one another and can be used effectively, given the experience of the individual (or, as Pettinger puts it, the 'expertise to the level of being a true expert' in determining the future strategic direction of an organisation. Experience and knowledge are the key to effective decision making and the exercising of judgement and/or use of intuition.

Individuals learn from their experience; however, what is learned is not necessarily what *should* be learned from any given situation. This is usually due to a number of factors limiting the extent and quality of feedback, namely:

- delayed outcomes not being attributed to action;
- reliability of the feedback;

- lack of information on alternative outcomes based on different decisions having been taken;
- lack of effective learning experience.

Not only is experience important but also the way in which experience is reflected upon. It is perhaps the experiential reflection within the decision-making process that enables individuals to determine when and to what extent judgement and intuition can be used. By reflecting on past decisions, individuals can develop a greater conceptual understanding of the decision-making process and thus become eventually more expert in making decisions.

Final thoughts on judgement and intuition

There is no right or wrong when trying to decide if judgement and/or intuition are appropriate when making decisions. Individuals will make decisions in a way that best suits them within a given situation. If an individual is comfortable using intuition and suitable outcomes are achieved, the issue as to the appropriateness of its use may be irrelevant. However, it needs to be recognised that the outcomes achieved may have been down to sheer luck and that complacency with regard to the fallibility or otherwise of their own intuition should not cloud their judgement as to the efficacy of its future use.

In the final analysis most managers develop intuition about what decisions to make and how to make them. Such intuition tends to be subjective in nature and is developed through years of experience within an organisation or industry; experience in this sense provides managers with what can only be referred to as 'insights' (Harper, 1988). Intuition is recognised as an important element within decision making, but perhaps most managers tend to emphasise the more 'objective' decision-making tools, such as probability theory and decision trees. They therefore miss out on an aspect of decision making that, while it should not replace such methods, could at the very least add to the decision-making process.

Summary of the chapter

- The classical approach to decision making tends to preclude the use of judgement and intuition.

- The degree of uncertainty and information available plays a part in determining whether or not judgement can or should be exercised.

- Judgement and its effective use is dependent on experience.

- Judgement can take a number of forms, dependent upon the degree of ambiguity, measurability of performance, known outcomes and the extent of repetition involved in the decision-making situation.

- Bias can influence judgement and therefore there is a need to de-bias judgement.

- Intuition is part of the subconscious element within decision making and is linked to experience.

- Intuitive decisions are not necessarily random or irrational.

- There is a need to achieve a balance between the use of rationality, judgement and intuition when making decisions.

Case Study 7: Problems at Batus Boats

The new manager of Batus Boats is in trouble. Since John Sander took over as manager of the company in 1995 the shareholders have seen a decrease in returns and the overall profitability of the company has declined sharply. No new initiatives with regard to new designs or the adoption of new boat-building materials have been taken recently, except for an attempt to diversify into the manufacture and sale of surfboards.

This later decision has only succeeded in detracting from the main business of the company, namely building boats to personal specifications laid down by customers, and has diverted both management attention and money. Batus Boats has now decided to sell its surfboard business, if it can find a buyer.

Not only has the surfboard venture been a failure, but also the company has not built or designed any new boats since the middle of 1996. In fact, the boat designs that the company is currently using date back to the late 1980s and do not fully reflect the advances made with boat design and the development of stronger and safer composite materials.

John Sander has in the past defended his decision to diversify in the way that he did because of the increasing threat from home-grown boat builders and competition from EU-based companies. He is actually quoted as saying on one occasion that, 'If I made a mistake it was in following other companies and their diversification strategies. I ignored 24 years of experience in the industry.'

Questions for discussion

1 *As John Sander was making his decision to diversify into the manufacture and sale of surfboards, he would need to be aware of all elements in the decision situation, both internal and external. For example, does Batus Boats have the finances and expertise to diversify, and has the company analysed the market trends? To what extent do you think that reason and sound judgement must determine the way John Sander will approach his decision?*

2 *John Sander must remember that judgement is an essential adjunct to the effective use of any decision-making tool. Do you agree with this view, and what is the purpose of using non-judgement-based decision tools?*

Case Study 8: Shire Police Criminal Task Force

Shire Police Force has had in operation since 1994 a special Task Force charged with reopening and re-examining unsolved criminal cases. To date the Task Force has managed to clear up 34 previously unsolved cases, which had been on the books for more than two years and which had been given up as unsolvable. The Task Force is composed of five detectives and two administrative staff. Each of the detectives have at least nine years' experience and in fact their cumulative experience amounts to 53 years, which is one of the reasons given for their success rate in clearing up old unsolved crimes.

Each detective was chosen very carefully from a long list of potential candidates. The main selection criteria were: length of service with the Criminal Investigation Branch (minimum requirement being four years); being able to work successfully as part of a team; and a good track record for arrests and convictions. The candidates chosen were considered to be, with regard to their personalities, dogged and have a never-say-die approach to a case.

Most of the cases handled by the Task Force were considered to be unsolvable because there was a either a lack of evidence to secure a conviction or the evidence trail had gone cold. In fact most detectives would possibly regard the cases as simply unsolvable because of the time that has elapsed between the crime being committed and the case being re-examined. The Task Force, however, believes that time is on its side because of a number of factors, the most important being that over time people become more prepared to talk about a crime, especially if there has been a falling-out between those involved or linked to the case.

The other factor that has contributed to their success, at least claimed by the detectives, is that they follow their gut instinct. They claim that this is one of the most basic skills that detectives need in order to be successful. They also argue that there is a need to be creative and to brainstorm when looking for solutions and when attempting to make links between items of evidence. Their track record of being able to do this has been very successful – hence their clear-up rate of 34 cases since 1994. They pride themselves also on being able to think laterally in order to come up with new leads and avenues of investigation without ever having been on any type of decision-making or problem-solving course! In short, they believe that, based on experience, they have developed a 'nose' for what to look for and how to pursue a case. Instinct is therefore the key.

Questions for discussion

1 *Define the problems faced by the detectives. How do they make decisions and could they make their decisions using any other methods?*

2 *Discuss the role and value of intuition within the context of the Task Force's brief to clear up unsolved crimes.*

3 *What, if anything, can be learned by organisations from the way in which the Task Force makes decisions?*

References

Agor, W. (1986) 'How top executives use their intuition to make decisions', *Business Horizons*, 29(1), January–February, p. 6.

Bazerman, M. H. (1990) *Judgement in Managerial Decision Making*, 2nd. edn, Wiley, New York.

Braybrooke, D. and Lindblom, C. E. (1963) *A Strategy of Decision*, Free Press, New York.

Campbell, D. T. (1958) 'Systematic error on the part of human links in communication systems', *Information and Control*, 1, pp. 334–69.

Cyert, R. M. and March, J. G. (1963) *Behavioural Theory of the Firm*, Prentice-Hall, Englewood Cliffs, New Jersey.

David, F. R. (1991) *Strategic Management*, Macmillan, Basingstoke.

Drucker, P. F. (1982) *Management*, Pan.

Dale, E. and Michelon, L.C. (1966) *Modern Management Methods*, Penguin, London.

Eyre, E. C. (1984) *Mastering Basic Management*, Macmillan, Basingstoke.

Harper, S. (1988) 'Intuition: what separates executives from managers', *Business Horizons*, 31(5), September–October, p. 16.

Hofstede, G. (1981) 'Management control of public and not for profit activities', *Accounting Organisations and Society*, 6(3), 1981, pp. 193–211.

Hogarth, R. (1980) *Judgement and Choice*, Wiley, New York.

Isenburg, D. J. (1984) 'How senior managers think', *Harvard Business Review*, November–December, pp. 80–90.

Lawrence, P. and Elliott, K. (1985) *Introducing Management*, Penguin Business, London.

Lindblom, C. E. (1959) 'The science of muddling through', *Public Administrative Review*, 19, pp. 79–99.

Mescon, M. H., Albert, M. and Khedouri, F. (1988) *Management*, Harper & Row, New York.

Mintzberg, H., Quinn, J. B. and Ghoshal, S. (1998) *The Process Strategy*, Prentice-Hall Englewood Cliff, New Jersey.

Morgan, G. (1996) *Image of Organization*, New edition, Sage Publications, California.

Nelson, R. (1985) 'How to be a manager', *Success*, July–August, p. 69.

Peters, T. J. and Waterman, R. J. (1982) *In Search of Excellence*, Harper & Row, New York.

Pettinger, R. (1996) *Introduction to Corporate Strategy*, Macmillan Business, Basingstoke.

Porter, M. E. (1985) *Competitive Strategy*, Free Press, New York.

Quinn, J. B. (1989) 'Managing strategic change', in Asch, D. and Bowman, C. (eds) (1989) *Readings in Strategic Management*, Macmillan, Basingstoke.

Raudsepp, E. (1960) 'Can you trust your hunches?', *Management Review*, 49(1), p. 7.

Simon, H. (1951) *Administrative Behaviour*, Macmillan, Basingstoke.

Simon, H. A. (1987) 'Making management decisions: The role of intuition and emotion', *Academy of Management Executive*, 1, pp. 57–64.

Stoner, J. A. F. (1982) *Management*, Prentice Hall, Hemel Hempstead.

Vickers, G. (1983) *Human Systems are Different*, Harper & Row, New York.

Part II

FRAMEWORKS FOR THE ANALYSIS OF OPTIONS

It is reasonable to assume that decision makers are subject to ever-increasing environmental pressure to improve the quality of their decisions. For example, information technology improvements are likely to make organisations more transparent while ever-more numerous and outspoken stakeholder groups demand that they are accountable for their actions.

Decisions are constantly being taken by individuals, groups, and organisations. Of these decisions some are perceived, rightly or wrongly, as simple and others seen as complex.

Simple decisions are seen as clearly structured in terms of cause and effect. Such decisions are usually to do with the day-to-day operation of the organisation and thus, not expected to be of long-term critical importance. These decisions tend to be taken quite easily. Strategic or long-term planning decisions, on the other hand, are complex. Complexity implies both lengthy and expensive process and uncertainty of outcome. Clearly, while the former implication may be justified, given the critical nature of such a decision's importance to the organisation, the latter calls into question the value of the whole process.

While some of this complexity is regarded as unavoidable, for example it may be impossible to reduce the number of stakeholder groups, the decision may be made easier, and the outcome better, if the decision maker employs appropriate processes and technique.

This part of the book will examine the case for adopting a holistic, rather than a fragmented and sequential approach to making decisions. It will also include an applied consideration of several quantitative techniques that can identify key elements of complex problems so that such problems may be reduced to a more manageable form.

CHAPTER 5

An introduction to quantitative and financial decision making

Learning objectives

At the end of this chapter you should:

- be able to apply a number of quantitative techniques to decision-making situations;

- appreciate the influence of personality type on the interpretation of the results of quantitative methods;

- understand the nature of relevant costs;

- be able to apply the concepts of marginal cost and contribution;

- appreciate the qualitative issues within quantitative method;

- understand the importance of timing of future cash flows; and

- be able to apply, select and apply investment techniques.

Introduction

This is the first of two chapters that will be concerned with numerical analysis in decision making.

In this chapter we shall explore and develop some of the commonest quantitative techniques, and apply them to specific problems, so as to demonstrate their potential usefulness to a decision maker. No prior experience of statistics will be assumed, and little more than a basic level of numeracy will be required to apply the techniques encountered. Indeed, it is in the interpretation of the problem and the application of the technique where complexity and sophistication often emerge.

Several examples will be used to illustrate the techniques introduced in this chapter, so that the techniques can be practised and some of the nuances within each method can be demonstrated.

The usefulness and importance of quantitative methods (QM) in management today

The importance of any manager being familiar with QM can be justified in terms of benefit to the organisation and to the individual manager. If one takes, as an example, the management task of monitoring and interpreting the organisation's external environment, such techniques may enable an analyst to organise large amounts of complex data into a systematic form. Economic data is a case in point. Large amounts of numerical data are processed to give straightforward trends in, say, national rates of inflation or the balance of payments, which can provide a useful basis for organisations to forecast their external environment. Objective interactions, or linkages, between variables may emerge, making primary conclusions clear.

Such quantitative findings may form useful parameters that may be combined with, and guide, qualitative debate. For example, an investment option may be quickly dismissed from a discussion if it is unlikely to be profitable, regardless of the qualitative issues that may be involved. The choice of Stanstead, as the third London airport, in preference to Foulness Island on the Essex coast provides a good example of this: the cost of building and operating the airport on an extremely remote, coastal location was seen as prohibitively high, even though the site had advantages such as a small resident population and therefore few people to be affected by noise pollution. Thus, the primary conclusion, regarding costs, enabled the Foulness option to be removed from consideration, leaving secondary conclusions, for instance about noise pollution, to be drawn about the remaining possible sites.

One of the main advantages of using numerical data in support of decision making is that it appears to add objectivity to the decision. For example, suppose a company is faced with choosing one of three possible new projects. Each project requires £200 000 of investment. Project A is very risky, carrying a 15 per cent chance of success, but the rewards would be huge; Project B carries an 80 per cent chance of success, but with moderate rewards. Project C, on the other hand, is virtually certain to succeed, but offers correspondingly small rewards. With the limited information available, we may not be able to make a very objective decision. It is possible that the decision will be made simply on the basis of how much risk we are prepared to accept. It may also depend on other factors; an organisation on the verge of bankruptcy might logically throw everything into Project A because neither of the other two would yield sufficient reward even if they were successful. In different circumstances, the guaranteed return of Project C might be appropriate. However, most decision makers would require more figures before coming to a decision. Their information requirements might include:

- the likely return if each of the three projects was successful;
- how much of the investment could be retrieved if each project were to fail; and
- whether the figures indicating the probability of success are reliable.

Even before we have considered how we might process numerical data so as to improve its value for decision making purposes, it is easy to see its relevance to the decision maker. However, it may be worth sounding a note of caution at this stage, that numerical data rarely makes the decision for us! There are many circumstances in which figures alone can give a distorted picture, and to rely solely on such data as the sole basis for making a decision would probably be no more rational than to ignore the numerical data altogether.

One final justification for the inclusion of a quantitative dimension in decision making is that individuals must take full advantage of any information that is available. If they do not, they risk rival organisations gaining an information advantage over them. It is probably no longer appropriate to delegate all numerical analysis automatically to the specialist; the decision maker needs to understand (though not necessarily be expert in) all aspects of the decision. Furthermore, understanding the output of such specialists is likely to be enhanced if one has some knowledge of how that output was prepared.

Information Technology in quantitative decision making

Some quantitative techniques do require a fair amount of data processing. However, many of them are greatly simplified by the use of computers. Whilst anything more than brief mention of computer software applications would be outside the remit of this book, it is as well to be aware of their availability, and the extent to which they will facilitate data processing.

For almost any decision, the manager(s) involved will no doubt have to handle a considerable amount of information relating to the likely costs and benefits of the different possible outcomes of the decision. All of this information will be the result of trend projections, historic events analysis, pilot studies, or simply judgement. It is essentially data about some future event and, therefore, subject to considerable uncertainty; it is to be treated with caution and suspicion. Hence, it is important that the forecast outcomes should be tested. For example, you might be considering opening a restaurant and your calculations tell you that, in order to earn your target income, the restaurant must serve, say, two hundred meals per day. You will need to know whether you have the space, staff, and customers to do this.

The use of computer packages allows managers to vary some, or all, of the input data and see the follow-through effect on the conclusion. For example, an organisations profit will depend (among other things) on market size, market share, selling price, and costs of production. It may be assumed that the organisation has estimated 'best case' and 'worst case' scenarios for each. Use of a spreadsheet would enable the analyst to substitute the best and worst case values into the profit calculations in order to determine their effect.

The latter example is one use of a particularly helpful application of Information Technology, namely 'sensitivity analysis'. This is an analytical process to determine how sensitive the final conclusion of the primary analysis is to changes of the variables – for example, what would the effect on profit be if sales were 10 per cent higher, or 10 per cent lower?

Quantitative method and personality type

Although quantitative approaches to decision making might sometimes appear to be more objective than qualitative approaches, such faith in figures can sometimes be misplaced. Quantitative analysis is often based on estimates of costs and revenues. If this is the case, the projections and forecasts we make can only be as accurate as the figures we put into our calculations. Moreover, there are so many external influences on the eventual outcome that it is scarcely possible to create accurate models. Nevertheless, this need not be taken as an argument against the use of quantitative techniques, since the latter are useful in generating scenarios.

| Exhibit 5.1 | **A holiday company and the weather** |

Consider an example of a company whose fortunes are, to an extent, governed by the weather. The company is considering building a new facility at a holiday complex that it owns. The proposals are either a swimming pool, tennis court, or a restaurant. After examining available data the pay-off matrix in Table 5.1 is predicted.

Table 5.1 Example payoff matrix (Profit, £000s)

| Strategy | Weather (the chance factor) | | |
	Cool	Average	Hot
Swimming pool	50	100	150
Tennis court	30	180	90
Restaurant	170	100	40

So which facility should the company select? Clearly, there is no clear-cut solution, and the figures given in the table – assuming they are accurate – will merely provide information support for the eventual decision. Which of the three facilities is chosen may depend on the decision maker's personality and attitude towards risk.

Some individuals will instinctively focus on the maximum possible benefit; that is, they will seek the maximum benefit for the maximum amount of time. Such a person might therefore ignore the likelihood of each pattern of weather, and concentrate on the fact that a tennis court could give the greatest return on investment (see Table 5.2a). Alternatively, a more cautious person may look at the worst case scenarios and try to optimise his/her choice from this perspective, namely to maximise the worst or minimum payoff. Such a person would, in this example, favour investing in a swimming pool (see Table 5.2b).

It may be argued that these two views of personality are simplistic extremes, and that few people are so consistent in their behaviour that they behave in a simi-

Exhibit 5.1
Continued

Table 5.2 Example alternative views on best option

(a) Maxmax view

	Cool	Average	Hot	Max
Swimming pool	50	100	150	150
Tennis court	30	180	90	**180**
Restaurant	170	100	40	170

(b) Maxmin view

Swimming pool	50	100	150	**50**
Tennis court	30	180	90	30
Restaurant	170	100	40	40

lar way all the time. While both comments have some justification, the analysis may have some credibility if one accepts that people have a *tendency* to behave in a certain way. In other words, a particular individual may not always, for example, be a risk taker but may generally have an inclination in that direction; or someone may not always be conservative and cautious in approach, but would generally take that view.

When choosing the preferred course of action, the likely approach for a particular individual or organisation may be revealed by behavioural indicators such as what they say and how they have behaved elsewhere. For example, they may have shown conservatism, innovation, ambition, aggression, altruism, selfishness, etc.

Relevant costs and benefits for the decision maker

Costs will have an important bearing on many decisions. It is important, however, to distinguish between those costs that are relevant to the decision and those that are not. In distinguishing between these two categories, there are three basic rules to be followed:

1 *Only movements of cash, either in or out, are relevant.* We are not interested in accounting adjustments. Therefore, *include* capital costs and expenses, but *do not include* non-cash items such as depreciation and general provisions for doubtful debts. Depreciation reduces taxable income; it is therefore important as a tax shield, and will enter the appraisal as part of the tax considerations. *Include* specific bad debts, since they represent cash flows that should have been received; but *do not include* any general provision for bad debt, which is nothing more than an estimate and does not involve movements of cash.

2 *All cash flows that are affected by the decision must be included.* This refers to all costs and revenues that are expected to change as a result of the decision. To expand on this:

- *Do not include* sunk costs, i.e. those that are past, representing expenditure to bring the organisation to where it is now. So, if the company has spent £100m building a factory, it then has to decide whether to open it or not. Thus while costs of labour, energy and materials both to operate and to not operate the factory will be relevant, the building costs will not be.

- *Do not include* allocated overheads since they are notional costs. The one exception, however, is if allocated amounts vary with output. Many overhead expenses, for example the salary of the managing director or the insurance costs of the premises, may be essential but they are not directly attributable to a particular unit of output and, consequentially, tend not to vary with the level of production; indeed, they may be paid even if output is zero. Thus, the decision to embark on a particular course of action, e.g. to fix production at a particular level, has nothing to do with these costs because they will be paid anyway. Some overheads, e.g. stock insurance or perhaps postage and telecommunications, may vary to some degree with output, although not directly. Include these variable overheads because they may change according to outcome and thus be relevant to the decision.

- *Include* scrap or residual realisable value of assets because these will be real cash flows at the end of an investment's life.

- *Include* all incidental or 'ripple' effect costs and benefits, e.g. how is investing for product *A* likely to affect the perception of stakeholders interested in product *B*? Obviously these interactive effects may be positive or negative.

- Work to quantify qualitative considerations – for example, what might be the cost to you if your principal suppliers reduce their product quality?

3 *The timing of the cash flows must be considered.* A particular sum of cash is worth more to us now than the same sum in a year's time, and therefore it is appropriate to take account of when cash would be received or paid by introducing a discounted value. This notion will be dealt with later in the chapter.

Let us now consider some possible applications of the first two rules.

Marginal costing

This is a decision-making technique based on the principle that, in the short term, individual costs may be categorised as either 'fixed' or 'variable'. In the long term, all costs are variable; however, in the short term, output will be constrained by the limited availability of one or more resources, for instance the supply of suitable factory space. These limited resources will be the fixed costs, and will be the critical constraints determining the level of maximum output. Variable costs, also known as marginal costs, are able to change with activity or output, even in the short run. The decision maker has to decide how different outcomes will affect marginal costs and, consequently 'contribution'. Contribution is defined as the difference between selling price and marginal cost per unit of output, over all units of output; this difference applies first to fixed costs and then to profits.

The following examples indicate the potential usefulness of these concepts:

Exhibit 5.2

Discontinuing a product line

The following example illustrates how it may be logical, at least in the short term, for a company to continue producing a product line even though it is making a loss. This is because the product still makes a positive contribution. (Contribution = Sales Revenue – Variable Costs) If the product more than covers the variable cost of producing it, it will be contributing towards paying off the fixed cost of production. When sufficient items have been sold to cover these fixed costs, the contribution will add to the company's profits.

The cost statement in Table 5.3 illustrates the notion of contribution:

Table 5.3 Example cost statement showing product contributions

	Dishwashers £000s		Videos £000s		CD Players £000s		Total £000s	
Sales Income		180		260		250		690
Less Costs:								
Variable	120		180		230		530	
Fixed	90		100		70		260	
Total		(210)		(280)		(300)		(790)
Profit/(Loss)		(30)		(20)		(50)		(100)
Contribution		60		80		20		160

In spite of all product ranges making an accounting loss, they all make a positive contribution to fixed costs. Discontinuing any of them would make the company worse off; if production of dishwashers were stopped then the company would save 120 units of variable costs but lose 180 units of income, i.e. a net loss of 60 units.

Exhibit 5.3

Pricing for special orders

A manager may wish to attract new customers by offering special low prices, perhaps on an introductory basis. Alternatively, the organisation may have spare capacity that it may wish to fill – for example, a holiday company may seek to sell off-season holidays, or an energy company may be looking for off-peak sales. If the companies can offer their products at substantially discounted prices, it may persuade customers to buy at times other than those at which they would normally do so, and such sales thereby fill up the spare capacity.

The company may vary its normal price downwards to the point at which price equals marginal cost. All prices above this level are attractive because they yield positive contribution. Prices below marginal cost will yield a negative contribution, i.e. the company will actually make itself worse off by selling at such prices.

Clearly, for sustained existence the company must cover fixed as well as variable costs and will presumably ensure that it does so with its 'normal' or regular business. By implication, if a company heavily discounts its price to one group of customers, it must ensure that these customers are appropriately separated from other groups. Other dangers may arise from the reaction of their competitors if they drive prices, and profits, still lower. Alternative action for the company may be to consider other uses for the spare capacity.

Exhibit 5.4

Make-or-buy decisions

A company may be faced with the option of either buying products in (perhaps components of an end product) or making them itself. Analysis of marginal costs can inform the decision.

Suppose a company makes four products, A, B, C and D, with the costs as set out in Table 5.4.

Table 5.4 Example manufacturing production costs

	A (£)	B (£)	C (£)	D (£)
Variable production	17	13	15	12
Fixed production	8	9	6	10
Total production cost	25	22	21	22
Other variable costs	2	3	1	1
Other fixed	4	2	3	2
Total costs	31	27	25	25

The company can alternatively buy the products from outside at the following prices: A at £20; B at £15; C at £14; and D £24. So, should the company buy in all or some of the products?

For each product the Total Variable Costs of manufacture are: A at £19; B at £16; C at £16; and D £13. These are the costs that would be saved if the products were purchased, rather than made. For product A, variable costs saved are £19, but buy-in costs are £20, which means a potential loss of £1 per unit, so the company should continue making A. Only for B and C is buying cheaper than the marginal cost of production, and these are therefore the two products that should be bought in by the company.

Contribution and break-even analysis

A simple calculation can be used to determine the level of output at which a firm will just cover all its costs (both fixed and variable). This break-even output will occur when the firm's total contribution from all products exactly matches its fixed costs. In other words,

$$\text{Break-even output} = \frac{\text{Fixed costs}}{\text{Contribution per item produced}}$$

Suppose Turner & Co manufacture cricket bats and their fixed costs are £15 000 per annum. Their bats sell at £48 each, and variable costs per bat are £36. Contribution, therefore, is £12 per bat. Thus to break even, Turner & Co must produce and sell

$$\frac{15\,000}{12} = 1250 \text{ bats}$$

Opportunity cost

Opportunity cost is a management accounting concept that can be useful in appraising a decision. Opportunity cost is the value of the forsaken alternative, or the net value of sources of income that will be lost if a project is not adopted. It should be included in the calculation as a lost benefit or cost.

To illustrate the concept, let us consider the following example.

Exhibit 5.5

To be or not to be a shopkeeper?

Projected figures per annum may be calculated in this example as set out in Table 5.5.

Table 5.5 Example cost of setting up in business

	Historic accounting (£000)	Management accounting (£000)
Sales	160	160
Less: cost of sales	(120)	(120)
staff salaries	(20)	(20)
other expenses	(5)	(5)
Imputed: Salary	–	(15)
Interest on capital (say 10% of £50 000)	–	(5)
Profit/(loss)	15	(5)

The opportunity costs will be salary, £15 000 and interest on capital £5000

If these are included in our decision, a reasonable profit, of £15 000, is transformed into a loss of £5000.

It should be remembered that opportunity cost depends on individual circumstance – for instance, perhaps for a newly graduating student about to embark on full-time employment, opportunity cost will be low.

Let us now consider a slightly more sophisticated example.

Exhibit 5.6

Manufacturing choice

Suppose that a company is making 40 000 units of product A. To buy the product in would cost £15 per unit; to manufacture it, costs are as set out in Table 5.6:

Table 5.6 Example unit costs

	Unit cost (£)
Direct materials	7.20
Direct labour	3.30
Variable Overheads	2.00
Fixed Overheads	5.50
Total	18.00

The company discovers that its production facilities could be used to make 25 000 units of B at a marginal cost of £8, and B could be sold at £14 per unit. What should the company do? The financial options are set out in Table 5.7.

Table 5.7 Example cost options

Manufacture of A:	£000	
Marginal costs	500	(40 000 × £12.50)
Opportunity cost – loss of contribution from B	150	(25 000 × £14–£8)
Total Cost of Manufacture	650	
Cost of Purchasing	600	(400 000 × £15)
Loss by Manufacture	50	

Thus, we should buy product A and manufacture product B instead.

Further uses of contribution

In the previous examples we applied the concepts of marginal costs and contribution to achieve a break-even output for a firm that has both fixed and variable costs of production. Let us now take another example.

| Exhibit 5.7 | **KEEP** |

KEEP

If a company produces electric kettles, and has a selling price per kettle of £20, a variable cost for each unit of production of £12, and fixed costs per year of £20 000, the contribution made by each kettle will be £20 – £12 = £8. If the sale of each kettle contributes £8 towards covering fixed costs, the company must sell 20 000/8 kettles per year to fully cover its fixed costs; in other words, 2500 kettles must be made and sold each year to break even. Each additional kettle sold beyond this number will contribute £8 towards profit for the company. Thus, if 4200 kettles are sold, the profit made on these kettles will be (4200 – 2500) × 8 = £13 600.

This all seems very straightforward, but such application of contribution ignores certain realities of production and decision making. Firstly, organisations will rarely produce just one product. Secondly, there may be all kinds of resource constraints affecting production of different products, not to mention variations in demand, which will mean the company cannot simply sell however many kettles (or any other products) it chooses to make. Let us, therefore, complicate the production decision a little.

Knodishall Efficient Electrical Products plc (KEEP) make kettles, coffee percolators and steam irons which use less electricity than most rival products. These goods are then sold to wholesalers or large retailers in boxes of ten of each product. KEEP has total fixed costs of £300 000 per annum, and a variable cost and revenue structure for the three product as set out in Table 5.8.

Table 5.8 KEEP costs and revenues

Per box of 10	Kettles (£)	Percolators (£)	Irons (£)
Unit price	180	210	240
Productive labour	(45)	(48)	(60)
Materials	(75)	(90)	(120)
Variable expenses	(18)	(27)	(27)
Contribution	42	45	33
Machine hours	4	5.5	4
Demand	5000	6000	2000

If there are no constraints at all, KEEP would prefer to sell only coffee percolators, since they bring in the largest contribution. Their second choice would be kettles, and steam irons would be third. However, demand for each product, at the price charged, is limited. Therefore, if KEEP were to supply all the products demanded, the total contribution would amount to that shown in Table 5.9.

▶

Table 5.9 KEEP product contributions

Product		Contribution (£)
Kettles	(5000 x £42)	210 000
Percolators	(6000 x £45)	270 000
Irons	(2000 x £33)	66 000
Total contribution		546 000

Hence, the profit gained from the sale of all products (after fixed costs are paid) will be £246 000.

Now let us examine the effects of a constraint of each of the resource inputs in turn.

(a) A constraint on materials

Suppose there is a constraint of £800 000 of materials available. If the availability of materials is the determinant of how much KEEP can produce, it must try to gain the maximum contribution from each £1 spent on materials. Comparisons can be made between the three products by dividing the contribution gained on each product by the cost of the materials taken to produce that product. This may mean that priority in production is not given to the product which gives the highest overall contribution.

This effect can be seen in the resultant figures, where the contribution made by each product per £1 spent on materials is as follows: Kettles £0.56 (£42/75); Percolators £0.50 (£45/90); and Irons £0.28 (£33/120). We can see from this that, with a constraint on materials' availability, the company would initially give priority to producing kettles, then percolators, and finally, irons.

In our example, KEEP would have enough materials to satisfy demand for kettles, part of the demand for percolators, but none of the demand for irons. Production of 5000 kettles uses 5000 × £75 of materials = £375 000. This leaves £425 000 of materials for use elsewhere. To fulfil demand for percolators we would need 6000 × £90 of materials = £540 000, which is more than we have available; we have only enough resources to produce $\frac{425\,000}{90}$ = 4722 percolators.

The total contribution when the company has such a constraint on materials will be as set out in Table 5.10. With fixed costs of £300 000, this leaves KEEP with a profit of £122 490 in these circumstances.

Table 5.10 KEEP contribution under constrained material resources

Product	Quantity produced	Contribution per item (£)	Total contribution per product (£)
Kettles	5000	42	210 000
Percolators	4722	45	212 490
Irons	0	33	0
Total contribution			422 490

(b) A constraint on productive labour

Imagine there is now only £480 000 of productive labour available. This time, we are interested in maximising the contribution of each product per £1 spent on productive labour, and in our example we have the following figures: Kettles £0.93 (£42/45); Percolators £0.94 (£45/48); and Irons £0.55 (£33/60). KEEP's first choice will now be to produce percolators, then kettles, and finally irons. Once again, there is enough of the scarce resource to produce all of the first-choice product, some of the second, but none of the third. Production of percolators will use 6000 x £48 = £288 000 worth of labour. This will leave £192 000 worth of labour for use in producing other products, and this is only sufficient for $\frac{192\,000}{45}$ = 4266 kettles and nothing more.

Total contribution will now be as set out in Table 5.11 and, with fixed costs of £300 000, this leaves KEEP with a profit of £149 172.

Table 5.11 KEEP contribution under constrained labour resources

Product	Quantity produced	Contribution per item (£)	Total contribution per product (£)
Percolators	6000	£45	£270 000
Kettles	4266	£42	£179 172
Irons	0	£33	0
Total contribution			£449 172

(c) A constraint on machine hours

Suppose there is now a constraint of 50 000 machine hours available. The contribution per machine hour for each product will be: Kettles £10.50 (£42/4); Percolators £8.18 (£45/5.5); and Irons £8.25 (£33/4). The order of preference for producing the three products will now be kettles, then irons, and then percolators, and the contribution from the production of each product will be as set in Table 5.12. In this case KEEP will make a profit of £156 000.

Table 5.12 KEEP contribution under constrained machine resources

Product	Quantity produced	Contribution/ item (£)	Machine hours used	Total contribution per product (£)
Kettles	5000	42	20 000	210 000
Irons	2000	33	8000	66 000
Percolators	4000	45	22 000	180 000
Total contribution				456 000

Through these examples, we can see how a constraint on one of the resource inputs to the production process can affect not only the contribution and profits of a company, but also its preference for which products to produce.

Qualitative aspects of the decision

Although the analysis above shows clearly which of the three products under consideration would yield the greatest contribution and profits when there are resource constraints, it is still not certain that managers will opt for the most profitable production programme. Firstly, it is possible that there will be a degree of product interdependence, whereby some customers will only buy from the company if they can obtain the full range of products. Therefore, a less profitable line may be maintained in order to retain customers for the more profitable products. Secondly, resource constraints are often temporary – for example, KEEP may require more labour or materials, but cannot obtain them for a month or so. In these circumstances it would be logical to manufacture some of each of the products in order not to lose the customers for the least profitable product line.

Multiple constraints on production

A company may sometimes find that there is a shortage of more than one resource input at the same time. This situation is considerably more complex than those demonstrated so far, and will require the use of a computer spreadsheet with a linear programming function. This, we consider, is beyond the scope of this book, but the technique should be covered in a Quantitative Methods course.

Timing of cash flows and investment appraisal techniques

When considering an investment the manager will seek to estimate not only the size of the expected returns but, also, when they are likely to happen. For example, does the profit attributable to the proposed investment happen evenly over the investment's life, or is it bunched, perhaps towards the end? This kind of consideration matters for several reasons. Firstly, basic liquidity management means that any organisation will usually seek revenues now rather than later, in order to maintain the solvency of the business. Secondly, money may be said to have a time value, in that £1 now is preferable to £1 next year. This thinking refers back to the third basic rule (described above) relating to considerations of costs and benefits in a decision: 'The timing of the cash flows must be considered'.

Supposing an organisation, let us say a garage, sells a car to a customer at a price of £10 000. Naturally, the garage will prefer to be paid immediately rather than waiting a year or two for its money. If the garage owner does have to wait a year, there will be an opportunity cost involved. Perhaps an investment opportunity will have been missed, or simply the garage owner will have foregone a year's interest on the £10 000. This opportunity cost will rise if payment is delayed further. Thus, only if the £10 000 is received when due can maximum benefit be obtained from it.

This example illustrates that moneys received in the future should be discounted back to present-day values if they are to be compared with movements of cash that are happening immediately; hence the term 'discounted cash flow calculation'. Furthermore, the time value of money depends partly upon the *risk* associated with the future cash flows, such that the greater the risk, the smaller the present-day value.

Having established that the timing of cash flows does indeed matter, let us now consider some of the better-known appraisal techniques.

The Payback method

This is perhaps the simplest technique and has the practical merit that it is easy both to understand and to apply. Using nominal (that is, undiscounted) cash flows, the analyst simply calculates the length of time needed for the initial investment to be recovered. The shorter the time – known as the payback period – the better.

This method can be illustrated through the following example.

Exhibit 5.8

Alfred Smith's café

Alfred Smith operates a seaside café in Bellevue-on-sea. He has £2000 to invest in order to increase the profitability of the business. He is considering improving the facilities of the café by investing in a better soft-ice-cream machine; alternatively, he could spend the money on an elaborate promotion campaign that is intended to ensure that his café is featured in the publicity material of Bellevue and that of several major coach companies offering excursions to the town. As well as these options, Alfred is also considering the possibility of using the money as a down payment for the franchise of Yummy Burgers, but acceptance of this franchise would mean an expensive total conversion of the café.

Alfred has set about predicting the costs and revenues that might be expected for each of the projects. In relation to the ice-cream machine and franchise, as well as listening the data provided by the salespeople from the companies concerned Alfred has spoken to friends in the seaside catering trade who have embarked on similar projects. For the publicity campaign he has his own experience of previous similar campaigns to draw on. As a result of all this, the predicted costs and revenues of all the projects over a four year period are as set out in Table 5.13 (the figures in brackets being negative sums, i.e. costs, and 'Year 0' means the initial investment period, i.e. that made now).

▶

Year	Ice-Cream Machine (£000)	Publicity Campaign (£000)	Yummy Burger Franchise (£000)
0	(2.0)	(2.0)	(2.0)
1	0.4	1.0	(4.0)
2	0.6	0.8	(6.0)
3	1.0	0.2	1.0
4	2.0	0.1	4.0

Table 5.13 Smith's Café costs and revenues

The simple payback conclusion is that Alfred Smith should choose either the ice-cream machine or the publicity campaign because the payback periods of each are the same, namely three years.

However, there are a number of additional points that can be made from this predicted information:

- Liquidity is better maintained with the publicity campaign, with most of the projects revenues coming quickly.
- Project durability is better with the ice-cream machine, which appears to have expanding cash flows after three and four years, whereas the publicity campaign has run out of steam by this time.
- The franchise option is relatively expensive but seems to have good growth potential once it is properly running. Is Mr Smith prepared to wait five years or more to see his investment pay off?

Clearly, as this example illustrates, a simple application of payback may be misleading. The strengths of the Payback method, are that it is simple to understand and use, and it focuses on the liquidity issues of the project. However, it has significant drawbacks. In particular, the timing of cash flows is ignored within the payback period: there is no consideration as to whether they come at the beginning or the end of the year in question. Furthermore, cash flows after payback are ignored.

Accounting Rate of Return

On a continuum of complexity, this method is perhaps the second-least complex approach. It has the merit that all cash flows associated with a project are included.

Accounting Rate of Return (ARR) compares the average annual profit with capital employed over the life of the project. The method is alternatively referred to as the 'return on capital employed' and provides an example of decision making by 'ratio analysis', which is discussed further at the end of this section of the chapter. The ARR comparison is expressed as a percentage, and may be expressed as:

$$\text{ARR} = \frac{\text{average annual profit}}{\text{initial capital cost}} \times 100\%$$

The basic rule is that the larger the percentage the better, though organisations may impose minimum levels of acceptable return and reject all projects with predicted returns below this.

<table>
<tr><td>Exhibit 5.9</td></tr>
</table>

Alfred Smith's café (contd)

For the ice-cream machine the profits over four years totalled £4000. So the average annual profit is given by:

$$\frac{\text{total profit over the life of the project}}{\text{number of years of project life}} = \frac{£4000}{4} = £1000.$$

Initial investment was £2000, so ARR is calculated as

$$\frac{£1000}{£2000} \times 100\% = 50\%.$$

Similarly for the publicity campaign, average profit is £2100 ÷ 4 = £525, and so ARR is given by:

$$\frac{£525}{£2000} \times 100\% = 26\%.$$

The franchise cannot be considered over a four-year lifespan because the investment would not yet be in profit.

Thus, appraisal by ARR, in contrast to the indifference of Payback, reveals a distinct preference for the ice-cream machine, even though the publicity campaign shows stronger cash flows in the early years.

It may be commented that the approach is arguably inconsistent, in that it compares an investment's lifetime profit with capital employed at the beginning. For consistency the process should include average capital employed throughout the life of an investment. This may be most simply achieved by calculating an average of the capital invested at the beginning and at the end of the project.

Suppose the scrap or trade-in value of Alfred Smith's ice-cream machine at the end of four years is £250. Then the average capital employed is calculated as £2000 + £250 ÷ 2 = £1125, and so the revised ARR becomes $\frac{£1000}{£1125} \times 100\% = 89\%$.

Alfred's publicity campaign is an essentially intangible asset so probably has no scrap or residual value. The revised average capital employed figure in this case becomes: £2000 + £0 ÷ 2 = £1000, and so the corresponding ARR is calculated as:

$$\frac{£525}{£1000} \times 100\% = 53\%.$$

Each of these very straightforward methods of investment appraisal has its merits, though consistency of method is clearly essential for valid comparison between alternative investments. It would be perfectly valid to use both methods in order to gain more than one perspective of the alternatives, but each method should be followed through separately and comparison of the results made afterwards.

When appraising a number of options using ARR, we should be wary of simply selecting the highest percentage return. It should be remembered that an organisation's prime interest is real profit and cash, not percentages. Over-reliance on ARR can be misleading. This can best be seen in the context of another aspect of the example of Alfred Smith's café.

| Exhibit 5.10 | **Alfred Smith's franchise option** |

So far, we have not calculated an ARR for the franchise option. Let us predict some more data for the investment, so that investment for the whole project looks like that set out in Table 5.14.

Table 5.14 Smith's Café investment and cash flow profiles

Year	(Net cash outflows)/ net cash inflows (£000)	Capital invested at end of year (£000)
0	(2)	2
1	(24)	2 + 26 = 28
2	(26)	28 + 27 = 55
3	1	55 + 4 = 59
4	4	29
5	10	15
6	10	0

In Year 1 the net profit was £2000 but capital invested was £26 000 (yielding a net cash outflow of £24 000, as shown). In Year 2 the corresponding figures were £1000 and £27 000, and in Year 3 they were £5000 and £4000 respectively. There was no investment in subsequent years, and it is assumed that the residual value of investment falls to nothing by Year 6.

Total profit is given (in £000) by: 2 + 1 + 5 + 4 + 10 + 10 = 32, and average annual profit is 32 ÷ 6 = 5.33. Average capital employed is given by:

$$\frac{2 + 28 + 55 + 59 + 29 + 15 + 0}{7} = \frac{188}{7} = 26.86$$

So, ARR is given by $\frac{5.33}{26.86} = 19.84\%$.

While the ARR is lower in this than for the other investment options, the project yields £10 000 per annum when it matures. This is five times the best annual return of the other possible investments. It may therefore be argued that the investment is five times as attractive. But is this really the case? It must be remembered that, not only are the returns bigger but so are the costs, with an average of £26 860 invested per annum. Such an investment clearly requires considerable financial commitment, and a consequent personal one as well.

If it were a real situation it would be appropriate to incorporate qualitative issues into the decision-making process by considering factors such as the impact a project of this kind might have on the franchisee's overall lifestyle.

In summary, the strengths of ARR are that ARR is a conceptual improvement on the Payback method because it takes account of cash flows over the whole life of the investment; furthermore, it is simple to understand and straightforward in its application. However, the main weakness of ARR are that it does not take account of the timing of cash flows within lifetime of the project, and it measures in percentages, rather than financial terms.

Net Present Values: discounted cash flow

The Net Present Value (NPV) is, conceptually, probably the soundest technique for investment appraisal. Its main strengths are:

- all cash flows, within the project, are considered;
- the timing of all cash flows is specifically considered; and
- risk and opportunity cost are specifically considered.

The technique's only real weakness is lies in the potentially false assumptions that may be made. The implications of this will become clearer as we work through examples.

The principle of the Net Present Value calculation is to convert all future cash flows, whenever they occur, back to present-day values. This will involve calculating, for example, what £100 next year, or the year after, might be worth now. It may be that receiving £100 next year is equivalent to, say, £92 now; or £100 the year after next might be worth £85 now. This technique is based on distinguishing between *nominal* cash flows, meaning the actual sums of money that flow in and out as a result of an investment, and *discounted* cash flows, meaning the nominal cash flows that have been adjusted to allow for the reduction in value due to the passage of time.

The size of the discount factor for future cash flows will depend on the opportunity cost and the risk associated with the investment. So, if we are owed £1000 with the promise that this sum will be paid in one year from now, the present value of this future income will depend on factors such as the likelihood of the debt not being honoured, and what the £1000 might have earned for us over the course of a year if it had been paid now. As well as differing between investments, the rate may be expected to change, from one time period to the next, in response to environmental factors such as the level of economic activity, any 'feel good factor' that is perceived generally, and perhaps the demographic nature of the population. These ideas form the conceptual underpinning of the NPV method.

The NPV process involves, firstly, estimating all the cash flows associated with the investment under consideration, and when they occur. It is then necessary to reduce the value of these cash flows to account for flows that occur in the future. For the purpose of illustration, let us assume that the present value of cash paid or received is reduced by ten per cent for each year that payment is delayed. Therefore, £1000 next year will be worth £1000 − (0.1 × £1000) now, i.e. £900. To calculate the compound effect of this value reduction over several years, we should use the following formula:

$$PV_0 = \frac{FV_n}{(1 + k)^n}$$

Where n is the number of years into the future that the cash flow occurs,

FV_n is the nominal value of a future cash flow received in the nth year (i.e. actual money paid out or received in that year)

PV_0 is the present value of the future cashflow,

k is the rate of fall in value.

In our example, $k = 10\% \equiv 0.1$. The NPV formula can be rewritten as:

$$PV_0 = FV_n \times \frac{1}{(1 + k)^n}$$

meaning that the FV_n, the actual future cash flows are adjusted by $1/(1 + k)^n$; this fraction is known as the discount factor. It is a fraction that converts a future £1 into its present-day equivalents. So, at ten per cent, the present-day equivalent of £1, received at the end of one year, would be £0.909 and, if not received until two years from now, £0.826.

Although this compound formula for discounting has been introduced, it is more usual to discount using tables of Present Value Factors, which are included as an Appendix to this book. The different rates of discount are tabulated against a range of time periods (years) over which the cash flow will occur. By choosing the appropriate year and the relevant discount rate, we obtain a discount factor for that cash flow. This figure should be multiplied by the nominal cash flow amount in order to obtain its present value equivalent. For example, if we continue to assume a discount rate of ten per cent, and we are concerned with a cash flow of £3000 in three years' time, we can see from the discount tables that the discount factor is 0.751. When this figure is multiplied by the cash flow we have (£3000 × 0.751) = £2253 as the present value of the £3000.

Consider now the example of Alfred Smith and his café in Exhibit 5.11.

These examples illustrate a further attraction of the NPV method: there are clear criteria for basic acceptability of a project; it must offer a positive NPV over an acceptably short life span. Clearly the likelihood of achieving a positive NPV depends in part on the discount rate chosen. Indeed, it is possible that a project

| Exhibit 5.11 | **Alfred Smith's Café options by discounted cash flows** |

We can now discount the future cash flows, and reappraise Alfred's investment decision, taking account of *when* cash is either paid or received.

Table 5.15 Alfred's discounted cash flow

Year	(nominal cash flow) (£000)		Present Value Factor at 10%		Discounted (present value) cash flows (£000)
(a) Ice-cream machine					
0	(2)	×	1.0	=	(2.0000)
1	0.4	×	0.909	=	0.3636
2	0.6	×	0.826	=	0.4956
3	1.0	×	0.751	=	0.7510
4	2.0	×	0.683	=	1.3660
			Net Present Value		0.9762
(b) Publicity campaign					
0	(2)	×	1.0	=	(2.0000)
1	1	×	0.909	=	0.9090
2	0.8	×	0.826	=	0.6608
3	0.2	×	0.751	=	0.1502
4	0.1	×	0.683	=	0.0683
			Net Present Value		(0.2117)
(c) Franchise project					
0	(2)	×	1.0	=	(2.0000)
1	(24)	×	0.909	=	(21.8160)
2	(26)	×	0.826	=	(21.4760)
3	1	×	0.751	=	0.7510
4	4	×	0.683	=	2.7320
5	10	×	0.621	=	6.2100
6	10	×	0.565	=	5.6500
			at this stage the NPV	=	(29.9490)
7	10?	0.513			
8	10?	0.467			
9	10?	0.424			
10	10?	0.386			

The ice-cream machine thus shows an overall NPV profit of £976.20 (Table 5.15a). The publicity campaign project, however, shows a negative NPV when a ten per cent discount factor is applied (Table 5.15b), which means that, at this rate of discount, the project should be rejected as loss-making.

However, before we reject this project, it may be worth examining some of the assumptions we have made. Are the projected cash flows correct, and might the discount rate we have applied be high? Once again, it can be seen that quantitative analysis may not be entirely objective, and it is worth taking the time to question the fundamental assumptions of the appraisal.

▶

Now let us turn to the projected cash flows of the franchise option and see how they will be affected by discounting. This is, of course, a longer term project, so the cash flows will be more heavily discounted. The method of calculation is the same; and is shown in Table 5.15c. If we were to continue the projected cash flows further into the future past ten years (which would magnify the uncertainty of the forecasts), we would see that, with this level of business activity, it would appear that it would take Alfred Smith until year 14 to break even on his investment. Even if we assume – perhaps unrealistically – that accurate cash-flow forecasting is possible over such a long period, few organisations will be willing, or able, to wait such a long time for so little return. This NPV calculation shows that Alfred Smith should only accept this option if he can either achieve higher sales, or pay less for the franchise.

might have a positive NPV at one rate of discount, say ten per cent, but that this might become a negative value at a higher discount rate.

These two situations can be plotted graphically, NPV against discount rate, and are shown in Fig. 5.1.

Point A shows the highest possible NPV with a zero value discount rate, though this would be most unlikely in practice; point D is the preferred discount rate, which shows a positive NPV, and C indicates a rate that shows a negative NPV. The line $n_1 n_2$ shows all the NPVs for the various discount rates. From this it can be seen that at discount rate B the NPV is zero. This rate of discount is known as the internal rate of return (IRR), representing the discount rate at which the present value of all cash inflows exactly matches the present value of cash outflows. At a discount rate below the IRR, a project is judged to be viable; at a higher rate, it is not.

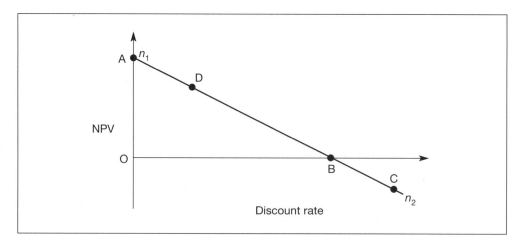

Fig. 5.1 NPV against discount rate

In general terms, the more pessimistic an analyst feels about the future and/or, the greater the opportunity cost associated with a particular investment, the larger will be the appropriate discount rate, and the smaller will be the present-day equivalents of its future cash flows. The risk perception may be about the economy in general, or this particular investment, which may for some unique reason be considered high-risk.

The effect of inflation on NPV calculations

Inflation might be defined as the erosion of the purchasing power of money over time. It is usually expressed as a percentage, so a seven per cent rate of inflation, for example, means that on average £100 today will buy roughly seven per cent less than it would have done last year.

If it is expected that there will be inflation in future years, this will have to be reflected in the discount rates we apply to the appraisal of potential investments. The discount rate that would apply in the absence of any inflation is known as the 'real' discount rate, whilst the 'nominal' rate is that which is actually used, and which takes account of inflation.

A number of economists have developed relatively complex methods of including provision for inflation in the discount rate. However, the formulas used by Brealey and Myers (1991) in fact give a very similar result compared with the much simpler method of adding the inflation rate to the real discount rate. Such a method as Brealey and Myers' may be needed if inflation reaches very high levels, but in normal circumstances (when inflation remains below ten per cent) the approximation method will give an appropriate nominal discount rate. Indeed, it may be argued that, given that estimation of the real discount rate is open to subjective interpretation, small differences in the nominal rate due to the method of calculation are quite acceptable.

It should not be forgotten that nominal cash flows will themselves be affected by inflation, so although the use of higher discount rates may tend to make a project seem less attractive, this should be balanced by inflated nominal returns on investment as time passes.

Estimating a discount factor

There are two elements to consider in establishing a real discount rate, opportunity cost and risk. Inflation will be included in setting the nominal rate.

Opportunity cost

If money is invested in a project, that capital will have had an alternative use. The opportunity cost of investing in a business venture is, therefore, based on what the same sum might have earned if used for a different purpose.

One obvious alternative is simply to have put the money into a savings account with a bank. In this case, the opportunity cost will be related to the interest the funds would have earned as savings. Alternatively, the capital raised for the business venture may have been borrowed. Here, the cost is very clear, since the borrower will pay interest on the loan. The interest, either paid on a loan or earned from savings, will vary according to economic conditions, and so the opportunity cost element of the discount rate will not necessarily remain constant. Indeed, it is likely to vary with interest rates within the broad monetary system.

Other factors that might affect the opportunity cost might include share price changes. Investment in another company's shares is an obvious alternative to undertaking a business venture. Therefore, a buoyant stock market will increase the opportunity cost of the project that might be undertaken since the alternative of the purchase of shares in another company will appear more attractive.

Risk

The risk element in assessing the present value of, say, £100 next year derives from the fact that the money may never be paid. The present value of this money essentially refers to the sum that would be acceptable now, instead of possibly receiving the £100 next year. If a trader is very doubtful as to whether the money will be paid, he/she might be prepared to accept a relatively small sum now in lieu of payment next year.

Of course, the smaller the sum such a person would be prepared to accept now, the higher the discount rate. It can be seen, then, that there is a direct relationship between the discount rate and the perception of business risk involved in a project.

Sensitivity analysis

When an organisation estimates the costs and revenues associated with a potential project, assumptions will be made about the market size, its likely share of the market, various costs, etc. These estimates may, of course, be wrong – sometimes by a considerable amount. The idea of a 'sensitivity analysis' is to gauge the effect of such inaccurate estimates on the outcome of the project. The technique can best be seen in the context of an example.

Exhibit 5.12	**A sensitivity analysis on cheese retailing**

Suppose we are thinking of opening a retail shop to sell speciality cheeses. The set-up costs of the venture are estimated to be about £100 000, and we would be operating within a catchment area of 150 000 households, of which we believe we might expect to serve two per cent. On average, those households that buy from us are expected to spend around £2 each week. We have estimated average margin (that is, gross profit as a proportion of sales) to be about 20 per cent. The rent will be £2000 per annum, wages £20 000, and sundry variable costs will amount to £3000 for the same period. We shall assume a project life of five years, and a cost of capital of 12 per cent.

We have allowed room for error by estimating, not only what we think will be the value of each of these variables, but also a range of values to correspond to the most optimistic and the most pessimistic scenarios we can imagine. All of this data is set out in Table 5.16.

The most likely, or expected cash flows have been projected for years 0 to 5, and from these, using discount factors appropriate for 12 per cent, a NPV of £42 000 has been calculated, using the normal method shown earlier in the chapter. The column of 'pessimistic' NPVs is calculated by looking at each variable in relation to the worst-case scenario. The 'pessimistic' NPV for each variable is calculated by using the worst-case value for that variable, but keeping the values of all the other variables at their expected levels. A similar process is used for calculating the 'optimistic' values.

Table 5.16 Forecast data and NPVs for a cheese retailing shop

| Variable | Range of values | | | NPVs in £000 | | |
	Optimum	Expected	Pessimistic	Optimum	Expected	Pessimistic
Market share	3%	2%	1%	160	42	(76.5)
Market size	170 000	150 000	110 000	73	42	(21)
Revenue	£3	£2	£1.5	160	42	(17.4)
Margin	25%	20%	15%	101	42	(9.8)
Wages and other variable costs	£19 000	£25 000	£28 000	64	42	30

The most critical variable would appear to be market share, since, in the worst-case scenario, this has the lowest NPV of a loss of £76 500, yet the optimistic forecast suggests that profits will be greatest if we achieve our maximum market share. Management attention must, therefore, remain focused on this variable so as to ensure that the expected value (or better) is achieved. All other variables that have possible negative NPVs warrant attention. Variable costs, on the other hand, are, according to our calculations, less likely to have a significant impact, and may warrant less attention.

The sensitivity process shown illustrates change in only one variable at a time. While this may be useful from the practical point of managing the calculation, it possibly oversimplifies the situation, in that more than one of these factors, whether or not they are interrelated, are likely to vary at a given time. The use of a computer will permit a more sophisticated, holistic analysis, but our example is nevertheless illustrative of the principle of sensitivity analysis.

Quantifying the qualitative issues

So far in this chapter, we have only considered the obvious (primarily financial) costs and benefits directly associated with a proposed investment. Here are a few examples of less obvious issues, which, although difficult to quantify, could have a significant bearing on an investment decision.

- A new production machine may result in a more reliable product, produced to finer tolerances. This might have a beneficial effect on customer loyalty, both for this product, and others in the organisation's portfolio.
- These higher standards may enhance the organisation's reputation and bring in new customers for products unrelated to the proposed investment.
- New investment may require structural change within the organisation. Staff reactions to new work systems could be positive, seeing them as an opportunity for personal development, or negative, in which case they may try to prevent the systems from working effectively.

Finance and other issues

This chapter has concentrated almost entirely on assessing the merits of proposed investments. It would be as well for any investment appraisal to include consideration of the following factors:

- whether profitability might have any consequent effect on expenses elsewhere in the organisation;
- what the perception and reaction are of existing suppliers and customers to new aspects of business;
- whether liquidity will be affected by the new venture, and what might be its effect on the level of debtors and creditors;
- whether there are systems in place to deal with any additional administrative workload;
- whether the proposed changes might make the organisation more/less attractive to lenders and investors; and
- how the raising of funds for new investment might affect gearing, the capital structure and ownership concentration (who owns what proportion of the shares) of the organisation.

Summary of the chapter

- The chapter introduced a number of quantitative approaches to decision making, most of which involved management accounting techniques. It was seen that management accounting techniques do not necessarily provide a complete solution, and that personality and organisational can have an impact on the decision made.
- Consideration was given as to which costs are relevant to a business decision. Three fundamental rules were introduced for assessing which costs are relevant.

- The importance of marginal costs and contribution in financial decision making were examined and applied to specific decision-making contexts, such as when a product line might be discontinued, and circumstances when a dual pricing structure might be applied.

- A range of investment appraisal processes was discussed, highlighting the fact that different approaches will often lead the decision maker in different directions. This examination demonstrated how these techniques could be misapplied to make inappropriate decisions if not treated with caution. Certain of the techniques had very specific merits, for example, if liquidity is a potential problem for the investing company, payback analysis may be particularly appropriate.

- Discounted cash flows were thought to give a more complete picture than other methods of investment appraisal, but even this method relied heavily on the accuracy of estimates of costs and revenues. This was demonstrated through the use of sensitivity analysis.

Case Study 9: Corpair Ltd

Corpair Ltd manufactures compressors for industrial use. Worried about likely increased competition from the emerging Pacific Rim economies, the company has decided to modernise its production machinery. Existing machinery cost £250 000 four years ago and had an expected life of eight years. It will now cost the company £5000 to remove, but it thinks that it may be able to sell all the equipment to a customer in Poland for £15 000. The costs of moving the equipment to Poland will amount to £5000 and will be born by Corpair.

The company is considering two possible options for replacing the machinery:

1 *Relco*. Relco supplied the previous machine and has traded with Corpair for the last 30 years. Relco machines have always been reliable and the staff of Corpair are used to working with them. The new machine would cost £350 000 and has been developed from the previous model, although the new version has some computer control so would need only two operators instead of four. (Each operator costs £25 000 per annum.) The machine would be able to produce the full range of Corpair products, and the annual demand for these is predicted to be 500 units for at least the next three years, with a likely reduction of 50 units per year thereafter. The material and other variable costs total £500 per unit. The selling price of each unit is £900. The firm's cost of capital is 12 per cent.

2 *Avma*. The alternative machine is available from Avma Ltd, the UK branch of Advanced Machines Inc., a California-based company that specialises in high-tech problem solutions. The Avma machine is completely automated, and will only require 10 per cent of one person's time to check and maintain it. The machine will produce to finer tolerances than the Relco model, reducing machining time and reducing variable costs by 20 per cent. The Avma machine is capable of producing a variety of different compressors, as well as those in Corpair's present range. This is attractive to the company because they have recently had several enquiries for bigger and more

powerful compressors. The selling price of these machines would be in the order of £2500, but the Avma machine is rather more expensive at £650 000.

1 *For each of the replacement options, calculate Payback, Accounting Rate of Return and NPV.*

2 *Discuss any qualitative issues that you consider relevant to the decision.*

3 *Advise Corpair as to what they should do.*

Case Study 10: Staystuck foam-based construction adhesive

Staystuck Engineering has been working on a new foam-based gap-filling adhesive for the construction industry. The product is to be sold in an aerosol can. In use it is squirted, via a narrow plastic pipe, into a cavity to be filled, where it combines with air to expand and set in a rigid foam.

So far the company has spent £500 000 to develop the product. Full production facilities will involve another £7.75m. The product is expected to have a life of four years. Depreciation is expected to be linear (i.e. the same proportion of the original investment each year), with the assets having a residual value of £100 000. Other factory overheads are expected to be between £1.5m and £5m, and probably around £3m.

The company's research suggests that the total market for such products may be ten million units each year, and Staystuck hope to achieve a 1 per cent share. At worst, they believe their share could be as little as 0.4 per cent, and at best, as much as 1.6 per cent. Competition from substitute products could drive the total market down to eight million units, although repeat orders could boost it to 11 million units.

Material costs will probably be £2 per unit, although scarcity of certain key ingredients could drive this cost up to £2.75. It is not thought likely that these costs will be less than £1.25 per unit. About 5–12 minutes, and probably 10 minutes, of labour time will be required for can assembly, filling and packing, per unit. Labour costs £12 per hour.

Your marketing advisor tells you that the normal selling price of such products is slightly more than £64, with the highest price being £73 and the lowest being £61. This person also advises you that a promotional campaign would enhance your market share. The directors tell you that their normal cost of capital is 16 per cent.

1 *What are the principal uncertainties associated with this project?*

2 *What is the maximum cost of capital that the project can tolerate?*

3 *How much could be spent on the promotion campaign?*

4 *Can the uncertainties be reduced by any action on the part of Staystuck?*

5 *Can you suggest any other factors that Staystuck should take into account?*

Reference

Brealey, R. A. and Myers, S. C. (1991) *Principles of Corporate Finance*, McGraw-Hill, New York.

CHAPTER 6

Some further quantitative methods for decision making

At the end of this chapter you should:

● **understand the concept of probability;**

● **be able to estimate or calculate likely probabilities of future events, including conditional probabilities;**

● **understand the nature of 'expected values' of future events;**

● **be able to model decision scenarios using decision-tree analysis; and**

● **have a basic understanding of scenario modelling using network analysis.**

Introduction

The previous chapter was introduced as the first of two dealing with quantitative aspects of decision making. The main focus of Chapter 5 was management accounting. The principal emphasis of this chapter will be on the uses of probability in decision making; that is, the likelihood of particular outcomes occurring. In introducing aspects of probability, it is our intention to focus firmly on its application to decision-making situations.

When faced with a range of options, an organisation will need to know not only the potential gain from each option, but also the likelihood of success. However favourable the desired outcome of a decision may be, it can be of little worth to the firm if it is unlikely to occur. Conversely, critical threats are only worthy of serious contingency planning if they are likely actually to happen. For many organisations, it is likely that effort will be concentrated on those possibilities that are most likely to occur. However, we shall also encounter in this chapter circumstances in which it may be rational for an individual or organisation to accept risky options, with low probability of success.

In a slightly different context, Vroom (1964) linked probability to worker motivation, suggesting that outcomes that are perceived as unlikely have little motivational significance for staff. High probability outcomes tend to have considerable significance. One concludes that probability estimation may have significant impact on human resource management.

Some applications of probability

Amongst the many applications of probability, one very useful context in which it can be used is in project appraisal. Project appraisal can be a complex process, particularly when there are many investment options from which to choose; and this complexity is compounded if there are several possible outcomes for each option. We shall address some of these circumstances later in the chapter, but for now a very simple example of the application of probability will suffice.

It is possible to use probability data to estimate the 'expected value' of a project. This expected value is calculated by multiplying the outcome value by the probability of it happening. Its prime purpose is to enable the decision maker to balance the relative merits of a risky project with high potential profits against a more secure venture with lower yield but less uncertainty. This is illustrated in the case of Penny Farthing, a student seeking temporary employment.

| Exhibit 6.1 | **Penny Williams gets a holiday job** |

It is Easter and, planning ahead, Penny is looking for a job during the long summer vacation. She has two possibilities. The first option is to work for a contract cleaning company, providing holiday relief for regular workers, at £140 per week. The job is available for ten weeks. The second option is to work for her Uncle Bob, driving a van at a wage of £180 per week, also for ten weeks. This is financially more attractive, but, unfortunately, she has not yet passed her driving test. Her test is scheduled for May, and she has heard that the pass rate of candidates in the driving test is 70 per cent. The contract cleaning company requires an immediate answer as to whether Lucy will accept its offer of a job. It seems unlikely that any alternative temporary employment will be found.

Option 1 will guarantee an income of (10 × £140) = £1400. Option 2 offers a 70 per cent (or 0.7) chance of earning (10 × £180) ≡ £1800. The expected value of the second option will therefore be 0.7 × £1800 = £1260.

On the basis of the expected values of the options available, Penny may decide to accept the job with the cleaning company. However, as with most quantitative approaches to decision making, the figures may not give a complete picture! Penny may, for example, believe she is a better-than-average driver, and may estimate her chances of passing the driving test as 80 per cent. In this case the expected value of the second option will be: 0.8 × £1800 = £1440 and will tip the balance in favour of her uncle's job.

The foregoing deals with the quantitative implications of her two options, but what of the qualitative aspects? She may also feel one of the jobs is likely to be more enjoyable, and therefore would not make her decision purely on the basis of the expected monetary reward.

As with many other statistical approaches to decision making, calculating the expected value of an option does not give us an instant solution to the decision we have to make. There will be other issues to consider, just as in the case of Penny

Williams and her employment options. This will be discussed further at a later stage; but suffice it to say that, if we all made decisions purely on the basis of statistical probability and expected values, none of us would voluntarily take out insurance, and nobody would play the National Lottery!

An introduction to probability theory

Since throughout this chapter we shall be using probabilities to forecast the likelihood of particular outcomes, it is as well to start with some of the basic rules of probability.

Total probability of an event by definition sums to 1, so that all individual outcomes within the event must have probabilities of less than 1, and these individual probabilities must sum to 1. For example, if four horses are running in a race, we know that one of them must win. Therefore, the probability of one of the horses winning the race is 1, that is, a certainty. The probability of each individual horse winning will be less than 1, and their collective probabilities will add up to 1. In the absence of any trend data, or evidence that one or more of the horses is faster than the others, we might estimate the probability of each winning as $\frac{1}{4}$ or 0.25. However, suppose the same four horses have run a similar race on ten previous occasions, and horse A has won only once; horses B and D have each won twice, but horse C has won the other five races. An informed observer would clearly estimate the probability of horse C winning as greater than the others – possibly $\frac{1}{2}$ or 0.5.

In this example, trend data was useful, but this will not always be the case. Imagine you are tossing a coin and want to know the likelihood of the outcome being a 'head'. You may have tossed the coin seven times previously with a head resulting on each occasion. This is irrelevant to a future outcome; the probability of the next toss achieving a head is still $\frac{1}{2}$. (This is quite different from the probability of achieving eight consecutive heads, the chances of which are very remote.)

In certain circumstances, probability cannot be calculated either on the evidence of past trends, as in the horse race, or on the basis of the known likelihood of a particular outcome, as with tossing coins. In such cases, an estimate has to be made, based on whatever incomplete knowledge is available to us. This is the least reliable means of determining probabilities, but unfortunately in situations where organisations must predict the likely success of a particular project there will often be an element of guesswork. In essence, therefore, probability estimates may be:

- calculated using prior knowledge;
- calculated by empirical research; or
- estimated by the judgement of the analyst.

The preferred method will depend on other circumstances, and not all three methods may be possible. In the interests of maximising objectivity, the third option of the three should perhaps be regarded as something of a last resort.

Probability and expected value

A very simple example of how probability can be used to determine the 'expected value' of potential projects was given at the start of this chapter through Penny Williams. Two further examples can now be used to illustrate slightly more complex situations involving probability and expectations.

Exhibit 6.2

Lee West sits his exams

Lee West is a student who is about to sit his final exams. The probability of his passing is 0.8 and so, by deduction, he has a probability of 0.2 of failing. However, he might pass with distinction (probability of 0.1), with merit (probability of 0.3) or gain a bare pass (probability of 0.4).

Lee's employment prospects hinge on the outcome of these exams. He has been offered a job regardless of his results. If he fails his exams he will be placed on a low grade at a starting salary of £9000 per annum; if he passes his exams he will initially be paid £14 000 per annum; and the achievement of a distinction will be rewarded with an immediate salary increment of £2000. Probability can be applied to these possible outcomes using Bayes' strategy which develops the idea of 'expected value'.

As described earlier in the chapter and shown in elemetary fashion in the example of Penny Williams, expected value combines outcome with probability so as to produce a weighted average outcome for a particular event, with each outcome being multiplied (that is weighted) by its probability. Lee's expected income can be calculated by first multiplying each of the three possible salaries he will be paid by the associated probability of achieving it, then by adding together these sums, as shown in Table 6.1. It is possible that Lee might use this information to weigh up the merits of one job offer against another.

Table 6.1 Lee's job options and their expected value

Salary (£)		Probability		Expect value (£)
9000	×	0.2	=	1800
14 000	×	0.7	=	9800
16 000	×	0.1	=	1600
	Expected income = 13 200			

The next example concerns a decision a firm must make, choosing between two investment opportunities.

A further point of principle to bear in mind is that expected values only have significance if the event is going to happen repeatedly, because they are *average* outcomes. Thus, if the event is not going to recur frequently or (worse) is unique, then this approach is of little relevance to successful analytical process.

| Exhibit 6.3 | **Two company projects** |

Project *A* is a contract that will yield an income of £5000, with a possibility (estimated at 20 per cent) of a little extra work worth an additional £1000. Project *B* involves investing in production of a new product, for which there is some uncertainty as to whether there will be a market. Ad hoc research, however, tells the owner–manager that there is a good chance (about 60 per cent) of making £7000 profit, and £5000 if things go only moderately well. Total failure, however, would result in a loss of £2000, and there would appear to be about a 10 per cent chance of this happening. The expected value of the two options is evaluated in Table 6.2 below.

Table 6.2 Expected value of two optional projects

Outcome (£)		Probability		Expected Value (£)
Option A				
5000	×	0.8	=	4000
6000	×	0.2	=	1200
Total expected value				5200
Option B				
(2000)	×	0.1	=	(200)
5000	×	0.2	=	1000
7000	×	0.6	=	4200
8000	×	0.1	=	800
Total expected value				5800

As can be same from Table 6.2, the expected, or average, outcome of Option *B* is £600 better than Option *A*. However, in terms of *actual* outcomes *B* has a much broader range of possibilities. The analyst must look at this range to see if they are all acceptable when assessing a proposal. Thus, although the average outcome will be a healthy profit of £5800, the actual outcome will range between a loss of £2000 and a profit of £8000. The firm must be sure that its liquidity position is strong enough to make such a range of eventualities acceptable in any one year.

Having now introduced and developed the notion of expected values, let us return to a problem encountered earlier (Exhibit 5.1 in Chapter 5), where an attempt was made to decide between three investment opportunities in new holiday facilities. Probability may be able to assist our decision making by adding a further dimension to the analysis.

Exhibit 6.4

The holiday company (contd)

As well as estimating likely profits from each facility under each weather type, let us assume that we have examined historical data for the region and can assign probabilities to the different weather options, as set out in Table 6.3:

Table 6.3. Payback depends on the weather

	Weather			Expected
	Cool	Average	Hot	value
Probability	0.2	0.7	0.1	
Facilities				
Swimming Pool	50	100	150	95[a]
Tennis Court	30	180	90	141[b]
Restaurant	170	100	40	108[c]

Notes
(a) 95=(0.2×50)+(0.7×100)+(0.1×150)
(b) 141=(0.2×30)+(0.7×180)+(0.1×90)
(c) 108=(0.2×170)+(0.7×100)+(0.1×40)

Clearly the option with the highest expected value is the tennis court, and so on average this would be the most profitable option.

The value of perfect information

Let us change the situation slightly by assuming that we have all three facilities built but that, for some reason, we do not want to have them all open at the same time. In fact we only want to open one of them on any given day, and must therefore choose which would be the best, given likely weather conditions for the day.

While this scenario may not provide the most convincing example of the use of perfect information, the management of retail units such as supermarkets provides a better contemporary instance that touches most people's lives. Such organisations are making use of what is now remarkably accurate weather information to enhance their very short-term, and even daily, product or promotion decisions. Whether, for example, it is decided to offer lettuce or cabbage, meat for a barbecue or for a stew, or ice cream or rubber boots depends substantially on the weather forecast. Use of such information minimises waste, maximises sales by having enough stock available, and increases the profitability of a retail unit.

| Exhibit 6.5 | **The holiday company (optimal results)** |

First, we must calculate the expected value of optimal outcomes for each condition of the chance factor, and this is shown in Table 6.4.

Table 6.4 Optimal expected value

| | Weather | | | | |
	Cool	Average	Hot	Optimal outcome	Expected value
Probability	0.2	0.7	0.1		
Swimming Pool	50	100	150	(Hot)	
				$150 \times 0.1 =$	15
Tennis Court	30	180	90	(Average)	
				$180 \times 0.7 =$	126
Restaurant	170	100	40	(Cool)	
				$170 \times 0.2 =$	34
				Total optimal expected value	175

This means that if one had perfect knowledge of when the different types of weather would occur, the expected revenue would be 175. The weather would be expected to be hot 10 per cent of the time, average 70 per cent, and cool 20 per cent, but *it would be known precisely when each would occur*. Profits would increase by 34 units with perfect information (from 141 units, as per Table 6.3, to 175 units as per Table 6.4), so this is what the information would be worth were it available.

Decision trees

Probability concepts may be usefully combined with decision-tree analysis. In their own right decision trees are useful analytical tools in that they offer a useful way of sorting out complex situations so as to clearly and logically interpret the decision options. By considering the probability as well as the value of each outcome, or decision-tree branch, the expected value of each branch's outcome may be determined.

When preparing decision trees, interpretation is made easier if certain conventions are adhered to. These are threefold.

1 Decision choices are shown as square boxes.

2 Outcomes options are shown as circles with a line or branch showing every outcome.

3 Trees are drawn from left to right with the first decision as the starting point.

| Exhibit 6.6 | **Innovative Bicycles Ltd** |

The company has developed a new racing cycle of which it expects great things. At the moment the company has two courses of action open to it: to test market or to abandon it. (See Fig. 6.1 for a decision-tree diagram of the narrative that follows hereafter.)

If the company tests, this will cost £120 000 and the market response could be either positive or negative, with probabilities of 0.5 and 0.5 respectively. If the response is positive, the company could then either abandon or market the product full-scale. If it markets full-scale, then the level of sales could be low, medium, or high, with profits (in units of £1000) of –300 (a 300 loss), 400 or 1200 respectively. The probabilities of these outcomes are 0.2, 0.5, and 0.3. If the test market produces a negative response and the company still goes ahead with full marketing, the likely outcome is losses of 700.

At point E in Fig. 6.1, Innovative Bicycles should market the product if the test is positive. The expected value is:

$$(0.3 \times 1200) + (0.5 \times 400) + [0.2 \times (-300)] = £500\ 000.$$

So at point C, the decision is to market or abandon: 500 units or 50? Clearly the answer is to market, with an expected value of £500 000. And at point D, the decision would be to abandon, earning monetary 50 units, rather than take the loss of 700 units.

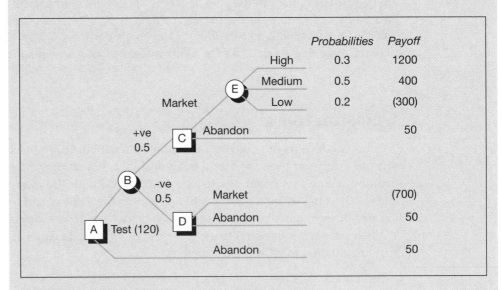

Fig. 6.1 Decision tree for Innovative Bicycles Ltd

At B expected value is $[(0.5 \times 500) + (0.5 \times 50)] = 250 + 25 = 275$. At A, if we test, expected value is $275 - 130 = 155$, and if we abandon expected value is 50 units. Clearly, 155 is greater than 50, and so the decision at A would be to test-market, and then go on to full marketing only if the test is positive.

Conditional probabilities, prior and posterior probabilities

Basic, or essential, probability of any outcome may be described as the 'raw' probability for that outcome. The evaluation of any raw probability is quite an easy and comfortable process when that probability is acceptably polarised. Thus, a raw probability that is perceived as large, say 0.9 and above, is likely to lead to the project being implemented, and a raw probability that is small, say 0.2 or smaller will mean almost immediate rejection of the project. Clearly, while the precise boundaries may vary from one analyst to another and may depend on the context of the decision, these figures will serve for the purpose of illustration.

The evaluation process becomes much less clear, and thereby less comfortable, when these raw probabilities are in the 'middle ground', say 0.8, 0.4, or worse, 0.6. When one remembers that the investment project may involve a great deal of cost to the organisation. Furthermore, the hesitancy that may be brought about by such indecisive probabilities may well have adverse consequences in terms of the timing and likely success of a project.

While an organisation may, understandably, be reluctant to fully commit its resources to projects with middle-ground probabilities, it is likely to be much more willing to commit on a limited, experimental basis, particularly if such an experiment could develop additional project information in order to modify the raw probabilities into something more polarised, and thereby make larger the expected value of the decision.

To understand the conceptual process consider the following illustrative example:

| Exhibit 6.7 | **Mick Smith** |

Mick Smith is an enthusiastic and ambitious yachtsman and is seeking commercial sponsorship to help him participate in a forthcoming transatlantic race.

Mick has approached several companies and, while they generally agree that the publicity benefits of a successful voyage will fully justify the sponsorship outlay, they have expressed concern about Mick's experience to date and consequent chances of successfully completing the voyage. Thus far Mick has only sailed in UK waters and the probability of him successfully reaching America have been assessed at 60 per cent. None of the companies wished to be seen to be supporting a venture that might subsequently be seen as foolhardy.

Mick has approached the race organisers for advice. They suggest that Mick should first undertake a shorter, but still ambitious voyage as a test of his ability. They suggest he sails from Portsmouth, the transatlantic race starting port, around Lands End and then across to the Fastnet Rock (which is off the south-east coast of Ireland), and back. Such a voyage, although relatively short, will fully test Mick's personal stamina, navigation skills and seamanship. The race organisers say that this has proved a most reliable test in past years and is 95 per cent certain to indicate a competent competitor. When Mick re-approaches his potential sponsors with this idea they agree that the test voyage, being of known reliability, will improve the quality of the information relating the transatlantic voyage. If Mick completes the test voyage the probability of his successfully reaching America can be reassessed at something higher than 0.6. Similarly, if he fails on the test voyage, the probability that he will fail to complete the transatlantic trip will become much higher than 0.4.

The sponsors agree to support Mick for the test voyage with transatlantic sponsorship being dependent on the test outcome.

The postulation is therefore as follows:

If we know that the probability of an event is very high, for example a test result accurately predicting the outcome of full scale project implementation, is it reasonable to use the test result as a basis for reassessing the project raw probabilities. If full scale implementation is made contingent upon first obtaining a favourable test outcome, can the probability of success be reassessed as significantly higher? Similarly, if the test outcome is failure does this mean that the likelihood of full-scale failure is significantly higher than suggested by the raw probabilities?

If the answers to these questions are yes and costs incurred by conducting the tests will be offset by reducing the wasteful deployment of resources. This improvement in the quality of probability calculation is achieved by making full scale project implementation dependent upon test outcome, that is by regarding the population of project outcomes as a subset within the population of favourable test results.

Consider a further example:

Exhibit 6.8

The Gold Exploration Company Ltd

The Gold Exploration Company Ltd (GECL) is considering mining at a particular site. Their chief engineer has assessed the probability, using past experience of such sites, of finding gold as 0.2. The value of finding gold is estimated to be £65m after costs, but if the mine is empty the company will have lost £10m in costs.

The company is considering engaging a firm of geologists to conduct a thorough survey of the site. This survey will cost £3m. GECL has used the survey company many times before, and has made the following estimates: if there really is gold there, then there is a 95 per cent chance that the report will be favourable. If there really is no gold on the site, then there is only a 10 per cent chance that the report will have been favourable. The problem probabilities can be sketched as in Fig 6.2 with the appropriate interactive factors.

An analysis of the information in Fig. 6.2, yielding some indication of what decision to make, depends upon clearly remembering the conceptual basis of probability:

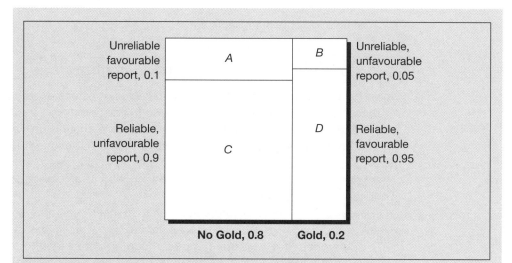

Fig. 6.2 Probability analysis of GECL finding gold

$$P(X) = \frac{\text{number of outcomes of } X}{\text{Total number of outcomes in the population}}$$

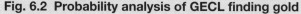

Populations of test outcomes are developed and in this case the survey can be favourable or unfavourable so there are two populations of outcomes. Within each population are, again, two possibilities, in that gold may be discovered or it may not. The postulations are that a favourable test result will significantly enhance the probability of actually finding gold, if full-scale mining were to be undertaken, and that an unfavourable test result would significantly enhance the likelihood of not finding gold. So the probability of finding gold, given a favourable survey, is given by Area D/(Area D + Area A), because the report needs to be both favourable and reliable and this means that Area D is the desired outcome with (Area D + Area A) being the population of outcomes if the survey report is favourable. So

$$P(D) = \frac{(0.95 \times 0.2)}{(0.95 \times 0.2) + (0.1 \times 0.8)} = \frac{0.19}{0.19+0.08} = 0.704.$$

P(A), representing the likelihood of a favourable but unreliable report, and thus no gold, is given by:

$$P(A) = \frac{(0.1 \times 0.8)}{(0.1 \times 0.8) + (0.2 \times 0.95)} = \frac{0.08}{0.08+0.19} = \frac{0.08}{0.27} = 0.296.$$

Notice that P(A) and P(D) do (as required logically) sum to one.

P(B), an unfavourable but unreliable survey, leading to gold being present for mining, is given by:

$$P(B) = \frac{(0.05 \times 0.2)}{(0.05 \times 0.2) + (0.9 \times 0.8)} = \frac{0.01}{0.01+ 0.72} = \frac{0.01}{0.73} = 0.014.$$

P(C), an unfavourable but reliable survey, not leading to gold, is given by:

$$P(C)= \frac{(0.8 \times 0.9)}{(0.8 \times 0.9) + (0.2 \times 0.05)} = \frac{0.72}{0.72+0.01} = 0.986.$$

Again, as expected, the population of unfavourable test outcomes sum to exactly one.

Thus, our calculations may be considered to have produced a somewhat mixed bag in terms of usefulness. If the report is favourable, there is only a 0.7 chance of finding gold; although this is more positive than a 0.2 chance! However, if the report is unfavourable, it is almost certain that no gold is there, with a prob-ability of not finding any of 0.986. The conclusion must be to only consider commitment if the survey is favourable.

In order to explore expected value consequences the entire scenario can be usefully expressed as a decision tree, as set out below in Fig. 6.3.

To summarise, if the company goes ahead and mines without a survey, the expected value will be £5m, which is a positive value and potentially attractive. If however, the company first obtains a survey and then mines, the expected out-come increases to £11.57m. The cost of the survey is £3m, and the net gain becomes £8.57m. For the company, the survey offering perfect information is worth up to £11.57m – £4m = £7.57m, and so to get the survey for only £3m rep-resents a bargain.

The problem may be then approached by being regarded as a developmental sequence of activities. Rather than choosing to do either one or other option on a full-scale basis immediately, a test or pilot study of each should be conducted.

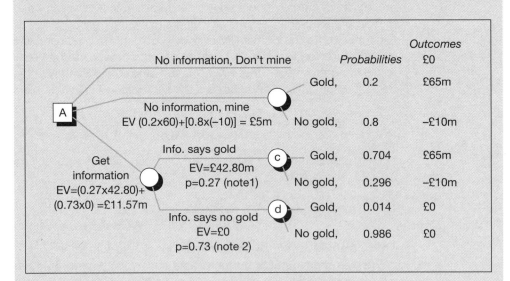

Fig. 6.3 Decision tree, for GECL's possible goldmine

Notes
1. 0.27 = (0.95 × 0.2) + (0.1 × 0.8)
2. 0.73 = (0.05 × 0.2) + (0.9 × 0.8)

Project management: network analysis

Project Management is another approach, in a sense similar to decision trees, in that it takes a complex problem and renders it more easily managed by translating it into a series of logical steps.

Projects may be both large and small; they are, however, all entities within the organisation in that they are something distinct that the organisation has created. As such they may be expected to have numerous process requirements, some sequential and some parallel, which need to be performed as efficiently as possible. Waste and delay are the enemies of business prosperity; projects need to be completed, to a proper standard, within budget and on time.

Project management is the process of breaking down the whole project into sequential dependent tasks. The reader is referred to Chapter 7 for a discussion of the importance of holistic decision making, and the inherent dangers of fragmentation. When a whole scenario is broken down, it is essential that this is done sensitively so that the synergy of the project is retained. Network analysis is a sound attempt at this in that it models the whole project, to show the interrelationships of the various jobs and what the critical aspects of the job are.

To prepare a network analysis, a manager must first identify all the tasks within the project and estimate how long they will each take to complete. The rules for drawing networks for a network analysis are as follows.

- Activities are drawn by solid arrows thus:

  The letter is to identify the activity and the number shows the duration of it, but the length of the arrow is not significant and does not indicate the duration of the activity.

- An event is a point in time between the finish of the last activity and the beginning of the next. It is shown as a circle thus:

- Dummy activities are shown by dotted arrows thus:

  Dummies consume neither time nor resources and are only used to maintain the rules for drawing networks.

- Every activity can follow only one 'tail event' and lead to only one 'head event.' Although an activity may share either the same head or same tail as other activities, it may not do both.

- An event is not completed until all preceding activities are completed.

- Activities move from left to right, so activity loops are not allowed and all activities must have a tail and a head; an activity cannot just be left hanging.

- Each event is subdivided into three sections thus:

In the top half goes the number of the event by which the event is identified (put into rough order). In the bottom left quadrant goes the earliest start time (EST) of each event. This is calculated by adding together the durations of the preceding activities. It is calculated by moving forward through the network. Where an event is shared between activities, i.e. it has two or more activities leading to it, the longest activity duration will be shown in the event circle. In the bottom right quadrant goes the latest start time (LST). This is calculated in each case in a similar way to EST except that the analyst starts from the end event and works backwards.

Consider the following example of making a cup of instant coffee, where the activities are set out in Table 6.5 and the corresponding network is shown in Fig. 6.4.

Table 6.5 Actions involved in making a cup of coffee

Activity	Activity description	Preceding activity	Duration
a	Fill Kettle	–	1
b	Boil water	a	5
c	Put coffee in cup	–	1
d	Pour water into cup	b,c	2
e	add sugar to taste	d	1
f	add milk	f	1

The critical path is the shortest time that the whole project can be completed in. It is shown to be the diagram route which connects the events with the same ESTs and LSTs. Activities that are not on the critical path will have some spare or float time. This is the time by which an activity may be delayed without affecting the total project. Total float up to a particular non-critical activity is calculated by subtracting the duration of the activity from the difference between latest head time, latest starting time of the next activity, and the earliest tail time of this activity (that is, its earliest starting time).

When first attempting to use this analysis, an individual manager may find that the most difficult thing to do is to ensure that the logic of the network is correct. The mathematical process is mechanistic, but requires care. It is a good idea to try

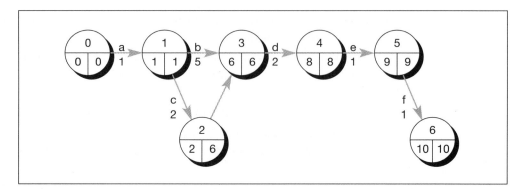

Fig. 6.4 Network of events for making a cup of coffee

developing simple models of familiar projects, such as lighting a bonfire or making a cup of tea, before moving on to more complex situations.

Summary of the chapter

- Probability estimations can enable the manager to prioritise effort and resources.

- Conditional probability calculations can enable an organisation to save wasted effort by polarising raw probability figures that are rather 'middle ground'.

- Complex projects may be more clearly and logically understood by use of analytical techniques such as decision trees or network analysis.

Case Study 11: Frustrated Fred

Fred has worked in the Accounts Department of a local engineering firm for many years. Last week the staff newsletter contained an announcement from the Personnel Department saying that the company is seeking employees who are prepared to accept voluntary redundancy. The basic terms being offered are a year's salary plus one week's pay for every year of service. Fred is currently earning £20 000 p.a. and has worked at the company for 25 years.

Fred is married to Shirley; they have a Building Society savings account that currently yields 4 per cent and that at the moment contains £10 000 of their money. They jointly own a house valued at £40 000. They have no mortgage.

Although both Fred and Shirley are quite happy where they live, Shirley has often said that she would like them to semi-retire in the sun by running a small hotel in Portugal. This would cost £50 000 to buy and set up but once in, their living costs would be almost nothing. If fully occupied (and there is a 60 per cent chance of this), the hotel would produce a net annual income of £25 000; otherwise the income is likely to be more like £6000.

Fred has to spend quite a lot of his spare time looking after his sick aunt. He is fond of her and is concerned because the doctors have said that she has a '50–50' chance of surviving the year. Her estate is unlikely to exceed £15 000. She would be the main reason for Fred not moving.

Although Fred likes Portugal he also likes Florida, where he has a brother. Fred's brother runs a garage and car dealership in Miami and keeps asking Fred to join him as a partner in order to take on a new franchise. Fred would have to put in £75 000 and Shirley is concerned that this would leave them homeless and almost without money. Fred's brother tells them not to worry, because their income should exceed £20 000 almost immediately; there is a 65 per cent chance of this – and Fred's income could be as high as £100 000 if a new car franchise really 'takes off', although the probability of this is assessed by Shirley to be only 25 per cent. There is also a 'small' chance of the franchise failing to produce more than £10 000, which would mean a rather low standard of living in Miami.

Question for discussion

Using a decision tree to analyse the information given, how would you advise Fred and Shirley?

Case Study 12: Gecap Ltd

Gecap Ltd is a venture capital company founded eight years ago by Peter George. The company specialises in providing funding to small and medium enterprises in the chemical industry. The company has recently been approached by Biofren Ltd, which is a company that develops and manufactures ecologically acceptable paints and varnishes, in relation to one of its new products.

Biofren thinks that it has created an anti-fouling paint for the protection of the bottoms of yachts and ships when they are immersed in water. Tests have shown that surfaces coated with this paint have shown no weed or barnacle growth even after being in water, at a variety of temperatures, for six months. Biofren has brought the product to a marketable state but need the financial help of Gecap in order to launch the product properly.

In their proposal document Biofren provides the following information. Biofren has conducted some basic market research and believes that UK sales could exceed 150 000 litres per month. However, customers are wary of environmentally linked products and the company fears that an unfavourable press review could cause sales to be as low as 15 000 litres. It is estimated that there is a 70 per cent chance of sales being high.

Development costs for the paint have been £5m and, if Biofren do not go ahead with it, these facilities would have a scrap value of only some £20 000. However, Biofren is now seeking to spend a further £20m on dedicated production facilities. The suggested selling price of the paint is £4 per litre, which will mean a margin of 75 per cent. The expected life of the product is at least ten years.

Biofren has mentioned in its document that it had thought about using a pilot marketing process to start the product. They propose working with a company called Whizz Campaigns. They have done this with several of their other product launches and found the results of the Whizz-devised campaigns to be an excellent indicator of how successful a full-scale product launch is likely to be. Whizz is asking £3m for its services, which are seen as 95 per cent reliable.

Biofren is concerned that, if the sales of the new product are low, this may affect customers for their other products and may reduce profits from other sales by £250 000. Biofren want to borrow £23m from Gecap, with repayment terms to be agreed.

Questions for discussion

1 *After full assessment of the Biofren proposal, how would you advise Gecap about the requested loan?*

2 *Should Gecap grant a loan, and if it normally charges 12 per cent interest per annum, how long might Biofren take to repay the loan?*

Case Study 13: George Smith

George Smith is considering building himself a house. He has estimated the activities involved to be those set out in Table 6.6.

Table 6.6 Activities for George Smith to build a house

Activity	Activity description	Activity precedents	Activity duration
a	obtain plans	–	2
b	buy plot of land	a	2
c	prepare site	b	5
d	buy materials	a	3
e	make foundations	a,c,d	3
f	build walls	e,d	10
g	make floors	f,d	4
h	make roof	a,d,f,g	3
j	install windows and doors	a,d,h	3
k	install plumbing and wiring	a,d,g,j	5
l	plaster walls	d,k	4

Question for discussion

By preparing a network analysis from the data in Table 6.6, how long will the house take to build?

Reference

Vroom, V. H. (1964) *Work and Motivation*, New York.

CHAPTER 7

Planning and decision making: the use of rationalism and holistic analysis

Learning objectives

At the end of this chapter you should:

- be able to outline why certain types of organisation may be expected to find formal planning a beneficial process, and how they might ensure that this process is effectively implemented;

- be able to evaluate the essential nature of organisational objectives, beliefs and culture;

- be able to outline the case for formal and rational planning from both strategic and operational perspectives;

- understand the concept of reductionism and outline its strengths and weaknesses as a decision-making approach;

- understand the concept of holistic decision making; and

- be able to understand and apply systems analysis and holistic analysis in order to develop potential solutions to a problem.

Introduction

Rationalism may assist organisational decision making by formally ensuring that deliberation and choice are as comprehensive as is appropriate within the context of the decision. Furthermore, rationalism may offer a structure to foster a feeling of teamwork amongst staff, hopefully leading to improved performance by facilitating commitment, communication and control.

This chapter is divided into two discrete sections. The first section will start by exploring, in some detail, the strategic and operational cases for rationalism as a decision-making model. The second section will suggest systems analysis as a technique for approaching a complex rational decision, which may be expected to help overcome the conceptual and practical difficulties that tend to manifest themselves when complex rationalism is attempted.

Generally, organisations are positioned along a continuum according to whether they see themselves as enterprising or conservative in their approach to business. Although this chapter may be useful to both, it is particularly relevant for organisations that consider themselves to be enterprising and actively seek opportunity.

The case for rationalism

Organisational objectives

When discussing the philosophical stance of the decision makers' strategic objectives it has, historically, been convenient to distinguish between private and public-sector organisations. It can be taken as axiomatic that private sector managers work to maintain their company's position in the marketplace: they will tend to be seeking competitive solutions, thinking laterally, and showing a readiness for innovative. In contrast, as Lindblom (1959) pointed out, included in the duties of public sector managers is the need to provide stability and maintain the status quo consistent with contemporary societal norms and values.

Two terms need definition early on in this context:

- *Incrementalism* is where planning tends to be 'bottom up', with managers responding to their departmental needs and acting within long-standing practices and assumptions.

- *Rationalism* provides a basis of evaluation for decisions already taken and those being considered and a stimulus for longer-term thinking.

Thus, 'incrementalism' (Lindblom, 1959) is arguably a conceptually sound approach for public sector organisations but potentially apathetic and therefore dangerous in the private sector. That said, Quinn (1980) found that incrementalism 'quite properly' played a substantial role in a number of large, mostly American, firms and that incrementalism and rationalism could, and should, be effectively combined. Accordingly, Quinn offers the concept of 'logical incrementalism'.

This is all fairly standard theory and, it is proposed, in need of some contemporary development. During 1996 the authors conducted some preliminary research to investigate planning styles within small and medium-sized building firms located within the county of Suffolk, UK. The findings suggested that planning styles depended, at least in part, upon the objectives of the decision makers: those with a prime wish to maintain their present lifestyle were substantially oriented to incrementalism; those who also sought expansion were constantly looking for opportunities of a more innovative nature and employed logical incrementalism.

Within the United Kingdom, in the period 1979–98, there have been profound political and economic developments impacting upon public-sector organisations, which have obliged them to become significantly more business-oriented. It is, therefore, proposed to dispense with public sector versus private sector in order to make distinctions, and to distinguish instead between organisations that may be described as being 'enterprising' and those considered conservative. The enterprising organisation is bold, ambitious and displays courage in its readiness to engage in innovative undertakings. It needs to recognise appropriate opportunity and to take successful action, in short, it needs to plan.

In these circumstances, there is a case for rationistic approach to decision making.

Planning and the need for rationalism

In broad terms, decision making may be categorised as either informal or formal. The degree of formality or otherwise can be determined by analysing four specific criteria:

- What is the procedure?
- In what way is the actual decision procedure organised.
- Who searches for options and how is this done?
- Who is involved in the evaluation of the various options and what is the basis of evaluation?

Formality versus informality is assessed in terms of the degree to which procedure is explicitly defined. The more explicit the decision-making procedure, the more it may be described as formal. Rationalism is an extreme manifestation of formality, which is decision making that involves defined search and evaluation procedures to be conducted by specifically identified staff.

If it is accepted that planning is important, then the essential reason for employing a formal approach is to ensure that the process is conducted in a clearly defined and thorough manner. For example, visionary leaders often seem to work intuitively, have clear ideas of what they want to achieve and, in broad terms at least, of how they will do it. To such people, planning can be achieved seemingly without conscious effort. It may be argued that such people would actually feel constrained by formal processes and would see such processes as tending to work against them. Clearly, vision and intuition have a substantial role to play within the process of synthesis and, indeed, they are likely to be the catalyst of it. However, only a few (often senior) managers are blessed, or perhaps cursed, with such natural abilities, and it is unlikely that any organisation can expect to have enough such gifted people to satisfy its planning needs.

Today, as organisations are tending to devolve their decision making downwards, all levels of staff are increasingly expected to employ such skills where appropriate to their work. There is an emerging and widespread need for staff to acquire and develop such skills because of the devolvement of planning. While it may be argued that, to their highest levels at least, vision and intuition cannot be taught, understanding and practice of them may be improved to a satisficing level if staff are aware of an appropriate procedure to achieve this. It is proposed that rationalism, the formal process of planning and decision making, may be such a procedure.

The nature of effective planning

Let us consider in a little more detail what effective planning involves. Effective planning requires a future orientation, interpretation and creativity so that organisations may develop proper identity and competitive advantage. It requires detailed analysis in order to ensure that, for example, the demands of the market are understood and acted upon. However, the essential yet most difficult point about effective planning is that it is more than simply analysis. It must lead to, or generate, synthesis; thus, effective planning is truly difficult.

The participants to the decision making are expected to answer unstructured questions about unique situations such as, 'Where do we go from here?' or 'What is the purpose of all of this?'. Past experience is not automatically helpful, even as a guide, and should be employed only with careful consideration and thought. Schon (1983) argues that caution should be generally observed when employing knowledge, and any situation should be regarded as potentially unique and consequently approached with thought and reflection rather than according to mechanistic processes.

It may seem somewhat surprising that rationalism is being advocated as an appropriate planning tool, given the tendency to depict the rational decision-making process as mechanistic. Rationalism is often illustrated using flow charts, which show the process as a series of seemingly simple steps. At a superficial level rationalism maybe seen as mechanistic. The process is usually depicted as a prescriptive sequence, basically recognition of a problem, analysis, evaluation, choice and implementation. However, in substance, this process will be appropriately conducted according to the specific nature and requirements of the problem in hand. What is evaluated, to what depth and how the elements of this are integrated will depend upon what is seen as relevant and important to the particular case in hand.

In practice, rationalism may provide unique and context-specific solutions, provided it is implemented appropriately. Clearly, success here is also likely to depend on extraneous factors – for example, an appropriately supportive organisational culture.

Operational issues

For all types of organisation, at an operational level of management thinking, it is possible that rationalism may improve communication within the organisation. A formal planning procedure should produce an articulated result whereby all staff become aware of what the implications of the plan are for them, what they can expect and what is expected of them. Clearly such articulation also provides an implied control procedure for the organisation.

Rationalism also implies an opportunity for all affected or interested parties to participate in the decision-making process, which may stimulate the commitment and productivity of those concerned. There is a danger, however, that the process becomes an end in itself. Staff may become complacent and unproductive if they become preoccupied with following organisational procedure or compliance with culture. If the corporate culture is to accuse and blame staff when things go wrong, then such a preoccupation amongst staff may be expected as part of their defence mechanism. Thus organisations, staff and particularly managers, having established an appropriate culture, must remind themselves of what the procedures are really for and what is important.

Is planning, and therefore rationalism, really useful? Thus far the discussion is theoretical and some may be wondering just how valid these conclusions are. Therefore what about the evidence? A useful summary is offered by Mintzberg (1994), who put forward that attempts to estimate hard strategic benefits have been beset by difficulties of measurement and researcher bias; the results are inconclusive. However, peripheral roles such as 'public relations, information, group therapy and direction and control' (original ref. Langley, 1988) have been found to be important. Furthermore Simons (1987, 1990, 1991 a and b) argued that 'interactive' analytical systems tend to provide an 'attention-focusing' mechanism to 'force analysis, and focus debate'. It is suggested that this latter point may be particularly appropriate within small and medium-sized organisations where, typically, staff are expected to perform a diverse range of tasks and work long hours as a matter of course. People become either too busy or too tired to think. It was found that the organisations that employed formal planning tended to be more prosperous than those that did not.

Rationalism is potentially attractive as a decision-making approach because it requires diligent, indeed exhaustive, exploration of the issues relating to the decision in question. It therefore encompasses both what is decided and why it is decided. Furthermore, rationalism attempts to regard decision making as a transparent process in contrast to certain other approaches, for example incrementalism, which views decision making as opaque and unfathomable.

It is not being claimed that this rationalism is ever likely to be an easy process; as Whittington (1993) says, were it so we would not pay our top managers so much. However, as Quinn (1998) states, formal planning does 'encourage managers to look ahead ... allows executives to blend analysis, organisational politics and individual needs into a cohesive new direction'. Clearly, such an approach contains the implied requirement of substantial effort by the parties involved and is therefore something not to be undertaken lightly. That said, at both strategic and operational levels of decision making the approach may have theoretical and (probably) empirical advantages that are likely to be useful and may be critical.

Developing rationalism as an approach to planning

It is proposed to introduce a number of cautionary points at this stage. Perhaps the most obvious is to keep a proper sense of perspective about the whole process. It is expensive and of little benefit to devote enormous resources to consideration of decisions that are relatively trivial. It is better to reserve the big effort for the big decisions. Even when considerable analysis and evaluation is appropriate, an organisation should retain a sense of realism regarding its endeavours. For example, is further scanning likely to produce better options or is it likely to be a waste of time in terms of improvement? If the answer to the latter question is 'yes', the organisation would be better off by not searching further, but instead employing their search resources on some other task.

More formally, March and Simon (1958) suggest that organisational behaviour is usually not to search endlessly for the optimal solution but to seek a satisfying option, one that is considered 'reasonably good', before those involved feel able to stop the search. A new search will be initiated if organisational performance falls below the desired minimal level.

Etzioni (1967) proposes a 'mixed scanning' approach whereby an organisation examines, in progressively more detail, fewer and fewer options. For example, if one were considering the siting of an airport, some of the options might be immediately and obviously unacceptable because perhaps there are already large urban developments nearby. Thus, there would be no need to consider the detailed financial implications of such sites because political considerations cause them to be rejected out of hand. Of the remaining options, perhaps some sites will clearly involve heavy capital investment because the land is poor, mountainous or waterlogged, and in turn these will be the next to be rejected. Thus the final, and very detailed, level of consideration will be applied to as few of the initial options as possible.

While these approaches are helpful, in that they reduce the scope of the problem, they do not help with the mechanics of solving the problem itself and something more is needed. Steiner (1979: 294) offers some pragmatic suggestions and, because they are useful notes for the reader, these are set out below as the ten most important pitfalls to be avoided in planning by management:

1 The assumption by top managers that they can delegate the planning function to the planner.

2 Top management becoming so engrossed in current problems that it spends insufficient time on long-range planning, and the process becomes discredited among other managers and staff.

3 Failure to develop company goals as a basis for formulating long-range plans.

4 Failure to assume the necessary involvement in the planning process of major line personnel.

5 Failing to use plans as standards for measuring managerial performance.

6 Failure to create a corporate climate that is congenial and not resistant to planning.

7 Assuming that corporate comprehensive planning is something separate from the entire management process.

8 Injecting so much formality into the system that it lacks flexibility, looseness and simplicity, and restrains creativity.

9 Failure of top management to review with departmental and divisional heads the long-range plans that they have developed.

10 Top management's consistent rejection of the formal planning mechanism by making intuitive decisions, which conflict with the formal plans.

In summary, Steiner states that managers should organise their organisation's planning process in a comprehensive fashion and the appropriate corporate culture should be fostered. All staff concerned must be specifically involved, managers to demonstrate the central role of formal planning to their function by preparing appropriate planning parameters, participating in the formal process, and remaining committed to the outcome. Let us assume that the organisation has allocated appropriate resources to the proposed decision process and that all of these are properly motivated and loyal – the sociological requirements for staff effectiveness are in place. What are the psychological issues regarding how can we expect staff to go about the process, for example, what cognitive dissonance can staff be expected to have, and can this be avoided or eased?

Cyert and March (1963) argue that, typically, managers demonstrate an abiding desire for simplicity; thus in order to complete their tasks with best economy in spite of their own cognitive limitations. Mintzberg (1994) suggests that although planning may be regarded as a procedure to produce an 'integrated system of decisions' it will, none-the-less, require 'decompositional nature of analysis-reducing states and processes to their component parts' in order to be achieved.

The need for holistic approaches to decision making

This decomposition of a problem into parts is surely at least a major conceptual flaw: it assumes that the researcher can understand the whole by somehow aggregating understanding of the component parts.

The reader is surrounded with the evidence that this is a fallacious assertion. At a physical level of thinking there are many examples such as water where, as Checkland (1984) puts it, 'the taste of water ... is a product of the substance water, not of the hydrogen and oxygen which combine to form it'.

Personality traits and leadership styles have been found to be determined, at least in part, by external variables such as behavioural context and organisation culture. So very little about us appears to be absolutely and always true. Most of what we are depends on where and when we are. In the 1970s the famous American consultants, McKinsey & Co. sought to develop an effective model for the development of corporate strategy. The outcome of this was the 'Seven S Framework' made famous in the book by Peters and Waterman (1982) *In Search of Excellence*. The model was developed out of a realisation that dissection was not the way for effective development of corporate strategy.

All elements, together with their relationships, must be considered as a whole. Putting all this another way, it is an argument for the concept of synergy; the whole may be greater than, or at least different from, the sum of the parts. It is not necessarily possible to analyse effectively the whole by looking at the parts separately. We, therefore, need a process that will enable us to view the decision as a whole, all aspects simultaneously. However this would appear to be in conflict with the fundamental problem, discussed by Cyert and March (1963), of cognitive limitation. While it may be possible to avoid this problem and achieve our ends by, perhaps, employing powerful computers or by seeking out intellectual geniuses, most managers instead seek to develop a way around cognitive limitation, by which the average manager may, simply, improve his, or her, performance

A further constraint emerges if we examine studies of how managers behave in practice. Mintzberg (1990) found that work is characterised by brevity, variety and discontinuity – and all at a relentless pace. Stewart (1983) suggests that managers live in a 'whirl of activity', switching their attention every few minutes between tasks. So, to be attractive to managers, the new decision process must be concise and readily perceived in order to be attention grabbing, as well as providing detailed analysis. Although not inevitable, there is potential for conflict between requirements here – for example the desire for brevity must not be at the expense of thorough analysis.

Summary of the requirements for effective rationalism in planning

Effective planning means involvement of appropriate staff and synthesis of proposals in order for there to be effective organisational strategy leading to operational advantage. Given the extensive nature of the preceding discussion, it seems appropriate at this point to summarise the requirements that have been identified:

- Effort should be commensurate with rewards.
- Simultaneous consideration of all the decision issues is needed.
- The process must be concise.

Systems analysis

Why systems analysis?

As Checkland (1984) points out, as members of prosperous Western civilisation we have very successfully employed scientific method in order to observe, understand and, we believe, improve our world. This has been achieved with spectacular result over the last few hundred years in particular. Unsurprisingly, we have tended to become culture-bound towards scientific thinking.

Scientific method may be defined in terms of its characteristics, that it is systematic and formulates knowledge from careful observation and experiment; hence repeatability and refutation. Science is also about reduction: what atoms are we made of, and what makes an atom? Systematic and consistent determination of the relationships between these parts, so as to form the whole, often poses severe problems for science if the relationships are complex. Organisations, and indeed their marketplace, being social phenomena, tend inherently to be very complex. Behaviour, both of the organisation and staff, may or may not be repeated even in the unlikely event of particular circumstances repeating themselves. This may be so because social phenomena tend to be open rather than closed in nature; they respond to stimulation and change in that their wants and needs tend to remain stable only in the short term.

Therefore, not only is it unlikely that science-based methods of tackling sociological problems will meet the three criteria set out above, but such problems imply a fourth constraint, namely the ability to deal with 'open', namely developing or unstable, situations. It should now be clear that the preferred approach is to reject science-based thinking in favour of some other; but why systems analysis specifically?

It is a meta-discipline in that it is a subject that discusses other subjects, including science. It is a way of approaching a problem, understanding it, and (hopefully) devising a solution to it. Systems procedure accepts the four criteria that have been identified. The analysis recognises wholes, that is entities that lose meaning or significance if reduced to their component parts. In its most general, and therefore most universally applicable, definition, a system may be defined as a collection of parts, with all of them linked by some form of relationship. These parts may be anything – for example, cogs in a machine, chemicals in a compound, or people in an organisation. The relationship may be similarly diverse: the physical distance between each cog, chemical reactivity, culture, structure, or the physical layout of an organisation's staff.

Clearly, at its most general level, systems jargon is extremely nebulous; specific content, and therefore the degree to which the concept is practicable, is sacrificed in favour of universal applicability. However, the suggested detailed model is not abstract but relevant and specific. The analyst is required to examine the actual elements and relationships, the 'things' that make up the decision that is under consideration, thereby performing a concrete, contextual analysis. The systems analysis process provides a useful framework for the practitioner to reach a point where that person can 'see the light', or, stated more formally, make the mental leap to a solution that synthesis requires. The difference between this and other analytical processes is that systems, with its sophisticated analysis, will, hopefully, enable one to leap more easily and in the right direction.

Although the practitioner will find that the process requires considerable mental effort, it is hoped that the concise format will strip away the mental clutter, what audio experts would liken to white noise, leaving one able to focus clearly on the salient issues. Surely, no standard process can be expected to do more than these things.

Figure 7.1 shows a suggested model of the systems process. The purpose of the model is essentially twofold:

1 to be conceptually sound by enabling the practitioner to employ formal processes and rationalism in the efforts to plan effectively; and

2 to offer an acceptably practical process, one that may be specific enough in content to be contextual.

The Systems Analysis model explained

Stage I: Identify or recognise a problem situation

Identifying an occasion for making a decision or becoming aware of the need for a decision is, obviously, common to all decision processes. Typically, decisions will be prompted by some sort of action, for example, an employee leaving, a customer complaining, or perhaps a change in the regulatory legislation governing the

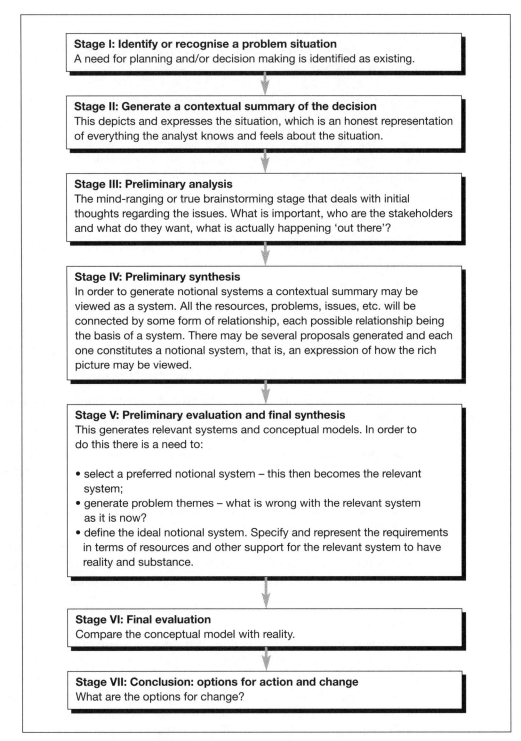

Stage I: Identify or recognise a problem situation
A need for planning and/or decision making is identified as existing.

Stage II: Generate a contextual summary of the decision
This depicts and expresses the situation, which is an honest representation of everything the analyst knows and feels about the situation.

Stage III: Preliminary analysis
The mind-ranging or true brainstorming stage that deals with initial thoughts regarding the issues. What is important, who are the stakeholders and what do they want, what is actually happening 'out there'?

Stage IV: Preliminary synthesis
In order to generate notional systems a contextual summary may be viewed as a system. All the resources, problems, issues, etc. will be connected by some form of relationship, each possible relationship being the basis of a system. There may be several proposals generated and each one constitutes a notional system, that is, an expression of how the rich picture may be viewed.

Stage V: Preliminary evaluation and final synthesis
This generates relevant systems and conceptual models. In order to do this there is a need to:

- select a preferred notional system – this then becomes the relevant system;
- generate problem themes – what is wrong with the relevant system as it is now?
- define the ideal notional system. Specify and represent the requirements in terms of resources and other support for the relevant system to have reality and substance.

Stage VI: Final evaluation
Compare the conceptual model with reality.

Stage VII: Conclusion: options for action and change
What are the options for change?

Fig. 7.1 A suggested model of Systems Analysis

organisation's product(s). Similarly, decisions may follow non-action – for example, the failure of a customer to place an expected order.

Let us assume that such an occasion has arisen. How is the systems analysis thinker to proceed?

Stage II: Generate a contextual summary of the decision

A contextual summary should be rich in meaning; it is a total view of how the decision maker sees the situation and feels about it. It should be an attempt to depict the situation as honestly and completely as possible. Practitioners should put down everything that they know or suspect about the decision; such as:

- Who are the stakeholders?

- What relationships do they have with each other?

- What are the hopes, aspirations and concerns of each group of stakeholders likely to be?

- What are the strategic issues of the decision, for example, what will be the effect on the organisation's reputation and position in the marketplace?

- What about operational resource issues?

- Does the organisation possess appropriate resources to deal with the decision?

In the broadest of thinking, all these issues may be divided into one of two categories:

1 *Hard issues* – those that can be measured, assessed and defined in an objective way. They belong to the realist ontological paradigm, that is, they have substance and reality of their own rather than only in the mind of the observer. They are quantitative rather than qualitative. Examples would include temperature, money, the length of the working week, sales targets formal disciplinary procedures, etc.

2 *Soft issues* – those involving forces, issues, relationships and concepts, the nature of which cannot easily be measured. They are subjective, within the nominalist ontological paradigm, that is, they do not have substance and reality of their own but only exist in the minds of the decision maker. They are qualitative rather than quantitative and may arise as a result of values, tastes and politics.

The relative descriptive abilities of the two concepts can be demonstrated by use of a few examples.

Feeling hot (soft issue) whether or not the ambient temperature (hard issue) is high or low; being considered wealthy (soft issue) regardless of how much money (hard issue) one has. Thus, when evaluating a job opportunity the hard issues would include the hours worked, rate of pays, holiday entitlement and aspects of the job task. Soft issues might include other aspects of the job task, for example, being polite or friendly when serving a difficult customer. Important issues like feelings of self-actualisation, respect, or liking for the line manager, and loyalty to the organisation would be examples of other soft issues.

It is apparent that hard issues are generally included in planning deliberations already. Our cultural predisposition towards a scientific approach to our problem solving renders us receptive to the hard issues because of their inherent objective and quantitative nature, which makes them relatively easy to deal with.

Soft issues are generally treated in one of three ways.

- Some attempt is made to quantify or harden issues.
- Judgement is used to resolve issues.
- Soft issues are simply ignored.

It may be argued that if an issue cannot be quantified, then it *should* be ignored. After all, if perfect knowledge is impossible anyway, why waste time on something that may have an indeterminate effect? In practical terms, to ignore something is no worse than to be unaware of it. While in practical terms this may be true, it is something of a 'head in the sand' approach. It assumes that if we do not perceive or acknowledge something, then it will not affect us.

Clearly this is in many instances a naive assumption. Indeed, one may argue that many of the soft forces may be very powerful and will certainly affect us, for example, whether one likes a person or not. Furthermore, soft issues, such as liking the job, may be more important and therefore more powerful than hard issues such as the rate of pay. It is sometimes argued that within some groups of workers such soft issues are exploited to the advantage of hard, for example, it is sometimes said that nurses tolerate 'low' wages because they are so committed to their job. One may, or may not, agree with this, but the example makes the point.

Thus, to ignore the most potent forces is hardly consistent with rationalism and is not an approach that is condoned here. It is intended that soft issues will be included in the contextural summary, together with suggestion of their relative importance and power. This may be achieved by qualitative devices such as their position, size, emphasis etc. Thus it is hoped that the practitioner will develop a proper perspective of the elements, for example, that *A* is more important than *B* in their effect on *C*, even if their precise quantitative effects cannot be easily determined.

The McKinsey model, described by Peters and Waterman (1982), provides an example of an analytical framework that includes both types:

1 *Hard issues*
   - *Strategy* – the route or method that the company has chosen in order to compete.
   - *Structure* – the way in which the company is organised.
   - *Systems* – the procedures by which the company operates.
   - *Staff* – the people who need to be challenged, motivated etc.

2 *Soft issues*
   - *Skills* – the key, fundamental skills that help the business excel.
   - *Superordinate goals* – the higher-order goals, the concepts, the vision, the values, the mission.
   - *Style* – the way the company conducts itself, symptomatic of the culture.

In a sense, preparing the contextual summary is the easy part of the systems approach in that the practitioner is required to prepare a representation of the situation as he or she sees it. Everybody, regardless of his or her academic ability, has probably had some sort of previous experience of picture making, at school for example, and so should be able to produce something; artistic merit is not important. However, experience has shown that such an unstructured process often intimidates. The very lack of convention or constraint means there are no reference points for proceeding with the process, with the consequence that it becomes difficult. The only possible response is that anything goes. Analysts should sketch or otherwise represent the situation as they see it.

One may use words, flow charts, hand-drawn images, computer-generated graphics, cartoons, whole or parts of photographs and even three-dimensional models to make the representation. Indeed, it is this flexibility that adds to the richness of the picture. The popular saying 'Its not what you say, its how you say it', exemplifies the concept: how you say something is as meaningful as what you say. Thus the choice of medium, format and layout may all be expected to contain and contribute meaning. Interpretation may be a consequent problem, and it is probably best if the picture's creator is willing to explain the work so that it can be properly understood. This should not be a serious problem in that such an explanation may be achieved by simple presentation.

How the systems practitioner lays out the parts says something about that practitioner's perception of the relationship between the parts. This relationship may be explicit, such as an organisation chart, or implicit, for example, the position of the item in the representation – is it in the centre or at the edge of the picture, what is it near or next to? Similarly, the relative importance of the different parts, along with their hierarchical relationship, may also be explicitly stated or implicitly suggested – for example, by the size, colour, position or emphasis given to the part.

What makes a good contextual summary? There are several requirements.

- It must be on a single page or sheet of paper and not be overlarge. In general, A4 size seems about right.

- The conceptual requirement is that the representation must be small enough to be viewed as a whole simultaneously.

- The depiction should be used to condense the information.

- The level of detail included is a matter of judgement, in that a balance must be struck between the level of detail and effective communication. Too much detail may render the picture 'messy' and confusing; it may also detract from the overview.

- The summary must be complete in terms of information relevant to the decision. The practitioner is seeking to depict the whole situation.

- All hard issues and soft issues should be carefully identified, together with their relationships. Position, emphasis, size and treatment given to the subjects must represent these relationships in some way.

- Artwork. The primary purpose is not to produce a piece of art, artistic ability – or lack of it – should not be an intimidating factor. Simple techniques, for example 'pin men', as a means of depicting people is perfectly acceptable. The work simply needs to be created in order to depict what is in the mind of the practitioner.

- Communication to others is probably helped if the work is also neat, simple and clear.

Exhibit 7.1

Ergo Computers Ltd

Gillian Lockhart founded Ergo Computers Ltd (Ergo) early in 1995. Gillian was then a newly qualified computer science graduate and was convinced that many of the personal computers then available were not very user friendly. Gillian believed that there was a large potential market for what she referred to as the 'ergonomically strong machine'. Gillian had several ideas for improving standard operating systems and keyboard design. Gillian also wanted Ergo's machines to be compatible with the operating systems of both Apple and Microsoft. This feature was both technically difficult and expensive to achieve.

Ergo launched their first machine, the Mk1, in 1996 and it sold well until 1998 when sales were down to one hundred a month which was some 10 per cent of the high point.

When sales were strong Ergo had a net cash inflow of £50 000 each month and had invested most of this in both computer research, for the next generation machine, and in voice recognition software to be available as a product in its own right. By January 1997 Ergo found that they faced competition from many similar small computer companies. It was apparent that most of the industry had moved towards adopting Microsoft standard operating systems. By September 1998 Ergo had £250 000 in the bank and access to £750 000 more from venture capital providers although this would be subject to the lenders being granted a seat on Ergo's board of directors. Ergo had a monthly wages bill of £15 000 which together with other overheads meant monthly outgoings of £20 000. Apart from Gillian, three people worked at Ergo, the secretary and receptionist Rachael who joined early in 1996, software engineer Jim Spencer who joined shortly after the company started, and hardware expert Pauline Smith who joined in late 1997. Both Jim and Pauline had moved their homes in order to join the company. Gillian has now decided to take stock of the position of Ergo. The Mk1 machine is now well behind the performance of competitors products. The proposed Mk2 computer would include all of the features of the Mk1 together with innovative capabilities that will put it far ahead of any comparable PC although it is not intended to have access to a printer because Gillian believes that future offices will be paperless. The Mk2 is ready now and the profit per unit sold would be high. Launching costs would be £50 000. The voice recognition software still needs eighteen months research, costing £850 000, but is expected to have global application by accepting all languages. Ergo has received an offer to buy the voice recognition development, as it now is, for £1m. Gillian has been approached by Comtech Ltd, a large American computer company who have offered £1m for her 80 per cent holding of Ergo. Comtech would run the company as a going concern but without Gillian.

Jim and Pauline each own 10 per cent of the company. They have offered to accept short term pay reductions 'if that will help the company', as Jim put it. Gillian is aware of the complexity of the decision and is having trouble deciding what to do.

Figure 7.2 is evidence that, for now, stages I & II have been completed with the representation being as complete as possible with the information available. Some assumptions have been made, concerning individuals contributions and expectations, but these are believed to be reasonable given the context. Although both hard and soft issues have been identified no attempt has been made at this stage to rank the various issues in terms of importance.

As the contextual summary suggests, the problems at Ergo have arisen from a combination of ambitious staff input and expectations and worsening market conditions facing the company. These factors have brought about both strategic and operational problems.

Preliminary analysis, stage III, reveals a number of problems to do with maintaining sufficient cash flow in order to introduce and develop the next generation of company products. However these cannot be properly addressed before the nature and purpose of the company is considered and made clear. This consideration, which is stage IV of the process, should produce several suggestions, each of which constitutes a notional system view of the company. Gillian and her staff need to look at all aspects of Ergo and their involvement with it in order to agree on what the core reason for the existence of the company is. This holistic thinking which leads to the development of notional systems together with subsequent selection of the relevant system may be regarded as being the heart of systems analysis. In the case of Ergo this stage of the systems process may be started by considering the nature of the central function of the company. From the information in the case this appears to be both technological development, selling, and, presumably, manufacture as well. Since each of these functions is likely to require at least some dedicated resources and structure, if they are to be performed successfully, each may be regarded as a notional system view of the company. It is also appropriate to consider the product range of the company. At present Ergo is working on both software and hardware which, although related, are obviously different products. At present, Ergo may be described as a small company that is trying to be six notional systems simultaneously; two product areas with three functions for each. The Ergo management appears to have a view of the company which is either very ambitious or ill defined. Either way, the modelling of that view, in terms of appropriate resource base for the company has been poorly done. It is not surprising that the company is in difficulties!

Stage V is the combined process of selecting, from the notional systems, a relevant system and then modelling it so that appropriate resources are made available for it to be effective. This part of the systems process is about determining priorities regarding the issues. Again, this should be attempted in a holistic, simultaneous way. Gillian, either alone as principal shareholder, or after consultation with Pauline and Jim and perhaps Rachael, should review their expectations, both hard and soft, in order to establish what they want the priorities of the company to be. This decision will depend in part on their likely future contribution and other resource constraints. It is also important to consider the impact of one issue on another, for example, how will the desire for a certain level of staff income affect the research and development capability of the company?

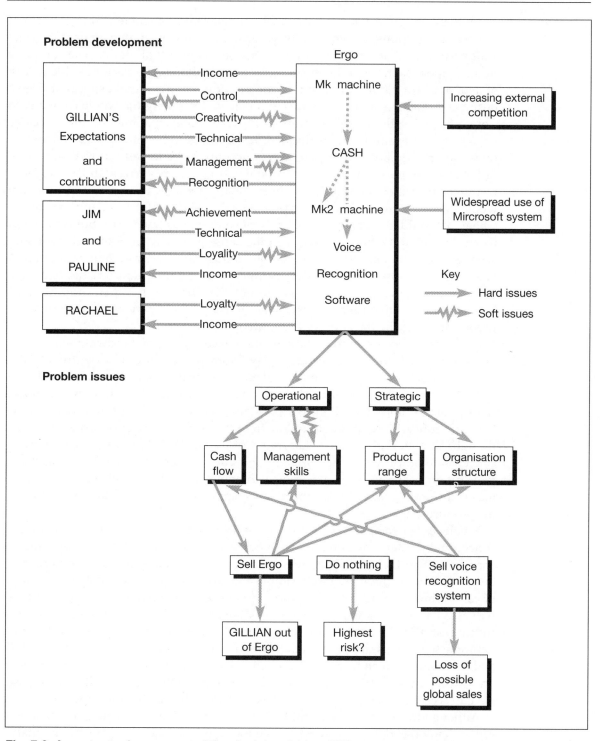

Fig. 7.2 A contextual summary of the decision facing Gillian as owner of 80 per cent of Ergo

All these considerations will establish the relevant system view of Ergo. Each of the decision options should then be comprehensively evaluated against the relevant system view in order to establish the best conceptual model. The company decides upon the hard and soft strengths and weaknesses of each possible course of action, again paying attention to the possible impact on all aspects of Ergo's business. Ergo appears to have three options, that is selling the whole company to Comtech, selling the voice recognition software alone, or doing nothing but carry on as now. For example, if it is decided that Ergo should retain all six notional systems, described above, then the best option might be to sell out to Comtech in order to have access to a large companies financial resources and managerial resources that such an ambitious choice would require. Such a course of action would clearly solve the hard issue problems of cash flow for Ergo and income for Gillian. It would also solve the softer problem of management skill but would also mean the loss, to Gillian, of Ergo with the consequent loss of powerful soft issues such as recognition and status due to the founder and leader of an organisation. A take-over by Comtech may be seen as Ergo acquiring the characteristics of a large company. Some existing customers might like that while others not, perhaps because they fear that Ergo will no longer offer a personal service. Thus Ergo needs to consider carefully the effect of Comtech on existing cash flow.

Selling the voice recognition system and concentrating on hardware would provide useful cash for future product development but would not automatically solve the functional management problems and further changes will be needed in order to prevent the problem re-reoccurring in the future. Also, loosing the global sales potential may deny Ergo the possibility of spectacular growth with all the hard and soft issues that would follow from this. Concerning appropriate function, it might be better, given the background of the present staff, for the company to concentrate on product development and allow others to manufacture and sell their products under licence. Some customers may welcome this specialism as a means towards quality, while others may complain about the incomplete nature of the product range.

Whatever is decided, the final stages of the systems process are to compare the conceptual model requirements with current practice and to make appropriate changes so that the provisions of the conceptual model become accepted practice. Such decisions as these are rarely simple and easy; they usually involve some form of compromise or trade off. If Ergo decide to sell their software development they will also have to decide how they will solve managerial issues such as ensuring future cash flow and the monitoring of market developments, particularly competitor activity. This may, for example, require the appointment of additional staff and/or require Gillian to spend more of her time on such issues and, therefore, less on her present preferences. If the company accepts venture capital Gillian will also have to accept a certain loss of control as another board member is appointed.

Although this example is a simple one in that possible preferences are identified rather than ranked, it is hoped that the important holistic content of systems analysis is now clear. Soft issues tend to be at least as important as hard and should not be ignored. Decisions, or parts of decisions, should not be made in isolation because each part impacts upon the others.

Summary of the chapter

- In broad terms, decision making may be categorised as either informal or formal. This means the way the actual decision procedure is organised, who searches for and evaluates the options, and how this is done.

- Formality versus informality is viewed in terms of the degree to which procedure is explicitly defined. The more explicit the decision-making procedure, the more it may be described as formal.

- A formal planning procedure should produce an articulated result whereby all staff become aware of, and committed to, the individual implications of the plan, what they can expect, and what is expected of them. Clearly such articulation also provides an implied control procedure for the organisation.

- Rationalism may be seen as an extreme manifestation of formality, with the potential operational advantages of formal planning being reasonably clear.

- The potential strategic benefits of formal planning do exist. Visionary leaders who have operated on an intuitive and informal basis understand what they want to achieve and are able to plan. These individuals may feel constrained by formal processes in that they would view such processes limiting their scope of operation.

- The fundamental problem with achieving the widespread practice of effective planning is to do with complexity of the subject.

- Effective planning requires a future orientation, interpretation and creativity so those organisations may develop a clear identity and competitive advantage. It requires meaningful analysis in order to be neither obsolete nor misplaced in relation to the needs of the marketplace. Even more than this, the essential point of effective planning is that it must lead to, or generate, synthesis. Managers are expected to answer nebulous questions about unique and unstructured situations, such as 'Where do we go from here?' or 'What is the purpose of all of this?'

- Given that these questions are asked by or within organisations, that is, in a social context, they are made the more complex because they involve people. Past experience is not automatically helpful and should not be employed presumptuously and without prior reflection.

- Cognitive limitation, combined with a culture-based predisposition in favour of scientific method, have led many analysts to employ reductionism as a procedural technique for dealing with these imperative but complex problems. Historically, however, the results of reductionism have not been consistently useful and, in part, this failure may be attributable to the essential nature of the analytical technique employed. Simplified or sequential analysis, leading to separate rather than holistic consideration of the decision issues, may lead to inaccurate or distorted conclusions and therefore be pointless, if not actually dangerous, for the organisation. An alternative approach is needed that is holistic and thus conceptually sound yet enables the managers to overcome their cognitive limitations.

- Systems analysis using formal processes may be a more useful relevant procedure for planning, given the limitations of human cognition.

Case Study 14: Paul's dilemma

One of your best friends, Paul Simmonds, comes to you and, after explaining his situation, asks for your opinion and advice.

Paul is aged 35 and married with three children: Tim aged 6, Vicky aged 10 and Susan aged 15, all of whom attend local schools. Paul's wife, Rachel, has her own retail hat business. The family home is a comfortable house valued at £150 000, and there is an outstanding mortgage of £8000 on the property. The family enjoys sailing their small boat around the local coast. Paul is passionate about computers.

Paul, after studying at university as a mature student and having worked in the building trade, works for Probgon Ltd. The company designs and supplies data processing systems for its clients. Paul is employed as a diagnostic engineer, which involves talking to clients in order to develop an agreed understanding of both what the clients needs are and how Probgon can help. Paul says that no two jobs are the same.

Recently Probgon has been feeling the effects of intense competition in its market, and it has been decided that the company must reduce its costs. Among other things, this will involve improving staff productivity together with some redundancies. The company is, at this stage, seeking voluntary departures, and staff have been offered an amount equal to a year's salary plus one week for every year of service. In Paul's case this would amount to £25 000.

Paul has been approached by a friend and colleague with the idea of starting their own firm, in partnership, and doing the sort of work that they do now, for which the estimated costs and revenues are as follows:

- Set-up costs: £100 000 (this includes premises, computers etc.) to be met by the partners equally.

- Running costs: £120 000 p.a. for staff wages, rent, telephone, etc. This excludes partner's drawings.

- Sales revenue: £160 000 for the first year but likely to grow at the rate of 100 per cent per annum for at least the following five years. (This estimation is based upon the Probgon clients who are likely to follow the partners.)

Questions for discussion

1 *What are the strategic options facing Paul?*

2 *What are the hard and soft issues?*

3 *After summarising and critically evaluating each option, how would you advise Paul?*

Case Study 15: Stays Engineering Ltd

Sidney Snetterthwaite and Susan Atkins are equal partners in Stays Engineering Ltd, a company that manufactures adhesives, mainly for marine use. The company is situated near Lowestoft in Suffolk, UK. Susan is a chemist with an outstanding record of applied research. She is 33 years old and married to Henry, who combines his time by painting landscape pictures and looking after their son William, aged 3. Sidney is 49 years old and a successful local businessman. He is also a local Labour councillor. Susan and Sidney first met three years ago at a local authority planning meeting, the agenda of which included a proposal to extend a local chemical works and Susan was attending as an interested member of the public.

Susan and Sidney started talking in a chance meeting over a cup of coffee. When explaining her background and interest in the meeting, Susan mentioned adhesive development work that she was doing and that her project was dying because of lack of funds. Sidney was impressed by Susan's apparent ability and became interested in her project. They formed a partnership in order to bring the results of her research to fruition. Since formation the partnership has prospered and last year Stays Engineering successfully issued shares to investors, who are friends.

The organisation now trades as Stays Engineering Ltd. Sidney now holds 30 per cent and Susan 38 per cent of the voting stock, with four other people each owning 8 per cent. Some of these smaller shareholders have now become managers within the company. The organisation chart is set out in Fig. 7.3 (the percentages in brackets show the person's shareholding if any).

Jenny is 28 years old and has been headhunted from a leading role within the marketing department of a national retail company. Sarah has a PhD in political science. She spent four years as a freelance journalist and two years ago made a career change into personnel. She is 37 and newly married. Jim is 26, has his AAT qualification and has been with the company since inception. George is 58. He is extremely proud of what Stays has achieved and is excited about what it can do for its staff and the nearby town, where George has lived for 30 years and brought up his family.

Two weeks ago the board of directors met for its monthly planning meeting. Stays have devised a new and very powerful adhesive that they are calling Wonder Resin Glue (WRG). Sidney has spoken to some of the company's main customers and thinks that weekly sales could exceed 130 000 litres. However, Jenny did say that she had reason to think that not all their customers would adopt the new adhesive and sales each week might average as low as 15 000 litres. She estimates that there is a 90 per cent chance of the former and 10 per cent chance of the latter event happening.

Stays have spent £50 000 on production facilities for WRG. Furthermore, direct material costs will be 25p per litre. The production line will require two people, each costing £14 000 per annum. The WRG facilities are expected to have a life of at least five years. WRG is expected to sell at £4 per litre.

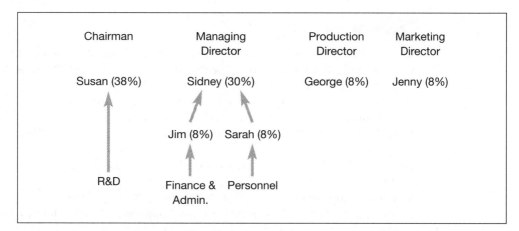

Fig. 7.3 Organisation chart for Stays Engineering

Jenny mentions that they have thought about advertising WRG. They think that a successful campaign might enhance sales by 100 per cent, although a poorly received campaign would only yield a 15 per cent increase. Additionally, a poor campaign might harm sales of the company's other products and reduce profits from those by £30 000. They think that the campaign would cost £50 000 and have a 60 per cent chance of success. Sidney challenged the substance of the marketing data; Susan attempted to bring the meeting to a conclusion but the issues remained unresolved.

Last Wednesday the two original partners had a working lunch so that they could discuss their futures. They wanted to discuss an approach by Bigbond, a California-based company that is considering making an offer for Stays. Bigbond is offering £600 000, which is equivalent to six years of current profits. This offer is subject to both Sidney and Susan remaining for at least two years. Sidney also mentioned that the previous week he was surprised to receive a telephone call from a firm of employment consultants offering him the post of Marketing Director with Glueco, with a total reward package of £45 000 per year. 'It all seems so complicated now', bemoans Susan. She feels that all the possibilities have them and the other directors feeling bewildered. She also knows that Jim and Sarah want more of a say in the running and the future direction of the company.

All the directors and shareholders are aware of the environmental trends – for example, employment prospects, market forces facing Stays Engineering Ltd, and other trends. They want to make the right decision.

| Matters for discussion | 1 *Critically evaluate the process of organisational planning that is demonstrated in the case.* |

1 *Critically evaluate the process of organisational planning that is demonstrated in the case.*

2 *Analyse the likely corporate, functional and individual objectives that are apparent in the case.*

3 *Critically evaluate the usefulness and suitability of the objectives of the different functional areas within the overall organisational plan.*

4 *Critically evaluate the hard and soft issues that are apparent within the case.*

References

Checkland, P. (1984) *Systems Thinking, Systems Practice*, John Wiley & Sons Ltd, London.

Cyert, R. and March, J. G. (1963) *A Behavioural Theory of the Firm*, Prentice-Hall, Englewood Cliffs, New Jersey.

Etzioni, A. (1967) 'Mixed-scanning: a "third" approach to decision-making', *Public Administration Review*, December, 385–92.

Langley, A. (1988), 'The roles of formal strategic planning', *Long Range Planning*, 21(3), pp. 40–50.

Lindblom, Charles, E. (1959) 'The science of "muddling through"', *Public Administration Review*, 19, 79–88.

March, J. G. and Simon, H. A. (1958) *Organisations*, Wiley, London.

Mintzberg, H. (1990) 'The manager's job: folklore and fact', *Harvard Business Review*, March–April, pp. 164ff.

Mintzberg, H., Quinn, J. B. and Ghoshal, S. (1998) *The Strategy Process* (revised European edition), Prentice-Hall, Hemel Hempstead.

Osborn, A. F. (1957) *Applied Imagination* (revised edition), Scribner's, New York.

Peters, T. and Waterman, R. (1982) *In Search of Excellence*, HarperCollins, New York.

Quinn, James Brian (1982) *Strategies for Changes: Logical Incrementalism*, Irwin, illinois.

Schon, D. (1983) *The Reflective Practitioner – How Professionals Think in Action*, Temple-Smith.

Simons, R. (1987) 'Planning, control and uncertainty: a process review', in W. J. Bruns, Jnr, and R. S. Kaplan (eds) *Accounting and Management: Field Study Perspectives*, Harvard Business School Press, Cambridge, MA.

Simons, R. (1990) 'The role of management control systems in creating competitive advantage: new perspectives', *Accounting, Organisations and Society*, XV, pp. 127–43.

Simons, R. (1991a) 'Strategic orientation and top management attention to control mechanisms', *Strategic Management Journal*, XII, pp. 49–62.

Simons, R. (1991b) *Rethinking the role of systems in controlling strategy*, Publishing Division, Harvard Business School, #9-191–091.

Stewart, R. (1983) *Managerial Behaviour: How Research Has Perspectives on Management: A Multidisciplinary Analysis*, Oxford University Press, pp. 96–7.

Whittington, R. (1993) *What is Strategy and Does it Matter?* Routledge Publishing, London.

CHAPTER 8

Strategic decision making

Learning objectives

At the end of this chapter you should:

- understand the differences between strategic and other types of decision making;

- recognise how corporate strategies lead to the development of strategies for different business functions;

- have an appreciation of the changing environmental context in which organisations operate, and the impact this will have on strategic decision making;

- understand the linkages between the environment, organisational aims and objectives and strategies; and

- understand why different organisations have different approaches to strategic decision making.

Introduction

There is probably no area of organisational theory that has attracted the attention of academics more than strategic management; and yet, at a practical level, it is a branch of management that is often misinterpreted or misunderstood.

What, we might ask, is the difference between a strategic decision and any other decision? Perhaps the fundamental difference lies not so much in the decision-making process as in the importance of the strategic decision, and in the fact that its impact tends to be felt across a broader span of the organisation. A strategic decision is one that governs the direction the organisation takes for the future. It is frequently said that strategic decisions are long-term decisions; but although this is often the case, 'strategic' is not, in fact, synonymous with 'long-term'. The timescale of strategic planning will vary, being determined by the business environment, and how well the organisation is, and has been, performing.

This chapter will begin by looking briefly at the nature of strategic decisions, who makes them, and who is affected by them. We shall then examine some of the often complex processes by which strategic decisions are made. The first part of this process will focus primarily on contextual analysis, which will, together with an assessment of the organisation's resource strengths, provide the rationale for the decision on the strategic direction the organisation might take. Finally, after describing an outline framework for arriving at strategic decisions, some brief consideration will be given to the relative merits of some alternative approaches to strategic decision making.

Strategic decisions and their context

Strategic decisions are not made in a vacuum; they are contingent upon a range of other factors – particularly the environment but also the extent to which the senior managers within the organisation wish to accept risk.

The importance of the environment can be illustrated by drawing an analogy between a large company and a cargo ship. If the ship is sailing in open seas in good weather, with clear visibility, and there are no other vessels within a great distance, the captain of the ship can safely set a steady course and progress rapidly ahead. However, he knows that changing the course of such a huge vessel is not easy; if the ship is travelling fast, it will take a considerable distance to alter its direction. Therefore, if there are adverse weather conditions, with poor visibility, and there is a risk that the cargo vessel might run onto rocks or meet another ship, progress will be slow and cautious. Just like the ship, the business organisation must consider the context of its operations, and adjust its strategic horizons accordingly. If, for example, the economic conditions are favourable for trading, and there is evidence that customers favour one company's products over other providers', then the context might be considered suitable for the exploitation of new opportunities – perhaps rapid expansion. The organisational equivalent of poor visibility or stormy weather might be significant competitive threats or economic recession. In such circumstances, a more cautious strategy – perhaps consolidation – would be appropriate.

Naturally, the size of the organisation may also have an impact upon its strategic horizons. To continue the nautical parallel for a moment, the cargo ship may be unable to alter its course quickly; yet a smaller craft would be able to respond much more readily to emerging obstacles. This is, perhaps, just as well, since it is unlikely that the small craft will have the same equipment or capability to recognise what is looming in the distance. The same is true of smaller business organisations, which, though they tend to be more flexible and respond to environmental change more quickly than large corporations, may not have the resources or capability to forecast far into the future. It is often the case, therefore, that smaller organisations do less formal strategic planning than larger organisations (Lee, Newman and Price, 1998). It is also true that many of the large companies are quite envious of the flexibility of the smaller firms to respond rapidly to environmental change, and they have put a great deal of effort into developing structures that are more responsive in a hostile environment.

163

Strategic decisions occur at different levels of an organisation. Corporate strategy refers to the chosen direction of an entire organisation. Consider for example, a brewery which currently brews and sells beer exclusively within the United Kingdom. Those working in the brewery may be content with products they produce and the customers they serve. So why change? First, patterns of consumption may reveal that there have been changes in consumers' tastes; continental style lagers are often preferred to traditional British ales. Second, the brewer's competitors have changed, as have patterns of distribution. Fewer small UK brewers are operating in the market, and the main competition now comes from larger companies, many of which are international. An increasing proportion of sales occur through the large supermarket chains that offer smaller profit margins for brewers. 'No change' may simply not be a strategic option for this company. The processes of strategic choice will be considered later, but for the time being, let us assume that a decision is made to both expand the company's product range through acquisition, and to extend its geographical market by brewing and selling in mainland Europe.

Having established the strategic objectives of expanding both our product range and our market coverage, and decided upon a corporate strategy of international acquisition, the next stage is for our organisation to set in place strategies for the different business functions. We will therefore need to develop financial strategies, marketing strategies, human resource strategies, etc. all of which will have to be commensurate with the corporate strategy. The parameters for decisions made at each of these functional levels are governed by the decisions made at the higher level.

It is imperative that the different functions all move in the same direction. Imagine that many members of an organisation are huddled in a group and bound together by a rope. The Marketing Department begins to move West, the Finance Department tries to move North, while Production heads South. The likelihood of any progress is, of course, minimal! If, on the other hand, it is decided, either by consensus, or by the leader alone, that the whole organisation will move in an Easterly direction at a pace that is agreed and communicated to the group, progress is possible. The better the co-ordination between the members of an organisation, the greater the likelihood of success.

Exactly the same is true of management strategy; our progress towards our corporate goals will be dependent upon the functional areas of the organisation adopting coherent strategies consistent with the corporate strategies. As we shall see later in the chapter, there is little point in one of the business functions forging ahead of the others, since a balance must be achieved between the functions if we are to succeed in our corporate strategic objectives. After all, if we are all bound together and moving in the same direction, there is little to be gained from one person trying to sprint whilst the others are jogging at a steady pace.

A framework for strategic decision making

If strategy is to do with setting an organisation's course for the future, the organisation will have start with realistic, achievable aims and objectives. There would be little logic in a new, small manufacturer of electrical components setting itself the goal of challenging the great multinational companies in its industry. Intermediate goals must be set before such dizzy heights could ever be contemplated. Once again, an organisation must consider its position in the context of its industry and the broader external environment before it can set itself realistic targets.

The first step in the process of strategic decision making for an organisation is therefore to establish where it stands at the present time. Of course, its current competitive position has much to do with its performance in the recent past, so it will also need to know how it reached the point it is at. For example, if our organisation has the third-largest annual sales turnover of all UK companies in its industry, and is beginning to trade in two other European Union countries, we may feel this represents a fairly useful position and it could be optimistic about the future. But what if five years ago it was the leader in its field, and has been overtaken by two young companies with driving ambition and a much stronger representation in European markets? There may be *other* businesses targeting our organisation as easy prey; clearly, the strategic position now looks altogether different. So it is easy to see the importance of recent history when making decisions about our future.

Once we have established both current standing and how an enterprise reached that position, we can begin to take stock of whether this is a situation that suits the organisation, in which case it is one which it might wish to defend. If not, the next task is to decide the position it would like to be in. Once again, realism must govern this decision, since, for example, turning around the fortunes of an organisation is not something that can be achieved at the whim of management; so, in such circumstances, plans for a staged recovery might be more appropriate.

Having conducted this fairly lengthy analysis of the current position relative to the situation the company would like to be in, it is now time for the decision makers to draw up their strategic plans. These plans will specify how we are to achieve the objectives we have set ourselves.

In summary, a framework can be created for making strategy decisions, and thus framework can be based on a four-stage process for stategic decision making. The four stages are:

1 Determine our current standing. *Where are we now?*

2 Establish how we reached this position. *How did we get here?*

3 Review our aims and objectives. *Where would we like to be?*

4 Decide upon a strategy. *How are we going to get there?*

Having established a framework for making strategic decisions, we will now develop some of the themes introduced in the framework.

Where are we now?

The people developing or reviewing organisational strategies will have a range of information requirements to support their decisions. A useful starting point would be an assessment of the organisation's purpose. This is likely to be reflected in its mission statement, and will give an indication of what the organisation's aspirations have been in recent years. If, as is the case with most commercial organisations, the organisational purpose leads to measurable financial objectives, these too can be assessed.

The performance of most organisations can be assessed in terms of their growth, profitability and efficiency. In general, in a competitive environment, strategic decision makers can be fairly optimistic if the organisation is outperforming its rivals in these three areas.

Growth may be measured by sales revenue, but it is worth bearing in mind that what matters is growth in *real* terms, rather than inflationary growth. Second, any measure of growth must be seen in relation to the growth of the relevant market. Ten per cent sales growth, for example, will indicate a more aggressive expansion if there has been no expansion of the market, since this means there has been an increase in our share of the market. By contrast, if the market has increased by 40 per cent, our company's share of the market will have diminished. This does not, of course, mean that our performance has been poor, even relative to our rivals, since a number of new firms may have entered the market, perhaps with no existing business, and achieved growth of more than ten per cent. Nevertheless, the fact that there has been rapid market growth does introduce perspective to our judgement. While the increase in sales throughout the market represents an opportunity, the entry of new firms must be monitored for the threat they may pose, particularly if there is a subsequent stabilisation (or even decline) of the market.

As part of a strategy of market penetration a successful company might sometimes increase its rate of growth by reducing its profit margin. Conversely, it is possible that an organisation might choose to sacrifice investment for a short period of time in order to temporarily increase its profit margins. While such a trade-off between the profit margin and growth may be feasible in the short term, most organisations will seek to balance the two over the longer term.

There is no hard and fast rule as to what might be an appropriate profit margin for a successful company, since this will vary considerably from one industry to another, but comparative measures will offer the most reliable picture. If an organisation is outperforming its industry rivals in terms of Return on Sales (profit before interest and tax/sales) without simultaneously sacrificing growth, it would appear to be successful.

Like growth, efficiency should be judged in comparison with other organisations. It may be measured against an industry average, since it is critical for the validity of our assessment that we are comparing like with like. Return on capital employed (ROCE) is a useful measure for this purpose.

Other financial data which may be of use in assessing the performance of an organisation might include gearing ratios. These may indicate the organisation's vulnerability to external changes, such as adjustments in interest rates, and are, therefore, important in assessing how robust the business is likely to be in the face of environmental turbulence.

How did we get here?

In order to understand the recent history of an organisation, its performance needs to be assessed in context. This requires an understanding of the business environment, which can be examined at three different levels. The first of these is the external environment, which is concerned with factors outside the control of the business but which will have an impact on the organisation. This will include the activities of governments and the economy as a whole. The second level might be termed the operating environment, and includes people and organisations with whom the company trades or competes, and whom it influences to an extent, without being able to exercise a direct control. This group will include customers and suppliers, other firms in the market, as well as potential new customers and competitors. The third level is known as the internal environment, and is essentially concerned with the operation taking place inside the organisation, such as the various business functions. While it may not be possible to exercise total control over the internal environment, it would be reasonable to regard it as entirely the organisation's own responsibility.

The external environment

The importance of the external environment can be amply illustrated if we take an example from the UK construction industry. There have been periods in this particular industry when demand for construction work has been so great, and prices have risen so rapidly, that even relatively poorly managed businesses have sometimes thrived. But, equally, when economic conditions have been unfavourable and little new building work is demanded, only the leanest and most efficient companies have survived. The peaks and troughs of economic activity have affected this industry more than most, with the cycle of boom and recession exaggerated in comparison with the rest of the economy.

Arguably, strategic vision becomes more important when the external environment is volatile. Recent research by the authors of this book (Lee, Newman and Price, 1998) revealed one East Anglian construction company that, in 1987 at the peak of the housing boom and following several consecutive years of economic growth, falling levels of income tax, and a government that promoted home ownership, was scarcely able to find labour, even at the highest rates of pay, to cope with the soaring demand for new homes. Building land had been purchased in advance of its requirement, so that the company could continue to expand; and the value of this asset was rising rapidly too. The management of this small company had been clearly of the impression that times had never been better. When interest rates subsequently doubled, demand plummeted and house and land prices fell as rapidly as they had risen, the same management was taught a brutal lesson. The asset value of its land holdings fell to around half the price that had originally been paid. The company limped along for a couple of years, largely on repair contracts, but eventually, in spite of its good local reputation, it was dissolved.

This particular company was ultimately defeated by its failure fully to understand its external environment. The external environment can fluctuate violently, and organisations have virtually no control over it. They must, therefore, anticipate what might happen in the future, and strategic decisions must take account of this.

A commonly used framework for scanning the external environment is the PEST (political, economic, socio-cultural, technological) analysis (see Fig. 8.1). PEST can identify key environmental influences on strategic decision making. For example, changes in the National Health Service over the past decade have been driven by a number of external factors:

- greater acceptance of market solutions to economic choice;
- an ageing population causing a rising dependency ratio; and
- improved technology, which has resulted in more complex medical choices (such as who should receive replacement hips, knees or organs), longer life expectancy, and greater survival rate of those with chronic medical problems.

Political	• Relations between countries
	• Trade policy (e.g. tariffs, import quotas)
	• Sanctions
	• Economic policies (e.g. EMU, monetary and fiscal policy)
	• Parties and power
	• Legislation (e.g. consumer protection, environmental protection)
	• Government relations with employers and trades unions
Economic	• The trade cycle of alternate boom and recession
	• Costs (including labour)
	• GDP and consumer spending
	• Government spending
	• Interest rates
	• Exchange rates
Socio-cultural	• Changing lifestyles
	• Values and attitudes
	• Demographic changes
	• Ethnic mix
	• Worldwide travel
	• Homogenisation of tastes across national boundaries
Technological	• Production techniques
	• New products from research
	• Competitors' developments
	• Reduction in product life cycles
	• Huge investment in joint ventures
	• Effects of technological development on labour

Fig. 8.1 PEST analysis

PEST can also identify the key *drivers of change*. For example, the globalisation of trade and the existence of multinational customers have led to an emphasis on economies of scale and cost-reduction strategies.

The operating environment

At the operating level of the environment, we can examine the extent to which an organisation's competitive position has improved or deteriorated. The first task would normally be to assess market share and whether the market has grown. A decline in market share, for example, will lead the company to question whether this represents a deterioration in its competitive position. If so, it will need to work out why it appears to have been overtaken by others within the market.

A variety of analytical frameworks and techniques are available for this purpose. One of the most effective is Porter's well known 'five forces' framework (1980). Porter identifies five generic sources of competitive opportunity or threat that merit managerial attention:

1 *Threat of new competitors entering the market.* This threat can be staved off by creating barriers to entry, perhaps by achieving economies of scale that will not be available to new but smaller firms, by product differentiation, or maybe by gaining control of distribution channels.

2 *The relationship with customers.* Ideally, customers will develop a loyalty to our organisation, ensuring we gain repeat custom. This is less likely if the customers are able to purchase similar products or services from a large number of other companies. The balance of power in the customer–supplier relationship will tend to rest with the customer if there are few customers, and their orders are large. Strategic decision makers, therefore, should try to ensure that their business is not over-reliant on one or two large customers.

3 *The relationship with suppliers.* This is the reverse of the customer–supplier relationship outlined above. Many large organisations pursue a policy of purchasing from small suppliers, for whom they are important customers. In this way, the large company is likely to be able to exercise more control over terms of business, such as product or service quality, delivery schedules and pricing.

4 *The likelihood that new, substitute products will be introduced.* In some markets, such as fashion goods, it is known from the outset that product substitution is likely to occur after a relatively short period. Where the product life cycle is known to be short, product replacement should be a part of the strategy. Product life cycles are shortening for many products, often because of technological change. Competitive strategies will therefore need to take account of product substitution. Other factors that strategic decision makers may need to consider will be cost-effectiveness of alternative products or services, and the extent to which the customer bears any cost of switching between substitutes.

5 *The competitive rivalry between firms in the market.* The intensity of rivalry between firms in a market will have an important bearing on a business's profitability and its ability to grow. Factors to consider here would be: the number of existing competitors in the market, the extent of similarity or diversity of competitors' products

(which will influence the likelihood of product or brand substitution), and whether or not the market is growing. If in fact the market is in decline, a key issue is likely to be whether there are barriers to firms leaving the market. For example, firms are sometimes reluctant to cease production because they have committed large amounts of capital to the project. In such cases, the intensity of competition will increase as organisations battle for a smaller number of customers.

The five-forces framework is one which has been widely used for assessing the operating environment, but before we leave this model, it is worth noting the importance of viewing this framework in its dynamic context. Porter's model is most useful for strategic planning and decision making when we recognise how the impact of each of the competitive forces acting upon an organisation is changing. In this way, we can judge whether our competitive position is becoming stronger or weaker. Some decision makers have been known to apply the five-forces framework using a scoring system on a scale of +5 to –5 for each of the five elements, where a positive score indicates an improvement in our position and a negative score a deterioration. Hence, if, for example, the size of the market is declining rapidly, and there are significant barriers to firms leaving the market, competitive rivalry might score around –4; a steadily improving relationship with our customers, with some indication of greater customer loyalty to our brands might conversely score, say, +2 or +3. The advantage of this sort of scoring system is that it forces a company to focus on its key competitive strengths and weaknesses, and to recognise areas where it is improving, or else losing ground, to rivals.

Porter's five-forces framework is given in diagrammatic form in Fig. 8.2.

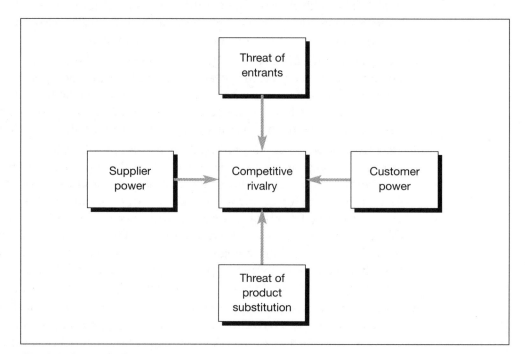

Fig. 8.2 Porter's five-forces model

The internal environment

The third level of the environment that needs to be examined is the internal environment, which is concerned with a firm's resource capability. The starting point for analysing an organisation's internal strengths and weaknesses will normally be a resource audit. This audit should take account not only of the *quantity* of resources but also their quality.

One approach to the resource audit would be to use generic categories of resources, which can then be subdivided as necessary. Four categories might be:

- *Financial resources*. These will include, not only the organisation's financial assets but also the systems for managing them, access to additional sources of funds, etc.

- *Human resources*. This is perhaps the most difficult area to audit, since human beings behave differently in different contexts. The human resources audit will cover skills and knowledge as well as a judgement of individuals' adaptability to new situations. This will, of course, be fairly subjective, but it is important to gain an impression of the likely consequences if major strategic changes were to be introduced.

- *Physical resources*. The most important consideration here will be depreciation, not just through wear and tear but also through technological obsolescence.

- *Information resources*. This intangible, but very important category of resources will include: product design, marketing information, and the findings of other research; it will contribute to the organisation's 'goodwill'.

To these four categories we might consider adding the organisational resources, which, whilst intangible, clearly have an impact on strategic capability. These might be summarised in terms of the McKinsey '7 S' framework (Pascall and Athos, 1982), which distinguishes between three 'hard' S's – strategy, structure and systems – and four 'soft' S's – staff, style, skills and shared values. Strength in the 'soft' S's might add flexibility to the organisation, which should enhance its ability to cope with strategic change.

Perhaps a slightly more analytical approach to evaluating an organisation's strategic capability is to apply Porter's (1985) 'value chain' model. The value chain is a tool for identifying potential sources of competitive advantage within an organisation. Its advantage over a straightforward resource audit is that it demonstrates the interrelationship between different resources and activities, recognising the importance of the linkages between them. The value chain framework recognises that value can be created in many different ways and at several stages of production. For example, when a customer buys a branded television set, that customer probably realises that a different make of television could have been purchased at a lower price. So why buy the particular brand? The customer is, in fact, probably paying 'extra' for the design, the reliability, the durability, the service support and the product's warranty. Many of these attributes are reflected in the brand name, which may indicate a package of benefits to the customer. What the value chain aims to do is to identify the different sources of value creation and achieve competitive advantage by outperforming competitors in as many of these activities as possible.

In his model, Porter distinguishes between 'primary activities', by which he means activities directly related to the production of goods or services, and 'support activities', which refer to those activities that smooth the passage of production, often rendering the overall process more efficient and hence contributing to the organisation's competitive position. Porter identified five primary activities:

- purchasing materials for production;
- manufacturing from them;
- marketing the products or services;
- distributing the products; and
- providing service support for product sales.

To these he added four support activities, which occur throughout all the primary activities:

- *procurement* – the purchasing of inputs for all primary activities, not just materials;
- *technology*, which is developed at all stages, and does not just involve the research and development of products and processes;
- *human resource management*, covering planning, staffing requirements, recruitment and selection, training etc. in all departments; and
- *infrastructure*, which covers general management, planning, finance, accounting procedures, and the company's response to legal and government affairs.

Of particular importance when assessing the organisation's strategic capability is a consideration of how well the different value-creating activities link together. For example, are production designers and schedulers acting directly upon customer information identified within the marketing function; and are information systems providing the right quantity of the right type of information in time for the organisation to adapt to changing external or market conditions? The effectiveness of the linkages in the value chain should give an indication of whether there is an appropriate balance between the different functional areas of the organisation.

There is no reason why all of the categories of activities identified in Porter's model have to be considered. Some may seem inappropriate to a particular organisation; and, indeed, other categories may be added. Some organisations might, for example, include design as a separate primary activity, and service organisations may exclude distribution. The point is that the model should serve to help assess strategic capabilities and need not be followed slavishly. The assessment will involve examining costs and performance for improvements in each value activity. If possible, comparisons should be made with competitors' costs and performance.

Having now considered the environment at all three levels, and in particular how the context of a firm's operations might have changed, it is necessary to examine the fit between the environment and organisation's current strategies. The company will need to review the objectives underpinning its existing strategies in order to assess whether they are still appropriate to the context. This is the stage that, above all, requires clear, logical thinking. Strategies may potentially have to be altered as a result of environmental changes, and it may now be necessary to adjust our aspirations.

Where would we like to be?

This stage of the strategic decision-making process will involve combining our organisational aims and objectives with an assessment of how the environment might change in the future.

The basis of environmental forecasting will initially be observed trends from the past. Since we know, for example, that no economy has ever grown at a constant rate, consumer tastes have always changed over time, and the skills required to maintain a competitive advantage have always had to be updated and renewed, it is fair to assume that these trends will continue in one form or another. The more information we can find to support predictions of the future environment, the better prepared we shall be to meet the competitive challenges of the future. If we know how soon economic boom might turn to recession, and when customers are likely to desert one product for another, we can plan our strategies accordingly. Of course, predicting the future is, at best, an inexact science; but on the basis that informed prediction is generally preferable to educated guessing, we should return once again to the three different levels of the environment.

The previous stage of formulating our strategic decisions involved monitoring what had happened in the past. We will now use that information for forecasting what the environment holds in the future. We may use some of the statistical and financial forecasting techniques used in earlier chapters for estimating rates of market growth, the payback period on investments etc. Other forecasts will involve objective judgements based on the information we have gathered.

The outcome of our forecasts should then be translated into a statement of opportunities and threats for our organisation. Suppose we perceive three different opportunities. They might each be evaluated using numerical techniques such as discounted cash flows, probabilities or decision trees. Ultimately, a qualitative judgement is likely to be made as to which best fits our organisational aims and objectives. The key stakeholders' attitudes towards risk may have a considerable bearing on the decision ultimately taken.

One of the most important aspects of the decision, however, will be the fit between our organisation's resource strengths and the opportunities available. For example, a manufacturing organisation may believe there are excellent opportunities for expansion into new markets. Yet they may fail to achieve that strategic objective because, although they may feel they have the production and marketing skills to make a success of the venture, they may lack the physical capacity to achieve the expansion without significant increases in costs. Other organisations have attempted to grow by increasing their productive capacity before they have evidence of market demand for extra output. In both these cases, insufficient care has been taken to ensure that the organisation has the capability to sustain its chosen strategy within all of its functional areas. Only when a fit has been established between an organisation's resource capability and the opportunities it perceives from its environmental forecasting will it be able to set the strategic direction for the organisation.

How are we going to get there?

At this stage it is necessary to establish the strategic direction for the organisation and the methods by which it will be achieved. This part of the strategic plan will identify what the organisation must do to achieve its objectives for the future.

Strategic direction has often been categorised according to whether the organisation intends to produce new or existing products, and whether it will serve new or existing markets. Four possible combinations of new or existing products and markets will be associated with different areas of key strengths within the organisation, and are as follows:

- *Existing product, existing market.* Consolidate current position, or grow through market penetration.
- *New product, existing market.* Product development.
- *Existing product, new market.* Market development.
- *New product, new market.*

These strategic directions should not be seen as mutually exclusive, since it is reasonable that an organisation might, for example, concentrate primarily on developing new products for its existing customers but find that as products are developed there are opportunities for the customer base to be extended. However, it is advisable for strategists to proceed with caution, since a blunderbuss approach lacks focus on customer needs, and the organisation may find it has a poor match between product and market.

One direction that is not covered in the bullet list immediately preceding is withdrawal from the market. An organisation might feel that the environment, at either the external or operating level, has become more hostile and that either there is insufficient scope to continue trading or its resource capabilities are no longer adequate to sustain its competitive position. Alternatively, a strategic decision may have been made to dispose of a particular business and focus on other opportunities.

A key question that strategic decision makers may ask themselves is whether or not growth should be an objective for the organisation. Growth is sometimes assumed to be desirable for all organisations; and while this may be true for many, there may be some – particularly smaller organisations – that are not happy with some of the implications of growth. Larger organisations will usually be less flexible than their smaller counterparts, and control is complex.

Whilst divisional structures are a possible way around these problems, the founders and owner–managers of some smaller organisations may not be prepared to lose their autonomy. This is graphically illustrated in Greiner's model of evolutionary and revolutionary growth (1972), which charts the changes in management focus, organisational structure, senior management style, control systems and management reward systems as organisations grow. Although the main purpose of Greiner's research was to demonstrate the critical points of transition as an organisation expands, it should be recognised that not all organisations will go through all the stages of growth identified in the model.

There follow some ways in which organisations can change their shape or direction in order to achieve strategic development and get to where they want to go.

Consolidation

Consolidation is to do with protecting market share in existing markets. It is primarily a defensive strategy, often appropriate when the environment is fairly hostile. It is important to recognise that consolidation does not mean 'doing nothing', since protecting market share can require resource capabilities to be strengthened.

Market penetration

Market penetration refers to an organisation's expansion of its share within its existing market through its existing products or services. Such a strategy might be most appropriate if the market is expanding, and the organisation attempts to capture new customers drawn into the market.

Attempts to achieve market penetration when the market is not increasing in size will almost certainly require an aggressive marketing strategy, and probably a short-term decline in profits if a policy of competitive pricing is used. In such circumstances, the organisation must have confidence in the relative strengths of its resources compared with those of rival producers.

Product development

The introduction of new products for existing customers is most appropriate where an organisation has either a loyal – or a captive – customer base, but new products are needed on a regular basis to keep them satisfied. A typical example of such a situation occurs in markets for fashion products. Buyers may have a favourite company from which they intend to purchase products regularly, as long as there is regular product replacement.

Organisations that are most likely to be successful with a product development strategy are those that have key strengths in research and development. The motor industry and consumer electronics are examples of industries in which product development is an important part of competitive strategy, since technological progress has been very rapid.

It is worth noting that an organisation that makes product development a key element in its strategy will, over time, inevitably have to develop new skills and competences to accommodate new technologies. We can see, therefore, the importance of updating resource capabilities, and not least, the support activities identified in Porter's value chain. Johnson & Scholes (1997) argue that the most successful companies following this strategy:

- have an excellent understanding of their customers' needs and preferences;
- develop products around key skills and strengths;
- are good at promoting the need for new product developments *within* the organisation; and
- involve people throughout the organisation, and even suppliers and customers too, in the process of developing new products.

Market development

Market development involves an organisation increasing its market coverage with its products. This can take several forms, the simplest of which is probably to find new uses for existing products. Manufacturers of breakfast cereals, for example, have encouraged customers to consume their products at other times of the day besides breakfast; Lucozade, once seen as a drink for sick children, is now promoted as a high-energy product for the very active, and particularly beneficial to sportsmen and sportswomen. Many industrial products have similarly found new uses.

The second type of market development occurs when an organisation that has previously served one segment of a market decides to broaden its customer base by serving new segments. This approach does carry risks, in that there is a danger of the image of the product being altered. One recent example from the late 1990s in the UK of successful market development of this type has been Tesco's introduction of a range of own-brand products with its simple but distinctive blue-and- white packaging, aimed at customers who tend to buy according to price rather than brand. This own-branded range altered customer perceptions about whether it was necessarily cheaper to buy from certain rival supermarkets that adopted price-cutting policies. As with many other companies that have pursued this type of market development, Tesco had to modify its products and packaging to some extent so that they could maintain some distinction between different market segments. It is interesting that, at the time Tesco first entered the low-price segment of the market, there were those who felt that their quality image in the higher-priced segment could be damaged. The fact that this proved not to be the case was probably due largely to the differentiation in the packaging of the different product lines.

A third type of market development concerns geographical spread from existing markets, often crossing national boundaries. Some ambitious organisations find that their local or domestic market simply does not offer sufficient scope for their desire to expand. Amongst the many examples of organisations that have successfully expanded in this way are the Scandinavian furniture retailer Ikea and the Dutch brewing company, Heineken. Ikea essentially maintained its original product concept as it expanded, initially throughout Western Europe and then (with some product alterations) into the US market. Heineken has recognised the different beer-drinking traditions and tastes in different countries, and has had to make adjustments to marketing methods and methods of distribution for different national markets. Both these examples, but perhaps particularly the latter, illustrate how market development through international expansion places new demands on an organisation's resource capabilities, requiring new skills to be developed internally or brought into the organisation from outside. This point will be developed further when we consider methods of organisational growth a little later.

Diversification

Although the term 'diversification' is sometimes used rather loosely to cover either product development or market development, we shall use the term only to describe a situation where an organisation opts for both simultaneously.

The motives for diversification are based on two fundamentally opposed philosophies:

- diversification for spreading risk (portfolio spread); or
- diversification for adding to competitive advantage (synergy).

The first of these motives would encourage conglomerate diversification rather than exploiting relationships between businesses. An example of this is Exxon's diversification into office equipment after the oil crisis of 1973–4 rendered its core oil business temporarily unstable. The principal advantage of such conglomerate diversification is that, with a range of very different business interests, an organisation is unlikely to experience simultaneous decline in all of them, especially as they are likely to have varying business cycles. The converse, of course, is that all strategic business units are equally unlikely to perform to their peak potential at the same time.

A second case for portfolio spread is based on escaping from dependence on an industry that is in long-term decline. BAT Industries, for example, appears to have recognised some time ago that the future for its core tobacco business is not bright. Although there is still profit to be made from tobacco, it has seemed prudent to it to diversify into a range of other businesses.

The second motive for diversification is based on exploiting relationships between businesses to gain synergy. In this case, diversification will be related to the organisation's core activities, and be 'concentric', or involve 'vertical integration'.

'Concentric' diversification occurs when an organisation's surplus resources are transferred into related product markets and sold to new customers. There may be a variety of reasons for this type of diversification:

- Managerial or other skills (particularly technical) may be transferable from one situation to another.
- Marketing assets may be used to boost a product's image in the new market (e.g. Woolwich has transferred goodwill built up in the financial services sector to its estate agency).
- Hotels and universities have both found that their physical resources are under-utilised at certain times of the day, week or year. Both have used their premises to attract conference trade, and universities have used student accommodation for holiday lets during vacations.

'Vertical integration' may be either backward (i.e. for a manufacturer, taking over its material supply source), or forward (i.e. in a manufacturing business, taking over distribution outlets). The benefits of vertical integration may be summarised as follows:

- Control can be gained, either of marketing functions or of vital supplies that may at times be scarce. Such control of supplies can also act as a barrier to new competitors' entering the market, thus, reducing the impact of one of Porter's five competitive forces.
- Forward vertical integration can help expand the market for existing products. Laura Ashley was initially a manufacturing organisation, but was able to

enhance the exclusivity of its product image and increase sales by establishing its own retail outlets.

- To be in control of technological developments, rather than purchasing technology 'off the shelf'. This allows the organisation to compete for technological leadership in its market. This was the likely motive behind Philips' investment in microchip manufacture and design even though the company has never quite achieved leadership status within its industry.

While concentric diversification or vertical integration may represent a possibly logical progression for an organisation, developing new products for new markets is undoubtedly a risky strategy, and one that many authors (e.g. Ansoff, 1974; Argenti, 1989) caution against. In general, a strategy of diversification might be more likely to succeed if there is some synergistic link with the existing business. Exhibit 8.1 illustrates this.

Exhibit 8.1	**Related and unrelated diversification**

In 1994, a Suffolk-based company dealing in seed testing and seed sales acquired a medium-sized farm, and began producing its own seeds, rather than buying from other farmers. The company's seed testing laboratory was then relocated from a small industrial estate to the farm and housed in a converted barn. Though such an expansionary strategy was clearly diversificatory, risk was minimised by the relationship between the businesses; and synergies were achieved by using spare farm buildings for the seed testing laboratory.

The same organisation, however, subsequently diversified in a less related manner, acquiring a tea-bagging business, which was also relocated to the farm. Whilst there is no direct link between tea-bagging and seed testing or sales, the tea-bagging plant required a good deal of space, partly for the production machinery, and partly for storage of the finished products. The farm site had space available in further out-buildings at much lower cost than had been the case prior to relocation. There was, therefore, a strategic logic in the acquisition of the tea-bagging business, though additional employees with experience of the product and the market had to be recruited to ensure that there was sufficient resource capability within the organisation.

According to Argenti, diversification is the wrong strategy for most companies for the following reasons:

- They are inexperienced compared with established competitors in terms of both product and market.
- Expansion of either the product range or the market coverage will be demanding on resources. By expanding both simultaneously, there must be a risk of an organisation overstretching itself.
- Diversification is often used by organisations with severe problems as an excuse for not tackling problems in the core areas.

Argenti does, however, suggest two circumstances in which diversification may be worth pursuing:

- if the organisation has surplus resources (not merely financial resources, but also people and skills) which are not needed in the core business; or

- if prospects for the existing business are very poor, and hence there is a danger of investing from a position of weakness.

In both these circumstances, Argenti argues for *closely related* diversification, so that the organisation might still exploit some of the expertise it has gained in its core business areas. Argenti does also, rather cautiously, support a third possible justification for diversification – to build a conglomerate, which he sees as a 'robust structure'.

Having now considered a range of possible strategic directions, and the circumstances in which decision makers might opt for each, we need to briefly consider the methods of achieving some of these potential strategic goals. In particular, we will examine methods of breaking into new markets through market development and diversification.

Methods of growth in new markets

Once an organisation has decided to expand into new markets, whether with its original product range (market development), or with new products (diversification), a decision will have to be made as to how this can be done. A range of options will be open to strategic decision makers. For instance, should they build new business units for the new market, or buy existing businesses? Should they pursue their goal alone, or find a partner and enter a strategic alliance? If they opt for a strategic alliance, should it be a formal arrangement, such as a joint venture, or a looser, networking type of arrangement, designed to tap the expertise of others only when it is really needed? This section will examine some of the choices and trade-offs underlying these questions.

Internal development or acquisition? The build-or-buy debate

Whether it is decided to break into new markets through acquisition or by using the organisation's own resources to build a new business will be governed by many different factors, such as the importance of speed of access to the new market, and the availability of capital for acquisition. Whichever method is chosen, it is almost certain that there will be trade-offs, in the sense that neither method of expansion is likely to be wholly advantageous over the other. In this section we shall, therefore, try to balance the pros and cons of building or buying a business, and relate each to the environmental context.

One of the advantages of *internal* development is the learning effect of employees' working to build up a new business unit. The hands-on nature of this type of expansion acquaints employees with the developing business and markets, and can be preferable to 'buying into' new products or markets with which the organisation is not familiar. It also avoids the sudden change associated with acquisition, whereby an organisation may be pitched into running a new business without having had any previous experience of that industry. Of course, a business may be purchased as a going concern, in which case experienced managers and employees will already be in place, but this brings a further potential problem in the form of matching the cultures of the different businesses. Internal development can also be seen as preferable in terms of its incremental requirement for capital.

However, the pace at which market access is achieved is always a likely potential disadvantage of internal development. Since internal development involves building a business from scratch, the process can be very slow, and it may be some considerable time before such a venture begins to repay the capital invested in it. In many cases, a strategic move into new markets must be executed quickly, or else others may seize the market opportunity first. An example of such a situation was seen in the brewing industry in Europe during the late 1980s and early 1990s. The industry was rapidly internationalising. Several large breweries were keen to gain a presence in several national markets, and speed of market entry became one of the most important considerations. Mergers and acquisitions became the norm, because internal development would have been too slow.

Porter (1980) suggests that when organisations enter a market by internal development, they sometimes fail to anticipate the full costs of such a strategy, since they need to consider not only the basic investment cost but also competitor reactions. He specifies two forms that these reactions might take:

1 Competitors may put up entry barriers, perhaps in the form of the production technology used. This may increase initial investment costs and require a substantial market share in order to achieve competitive cost structures. Alternatively, the barriers could come from competitors' strong brands, which might necessitate additional and costly marketing activity on the part of the new entrant.

2 Unexpected costs may be incurred to offset competitors' retaliation to market entry.

Porter also argues that, since internal development will create additional capacity in an industry, the circumstances in which it is appropriate are limited. Clearly, there will not be a problem if the market is expanding and can therefore absorb the extra capacity; but otherwise, according to Porter, internal development is only likely to be effective if:

- the incumbents in the market have specific weaknesses, such as poor management, or are financially weak;
- the new market entrant has some distinctive advantage, such as access to superior technology compared to incumbent firms; or
- a superior competitive position can be achieved through synergy with the organisation's existing businesses.

Before leaving the question of the relative merits of building or buying into new markets, it is worth exploring just a little further the issue of selecting targets for acquisition. It is advisable that potential acquisition targets should be assessed according to what they can contribute to the company's strategic objectives. This means that a business with *complementary* resources should be sought, rather than a very similar organisation. The other key issue in identifying an acquisition target is the culture match between the organisations to be united. In the search for business synergy when making an acquisition, it is easy to overlook the importance of potential incompatibilities between organisations. The integration of two organisations can be problematic because of differences in culture and management style. The differences may manifest themselves in terms of task or time orientation, the balance between salaries and performance bonuses, the number of formal layers of management, the balance between youth and experience etc. It is not difficult to imagine how two organisations that are culturally diametrically apart can fail to integrate successfully. Indeed, amongst mergers and acquisitions that ultimately prove unsuccessful, culture misfit is one of the main causes of failure.

Joint development or 'go it alone'?

There is no doubt that strategic alliances have become more important as a means of business expansion over the past two decades. The number of international joint ventures involving UK firms doubled during the 1980s, and has continued to grow ever since. Perhaps the most important reason for this has been the rapid growth of international trade. The globalisation of many sectors of the world economy has meant that many organisations are dealing in markets which are simply too large for them to compete in alone. Moreover, restrictions on direct investment in certain national markets means that partnership with a local organisation may be the only means of gaining access to these markets.

But perhaps the most obvious reason for developing strategic alliances is their potential for cost sharing when market entry is very expensive. Strategic alliances can offer an organisation the opportunity to gain access to expertise and valuable additional resources, yet without having to pay for full ownership of them. Astute organisations, recognising that the alliance may not be permanent, will try to learn from their partners, and so enhance their own strategic capability for the future. By minimising financial outlay, alliances clearly offer scope for strategic advantage for organisations which might not otherwise have the necessary resource base to compete in the largest markets. Furthermore, the shared costs of a strategic alliance will benefit each partner through the associated reduction of risk.

There are several forms of strategic alliance, some of which involve more permanent arrangements than others. Some of the commonest types of alliance are as follows:

- *Licensing of technology*, which is often used when an organisation has technical capabilities that have market potential beyond the scope of the organisation's own resources. For example, the UK glass manufacturer Pilkington has licensed its float glass process around the world, rather than investing in manufacturing facilities in international markets. Several other examples can be found in the brewing industry, such as Courage's production of Kronenbourg beer under licence in the UK.

181

- *Technical and marketing agreements,* where information and skills are shared for mutual benefit.

- *Joint ventures,* which are the most permanent form of alliance, where two or more firms create a new, separate entity in order to pursue a common strategic objective. The partnership is not necessarily one of equals, since one partner may contribute more than 50 per cent of the cost of the venture and may therefore have a dominant role in decision making.

Despite the increased popularity of strategic alliances, due in large part to the advantages they can bring to organisations expanding into international markets, they are not of course universally successful. Inevitably, entering into an alliance involves some loss of control, and this can be particularly difficult for organisations with strong cultures. International alliances can be particularly problematic in this respect, since an organisation's 'ways of doing things' can differ a great deal from country to country. A second problem that is not uncommon with strategic alliances is where one partner may not have the requisite skills to achieve the objectives of the union. This may sometimes derive from an alliance being formed purely for the purpose of gaining access to a market abroad. Mutual dependence tends to be a better basis for a successful strategic alliance.

Conflict between the partners is clearly a potential problem for a strategic alliance. Typical sources of conflict are:

- cultural differences between the partner organisations;
- one partner may attempt to dominate the relationship; or
- the partners may have divergent objectives – for example, on pricing policy, or with whom they should trade.

The best advice to strategists would be to avoid destructive conflict by taking preventive measures at the outset. Figure 8.3 summarises some of the general issues pertinent to setting up and maintaining successful strategic alliances. The recommendations are particularly applicable to joint ventures because of the more permanent nature of the alliance.

A brief critique of different approaches to strategic decision making

The methodology for making strategic decisions adopted in this chapter has been founded on a fairly rigorous approach of environmental analysis, assessment of resource strengths, planning, forecasting, and ultimately making a reasoned decision based on a balanced view of the information available. There seems to be a logic to such an analytical methodology, though its quasi-scientific credentials are, according to some authors (Whittington, 1993), somewhat questionable. This analytical approach to strategic decision making is based largely on judgements of what might occur in the future; but such judgements are clearly fallible and, some would suggest, so often inaccurate that they provide a poor basis for decision making.

Selecting the partner
- We need to understand what both/all partners want and expect from the alliance. In particular, we should ensure that our objectives are compatible.
- The partners' resources should complement, rather than replicate, each other.
- Ideally, the partners' individual strengths and weaknesses should be sufficiently different to encourage mutual dependency. Collectively, the profile of their strengths and weaknesses should be improved by the union.

Negotiating the alliance
- Negotiations should seek mutual benefits, not a better deal than the partner.
- Mutual agreement should be sought on policy issues; a majority decision, or dominance of one partner is likely to result in conflict at a later stage.
- The negotiating parties should have complementary, though not necessarily identical objectives. For example, the high-profile alliance between Rover and Honda, first established in 1979, offered Honda improved access to EU markets, while Rover gained from Honda's technological expertise.

Maintaining the relationship
- Written objectives offer the clearest guidelines from which both/all partners can work. These objectives may extend to a statement of the expectations of each partner, particularly in areas where there is a risk of conflict.
- A framework should be established for developing strategy and long term plans. This will ensure that one partner does not become progressively more dominant.
- Continually look for ways in which the partners' resources can complement each other, so as to achieve synergy in as many areas of value creation as possible. If the partners learn from each other, the alliance should be strengthened and conflict reduced.
- A mutually acceptable control system should be designed, which will give warning of any imminent difficulties.

Fig. 8.3 Some key factors for the success of strategic alliances

Ohmae (1983), in contrast, prefers to see strategic decision making as an art form, dependent on the inspiration of gifted individuals. While this may be true at the top of large organisations operating on an international stage, it may preclude a strategic role for humbler organisations, for whom analysis, planning and monitoring have their place.

A further criticism of the classical, analytical approach to strategic decision making is that the environment is apt to change so frequently, and in such an unpredictable manner, that technical analysis may not be appropriate. In this case, strategies may simply emerge from a more or less uncontrollable series of events (Mintzberg and Waters, 1985). This incremental approach to strategic decision making has many influential supporters and is appealing in its pragmatism. What is primarily required by strategic decision makers in this case is an instinctive understanding of what is happening in the environment, and a sufficiently flexible organisation to adapt to the incremental changes in the context.

Of course, that intuitive understanding of how the business environment is changing probably comes from the experience of monitoring and evaluating environmental change. We can reasonably conclude, therefore, that the analytical approach to strategy adopted in this chapter, whilst not offering a universal formula for making strategic decisions, is probably a sound basis from which we can begin to tackle this complex aspect of management. Experience, intuition and inspiration will undoubtedly help us to set our course for the future.

Summary of the chapter

- This chapter began by distinguishing between strategic and other decisions made in organisations. Although strategic decisions are made with respect to the various different organisational functions (marketing, finance, production, human resources, etc.), we saw how each of these needed to be consistent with strategy at the corporate level.

- Recognition was made of the paramount importance of understanding the environmental context of strategic decision making. The environment was considered at three levels: an external environment, over which an organisation has virtually no control; an operating environment, over which an organisation has some influence; and the internal environment, for which an organisation has complete responsibility and a good deal of control.

- A framework of four generic questions was used as a means of matching the organisational context to the strategic options available. This framework required a detailed analysis of the organisation's current and historical position, the aspirations of its key stakeholders, and how the organisational environment might change in the future. This led to a choice of strategic direction.

- Having established strategic direction, we considered methods by which an organisation's goals might be achieved. The main emphasis was on growth strategies, with consideration given to key questions of when internal development or acquisition might be more appropriate, and the merits of strategic alliances.

- Finally, the chapter concluded with a brief discussion of a few alternatives to the analytical approach we have adopted for making strategic decisions.

Case Study 16: The Wooden Toy Company

The Wooden Toy Company is located in the West Midlands of the UK and employs just over 60 people. Its products are of a high quality, and sell through specialist retailers exclusively within the UK. The company was formed in 1983 by Sally and James Davies, and grew steadily in the boom years up to 1989. After 18 months of successful trading, Imran Malik, a MBA graduate and former school friend of James, was brought in as Director of Finance and Administration. Sally assumed responsibility for Marketing and was the Managing Director, while James dealt with Production. In practice, however, the management structure was quite informal, and there was a good deal of cross-fertilisation of ideas in all of the functional areas.

From 1990 onwards, during the years of UK recession, trading became progressively more difficult for the Wooden Toy Company. However, they remained profitable until 1993/4, when they recorded a small loss, which was repeated in the following two years. Since 1996, they have been back in profit, although the company has never returned figures to rival those of the halcyon days of the middle and late eighties. Indeed, several aspects of the business have been giving cause for concern, and there are clearly some big decisions ahead for the organisation.

The location. The company is located on two sites. It has a factory and offices (leased) on an industrial park, and a storage warehouse (owned by the company) about a mile away, but with inconvenient access because it involves negotiating a busy one-way system nearby.

Capacity usage. Until 1990, about 80 per cent of the factory capacity was used, but this fell over the next five years to between 50 per cent and 60 per cent. At the end of 1997 factory capacity usage was back up to almost 70 per cent, but has subsequently fallen back again a little. The warehouse has had to be large enough to cope with storing toys in anticipation of a rush of demand before Christmas. Approximately 60 per cent of sales occur between the beginning of September and mid-November as retailers stock up for Christmas. In 1989 the warehouse was 75 per cent full at the end of August.

At a recent meeting Imran suggested that the company should reduce its capacity in response to the decline in demand. He based his argument on the likelihood that, if they were to reduce capacity, profitability would be more secure since some of their fixed costs would be eliminated. James, however, has been particularly reluctant to reduce productive capacity, especially as the trend over the last three years has generally been for demand to rise. He has asked the other two to consider whether it might be possible to cut costs without reducing productive capacity. For example, could the pattern of demand be altered to reduce storage costs?

Staffing. Imran has told Sally and James that, with 58 full-time and 6 part-time employees, the company is overstaffed for the present level of operations. Indeed, all three are agreed that they could probably manage throughout most of the year with 30 per cent fewer people. Nevertheless, the seasonal nature of their sales leads them to believe they should retain at least 85 per cent of current staffing levels in order to cope with peak demand. So far, however, they have avoided shedding any of the workforce, first because they are hopeful that sales will soon be restored to something approaching 1989 levels, and secondly because of the potential damage to the morale of their employees.

The market. Meanwhile, Sally has become increasingly concerned that the Wooden Toy Company might be losing its differential advantage, based so far on a fairly unique product range. She has been told of at least two French companies that are considering manufacturing similar products in the UK. The three directors have also realised that some of the wooden toys imported from the Far East and sold in major retail chains are cheaper than their own products, and yet are of a similar quality. Sally has begun to wonder whether they can fend off these competitive threats, or whether it is perhaps time to rethink their whole competitive strategy. One option Sally would like the three directors to consider is whether the company should itself expand into European markets, especially since there are no longer any barriers to trading within the EU. However, this particular option has not so far seemed particularly attractive to James or Imran. They feel that they have little knowledge of European markets, none of them speaks a foreign language, and the company has insufficient resources to expand without increasing borrowings.

Undeterred, however, Sally has been determined to explore the possibility of market development in Europe and has sought the advice of a friend who works in the International Marketing Division of a multinational company. The friend has advised that direct investment in Europe might be a better option than exporting.

A week ago, a social meeting between the three directors of the Wooden Toy Company led to a forthright discussion of the organisation's future. The central issue of debate was whether the company should 'draw in its horns' and cut down its costs so as to consolidate its position in its current market, or whether it should 'go for broke' and expand into Europe. Imran, the principal advocate of the more cautious strategy, found himself defeated by Sally's enthusiasm for expansion. James seemed to have abandoned his erstwhile prudence, and was lending support to Sally's arguments. Imran had serious reservations about Sally's formative plan, and privately he felt that James' support for Sally's position had as much to do with loyalty as logic. Imran regretted that this was the first time since he had joined the company that he, Sally and James had not been in full agreement over an issue of such importance. Nevertheless, he agreed to give further thought to the proposal, and as he left for home that evening, he felt determined that he would hold out for two conditions if they were to expand abroad:

- that the company should try exporting its products before taking on anything more ambitious;
- that they should not turn their backs on the their home market in pursuit of new customers abroad.

Questions for discussion

1 *What environmental factors might have contributed to the decline in The Wooden Toy Company's sales and profitability since 1989?*

2 *What strategic options do you think were open to The Wooden Toy Company at the end of 1998? Do you think there might have been a better option than expanding into European markets?*

3 *What potential difficulties might The Wooden Toy Company encounter in implementing a decision to expand into European markets?*

Case Study 17: J. Savage & Company

J. Savage & Company has been manufacturing children's clothing for almost 50 years. The company's heyday was probably during the 1960s when, under the guidance of its founder, Joseph Savage, the company grew considerably as the austerity of the postwar years gave way to a period of growth in consumer spending. Savage had served his apprenticeship under a master tailor, and was uncompromising in demanding the highest standards of workmanship from his employees. In return, however, Savage paid above-average wages and was always fair, even-handed and generous in his dealings with all who worked for him. Nor did he stint on the quality of materials used. Small though the business was, its reputation as a manufacturer of high-quality, durable products was considerable.

By the mid-1960s, Savage had recognised that the business had grown to such an extent that he was unable to maintain his former control over production as well as looking after customers and managing the firm's financial affairs. In 1965, after much deliberation, he decided to invite his son-in-law, Mervyn Hallam, to join the business as its production director. Hallam had obvious limitations, and was not a particularly effective communicator, but Savage felt he was fundamentally reliable. At the time, Hallam had recently left the Army, and was glad of the opportunity to join a thriving company with good prospects.

Hallam worked closely with Savage throughout the late sixties and early seventies, learning a great deal from his father-in-law. In many ways, Hallam proved to be a more authoritative figure than Savage in his dealings with the production staff. He was pleased to have made his mark on the company by significantly reducing the wage bill, as well as raising productivity – an achievement for which he felt Savage might have afforded him a little more credit. Nevertheless, Hallam recognised his debt to Savage, and was very fond of his father-in-law, even though he secretly felt Savage had grown a little soft in his dealings with the employees.

In October 1974, J. Savage & Company was deeply saddened to learn of the sudden death of its eponymous founder. The family was touched by the many tributes that had come from employees, former staff, customers and even from local people who had had little to do with the company but who had known Savage by reputation as an excellent employer. Hallam recognised that Savage's death represented a major loss to the company, but decided that the best course of action would be to make some radical alterations to the business. This, he felt, would establish him as the new man in charge, and would signal his intentions for the company.

Over the next 12 months Hallam installed a considerable amount of new production machinery, which effectively increased the factory's capacity by around 60 per cent. This was costly, though he had had little difficulty in raising loans from the banks, and in the long term he felt productivity savings would be made. He had already hatched a plan to steadily increase the proportion of part-time workers and to recruit more school leavers who would generally work for less money. He introduced a new tier to the management structure to ensure that the production staff were properly supervised, and appointed Terry Birkenshaw and Jack Spencer, two no-nonsense disciplinarians, to fill the posts created.

Financial management was an area of the business that had always been Savage's domain, so Hallam felt it would be prudent to appoint a specialist for this function. He interviewed a couple of accountants, but eventually decided to appoint his cousin, Bob Booth, who was a former Mathematics teacher, and excellent with figures. A reunion one weekend with some of his old Army colleagues led him to appoint Phil Marner as the new Director of Sales. Marner had left the Army a few years after Hallam, and had apparently done quite well in sales. Hallam was delighted that he had such a solid, reliable team in place, and looked forward to a period of further sales growth once the new production system really got going.

For one reason and another, the late seventies and early eighties was not a prosperous period for J. Savage & Company. Hallam had really done all that he could in reducing labour costs, but the mood of the times seemed to work against him. Most of the employees who had been with the company since Joseph Savage's day had now moved on. Some of the new people seemed downright lazy, and were stirring up trouble via the trade union. Absenteeism had increased markedly, and there was little evidence of the old loyalties shown in former times. Moreover, sales had not risen as Hallam had anticipated when he installed the new production facility. This brought about another problem. The new equipment should have enabled more garments to be produced at lower cost, allowing the bank loans to be paid off rapidly. But the factory was operating at not much more than half capacity, and prices actually had to be raised in order to cover the interest on the loans and other fixed costs. Marner had worked tirelessly to try to find new customers for their products, but somehow new business did not seem to come their way. Some of the retailers pointed out that foreign suppliers were now able to provide products at lower cost, but Hallam tended to dismiss this, arguing that the imports were clearly of inferior quality, and were not at all the sort of smart clothing Savage's customers wanted for their children.

The period from 1984 to 1989 brought considerable relief to J. Savage and Company. Interest rates fell steadily, and sales picked up quite well, though it was noticeable that Savage's share of a booming market was diminishing. Some of the company's products, particularly the summer wear, were not selling well, and stocks began to build up, with the result that the directors decided it would be a good move to concentrate production on winter garments.

The recession of the early nineties dealt a devastating blow to the company. Booth had always argued that loan capital was not necessarily bad for the business, and had allowed borrowings to increase during the boom years. The directors agreed that no one could have foreseen that interest rates would remain so high for so long; and Marner said it would be a long time before customers showed enough confidence in the economy for demand to rise by very much.

Things began to get a little better after 1994 as the trauma of the recession receded into the past, but the tensions of fighting for business survival had begun to take their toll on the relationships between Hallam, Booth and Marner. Each had his private doubts about the capabilities of the others, and one Monday afternoon in January 1999, the frankest of discussions took place about the current position and the future direction of the business. Booth had apparently spent much of the weekend discussing the state of the company with his daughter, Emily, an undergraduate at a top Business School. Emily had left him in no doubt that, despite his honest endeavours to increase sales, Marner had not the slightest clue about marketing. Moreover, she had called into question Hallam's competence as a strategist and manager of people, and in particular his ability to manage production efficiently and effectively.

Spurred by the weekend's discussions, Booth demanded a radical shake-up of both the production and marketing functions. In the circumstances, the response of Hallam and Marner was relatively controlled, though they were clearly put out by the tone and force of Booth's remarks. It became evident that they had been equally unhappy with Booth's management of the company's finances, and it was agreed that a major review of the company's strategic and operational performance was long overdue.

Questions for discussion

1 *Examine the changing environment (at all three levels) faced by J. Savage and Company, and consider what the main reasons were for the decline of the company's sales and profits after the death of its founder.*

2 *What were the principal flaws behind Hallam's decision to expand the productive capacity of the business?*

3 *Describe the process by which strategic decisions appear to have been made at J. Savage & Company, and make recommendations as to how it could be improved.*

References

Argenti, J. (1989) *Practical Corporate Planning*, Allen & Unwin, London.

Ansoff, H. I. (1968) *Corporate Strategy*, Penguin, Harmondsworth.

Greiner, L. E. (1972) 'A model of evolutionary and revolutionary growth', *Harvard Business Review*, July–August.

Lee, D. G., Newman, P. and Price, R. H. (1998) *How Useful Is Strategic Planning to Small and Medium-sized Enterprises?*, Working paper.

Johnson, G. and Scholes, K. (1997) *Exploring Corporate Strategy*, Prentice-Hall, Hemel Hempstead.

Mintzberg, H. (1987) 'Crafting strategy', *Harvard Business Review*, July–August.

Mintzberg, H. and Waters, J. A., 'Of strategies, deliberate and emergent' in De Wit, B. and Meyer, R., 1994, *Strategy: Context and Content*, West Publishing, Minneapolis.

Ohmae, K. (1983) *The Mind of the Strategist*, Penguin, Harmondsworth.

Pascall, R. T. and Athos A. K. (1982) *The Art of Japanese Management*, Allen Lane, London.

Porter, M. E. (1980) *Competitive Strategy*, The Free Press, New York.

Porter, M. E. (1985) *Competitive Advantage*, The Free Press, New York.

Whittington, R. (1993) *What Is Strategy and Does It Matter*, Routledge, London.

Part III

IMPLEMENTING DECISIONS

The final part of this book is primarily concerned with implementing decisions which will be acceptable to a broad range of stakeholders, as well as meeting organisational objectives.

Chapter 9 explores some of the ethical issues involved in making and implementing decisions, and asks the reader to recognise the impact an organisational decision can have on other parties, both inside and outside the organisation.

Chapters 10 and 11 consider the effectiveness of decision implementation, addressing some of the factors which can result in resistance within the organisation, and some of the means by which managers can assist the passage of change. Central to the effective implementation of decisions is the process of monitoring and control. To this end, Chapter 10 introduces a feedback model designed to encourage a comprehensive evaluation of managerial decision making.

CHAPTER 9

Ethical and socially responsible decision making

At the end of this chapter you should:

- understand the nature and purpose of business organisations;

- be able to identify stakeholders both internal and external to organisations;

- be able to understand the nature and historical development of ethical and socially responsible decision making;

- have an understanding of the fragmented nature of society and its consequent expectations regarding ethical and socially responsible decision making;

- be able to define ethical decision making;

- understand the need for ethical and socially responsible decision making.

- be able critically to evaluate the nature and role of business decision making within society; and

- appreciate the crucial importance of waste management as a contemporary management function.

Introduction

The previous chapters have concentrated on the decision-making process. This chapter takes the decision-making process further by discussing a conceptual framework against which the decision outcome may be evaluated.

The purpose of this chapter is to consider the potential impact of social and ethical issues upon the way in which individuals make decisions. As a means of providing a contemporary focus to the chapter, the final section deals with waste management. It is included because waste and the way in which it is managed is an area of topical concern for stakeholders both internal and external to organisations.

There is a clear need to consider the role of ethical and socially responsible decision making because of the pervasive role of business within today's global markets. Organisations are constantly involved in, and influence, almost everything that we do. It is proper, therefore, that organisations and individuals should consider their responsibilities, not only to themselves but also to those whom their decisions will affect either directly or indirectly.

The central contention of this chapter is that ethically and socially responsible decisions – those that are good in a value-based sense – are generally likely to be good in terms of outcomes not only for organisations but also for society as a whole.

A philosophical consideration of ethical and socially responsible decision making

There have been numerous assertions (of which Friedman (1971) is probably the most well known example) that discussion of ethics and social responsibility is inappropriate within business organisations. Friedman put forward that if managers pursue purely ethical objectives then that in itself may actually be unethical because to do so may require them to spend money that belongs to others. He wrote that a corporate executive has

> … direct responsibility to his employers … That responsibility is to conduct the business in accordance with their desires, which generally will be to make as much money as possible while conforming to the basic rules of society, both those embodied in law and those embodied in ethical custom.

Friedman is saying that managers should operate within the confines of the rules set by society, and that there is no need to go beyond those rules to be ethical for altruistic reasons unless it also makes sound business sense to do so. To make decisions purely on ethical grounds may actually act against the best interests of the organisation and its owners, namely the shareholders, to which the organisation is primarily responsible.

From an operational perspective, this viewpoint is rejected here because it is seen as an oversimplification of the issues relating to proper conduct of business and the way in which decisions are made. People today take more of an active interest in corporate activity and are willing to voice criticisms of organisations that are deemed to fall short of standards set by society. For example, aggrieved parties more readily resort to litigation in order to ensure that organisations take responsibility for their actions. Ethical and responsible decision making has assumed great importance not only for society but also for organisations as a means to avoid potential trouble in the form of adverse publicity and litigation. Organisations are also attempting to be more proactive in emphasising their ethical stance.

The philosophical point underpinning this chapter is that ethical and responsible decision making is consistent with the kind of bounded freedom that we all need in order to function and live our daily lives. Man, uniquely, has the ability to do this, to be bounded by a moral sense and to recognise when others are not conforming to the norms set by society. It appears that although other creature may share some of our basic skills and abilities, our nurture and education develops us to an unrivalled extent. Human beings are the only creatures who choose to live according to such a complex set of self-imposed rules and standards.

However, we are culturally inhibited from adopting an ethical stance. Buchholz (1993) outlines five basic attitudes that are at the heart of our culture, and our consequent thinking and practice, that limit the degree to which individuals are able to actually think and act ethically. These five are:

1 *A fixation on money.* We think of costs, benefits and value in monetary terms alone. Consequently, we justify policy changes in terms of efficiency rather than, say, quality of life. Perhaps the former sounds objective, forceful and strategic, while the latter sounds vague, nebulous, and soft.

2 *Technology has infinite capacity to solve problems.* Whatever we do now matters little because the future will take care of itself by more technological developments, as has happened in the past.

3 *Fragmentation is a valid approach to problem solving.* 'One step at a time' is a popular saying, which illustrates the belief that a complex whole can be regarded as the sum of its parts; that synergy does not exist. (Chapter 7 provides a critique of this view.)

4 *Force, rather than harmony, is the answer.* To get what we want from a situation, we must try harder. We tend to seek mastery of a situation instead of working in harmony with it.

5 *Economic growth is the bottom line for us.* While socially desirable consequences – for example improved health care and life expectancy – have followed growth in the past, it must be remembered that economic growth and social progress are not one and the same thing.

Evidence of contemporary managerial attitudes towards ethical and responsible decision making seems to support the idea of cautious acceptance. Ulrich and Thielemann (1993) found that although managers generally supported the idea that adhering to ethical standards is good business practice in the long run, they saw responsible thinking and market orientation as parallel philosophies rather than as being synonymous.

The conclusion is that although ethical and responsible decision making may be – and often is – regarded as an appropriate element within the decision-making process, it can be very problematic for individuals who wish not only to satisfy the needs of the organisation but also the ethical demands of society. This topic was mentioned in Chapter 3, and the next section will discuss it further.

Moral behaviour and freedom of choice

The implicit prerequisite for moral behaviour is freedom of choice. Freedom of choice, or rather the lack of it, has sometimes been put forward as a defence of immoral behaviour. For example, an employee might say that she had to do something or else lose her job. The validity of this type of argument, and consequences of actions based on it, is rather uncertain. On the one hand, the defence may be accepted and the immoral actions forgiven, and on the other it may be said that individuals always have a choice. It is sometimes a question of choosing between unpalatable alternatives.

If the actions under review are very serious, then exponents of the latter view are likely to take a rather intolerant line towards those who break society's ethical norms. Therefore is it appropriate to talk about pure, in the sense of being unbounded, freedom or some sort of constrained freedom? To be able to deal with ethical issues individuals need three things:

- *mental health* – to know who and what you are, to understand your priorities, to be responsible and have self-possession, to be 'happy within yourself';

- *information* – about the situation and its potential effect on the decision maker and other stakeholders; and

- *exterior limitations* – norms or constraints placed on the individual by society.

The scope for ethical and socially responsible decision making today

Ethical and responsible decision making is about much more than issues such as global warming, defining employee rights in the workplace or health and safety, important though these issues are. The intention of this section is to emphasise the broad potential for responsible thinking in today's market-based economies and to identify some aspects that are of particular interest and relevance. Ethical issues will be raised that relate to key concepts within the market-based economic systems that dominate today's global market economy.

Capitalism

Capitalism is an economic system based upon private property and free-market competition. Central planning is rejected, pursuit of self-interest and the uneven distribution of wealth tend to be the norms. Therefore a range of ethical questions need to be raised.

- Is the right to private property morally defensible and should there be restrictions on this right?

- Should all goods and services for which there is demand be produced?

- If capitalism works on the basis of competition, does this not imply hostile anti-social attitudes – for example, the marketing analogy to warfare?

- If buying and selling involves negotiation, should this include tactics such as bluff or misrepresentation?

- Does capitalism actually deliver as much freedom as it seems to promise?

- Can wealth justifiably coexist with poverty in the same country?

- Does capitalism encourage mass marketing and therefore focus on the common denominator within society. Does this mean proliferation of 'lower quality' pleasures?

As well as these general philosophical points relating to capitalism, other questions need to be raised in connection with corporations:

- What rights does calling a corporation a legal person imply?
- What are the responsibilities of corporations, and of their agents? What are the ethical implications of limited liability?
- Is insider knowledge defensible?
- What are the ethical issues of mergers, acquisitions and dealing with Third-World countries?
- Are the vast salary differences within companies defensible?
- Many executives are appointed partly because they are similar to existing executive members. Is this morally defensible?
- What are the rights of employees? Should work be efficient but boring?
- What are unethical sales practices?
- Should marketing communications take account of the audience's likely age or limited education?
- What is the difference between research and industrial espionage?

And again, yet more questions have to be asked in relation to society as a whole (see also the next section). They include:

- What should happen when a corporation breaks the law or contravenes ethical standards?
- Is it appropriate to allow fines to be passed on to consumers?
- Do future generations have rights now?
- Do developed countries have greater responsibility than less developed countries?
- Can a consumer-based materialistic society be justified?
- Do animals have rights?
- What exactly does it mean when a product is described as 'green' or 'environmentally friendly'?

The nature of society

It is only possible to develop a view of appropriate standards of ethical behaviour if one has some understanding of how contemporary society has evolved.

Only some 200 years ago most of mankind lived a very hand-to-mouth existence, as their ancestors had done before them. Travel was unusual. Families caught or grew most of their own food and made most of the things that they needed. Trade based on division and specialisation of labour was, for example, limited to employing the village blacksmith, or buying from the local baker or brewer. There was no need to consider concepts such as culture and ethics because they were taken for granted as part of everyday life.

With industrialisation came demographic movement off the land and into the cities. Production began to be organised on a large scale basis with the goods and services being traded for other products. Gradually economic activity has moved from being organised first on a local basis, then a regional one, then national, and now, finally, on a global scale.

It is not intended to suggest that conscious study of ethical behaviour is exclusively commerce based, but that ethical issues become relevant when people of different societies, or cultural background, seek to interact, in whatever context, religious, political, social or whatever.

Turning now to the nature of people's expectations. Should particular nations, regions, or races be regarded as ethically substantially unique; that there is little or no commonality between the ethical stances held by groups of people who are geographically and culturally different. If so, where are the boundaries of these differences? Alternatively, is it considered that people across the globe share sufficient socio-economic characteristics and thus have some ethical beliefs in common? Some differences are obvious and may be identified by simple travel abroad. Other differences are less obvious and may take time and effort to detect. Consider the nature of society in more detail.

Society can be viewed from a number of perspectives, for instance:

- unitarianism;
- separatism;
- modernism.

Unitarianism

The unitarian view sees society as a socio-cultural whole. Good examples of this approach are Marxism, which advocates communism and a classless society, and Catholicism, which teaches that we are all children within the family of God. Business organisations, like humans, are members of the same moral community.

Exponents of this unitarian view would argue that the rules of society do indeed apply to all. However, as Pratley (1995) points out, modern society is fragmented in the sense that it tends to be regarded as divided into different functional areas or social spheres. The process of earning one's living is one such example, and family life another. These comments are unlikely to apply equally to different societies around the world. Cultural differences will be reflected in the different weighting or importance attributed to each functional area by particular societies. Furthermore, there are some in which particular functional areas appear to be dominant, for example religion in some societies plays a remarkably central role in people's lives, guiding their actions both individually and collectively.

Any business manager should note and respond to such differences. Society may be regarded as unified only to the extent that some ethical standards should apply to us all, but the precise nature of those applicable to different groups will vary according to the rules of the group.

Separatism

This sees society as made up of independent and autonomous parts according to functional area. Extreme exponents of this view would argue that the only ethical standards that directly apply to business are those of the marketplace. In turn, society may use market forces to control business activity or may seek recourse to the law. Food production and distribution provides a good example of both controls, where many consumers will prefer free-range produce rather than battery or intensive production methods. While there may be other issues involved, this preference may be partly explained by customers translating their moral stance into buying behaviour. Similarly, the labelling of food has become more detailed and informative as a result of both customers' perceived preferences and legal requirements.

Although such examples show that societal ethics may indirectly have an effect, via market and legal controls, the separatist view of society is unsatisfactory because our individual needs – whether personal, social, or physiological – make us often dependent on each other. Such interaction involves numerous and diverse ethically based expectations on the part of individuals. As Jeurissen (1995) points out, it is unrealistic to expect all moral concerns to be covered by either customer behaviour or the legal process. A business, for example, may be unaware of some unethical activity being carried out in its name. Also, the desire to protect intellectual assets tends to push organisations away from transparency and public scrutiny, leaving the public unaware of the detail of what they are doing.

Modernism

Modernism recognises that contemporary society is fragmented by functional area and sphere (Pratley, 1995). The essential point here is that each area is relatively autonomous and has its own norms, procedures and rules. Modern man does behave differently depending on whether he is with his family, at work, or doing some recreational activity.

Contemporary hooliganism provides a vivid example of this. It emerges that some of the people arrested for this violent and anti-social behaviour hold responsible and well paid jobs. They may also have apparently stable family backgrounds. They are adept at compartmentalising their lives to an advanced degree.

The other fundamental attribute of the modernist view is the distinction between task and person orientations, which influence how we go about the different functional areas. These orientations may be described as overarching our conduct, and the two extremes are thus:

- *Task-oriented individuals* are concerned with behaving rationally, following procedures, achieving efficiency and meeting targets. They encompass functions

199

where objectivity is paramount, such as medical and technological research, business and bureaucratic administration. Those involved might be assembled into formal groups.

- *Person-oriented individuals* are concerned with the social and cultural sphere. They are concerned with informal groups and people bonding together on the basis of a common identification with ideas.

While our functional areas may overlap as illustrated in Fig. 9.1 (for example, we may go out for dinner with friends from work), it is not usual for our orientations to overlap in the same manner. Indeed, such overlap may be confusing for staff; for example, although an individual's boss is expected to behave courteously, this does not mean being over-friendly because such behaviour may be viewed with suspicion.

Part of ourselves, the person side, is much concerned with ethics but the other part, the task side is less so and these dichotomies span all the functional areas of our lives. Within each functional area the ethical stance is probably clear. The ethical debate centres upon the areas of overlap in that the expectations, between one area and another, of appropriate ethical behaviour are ill-defined. Clearly it is part of a manager's job to carefully investigate the nature of such expectations when the activities of their organisation affect either the private or political lives of stakeholders. International and even regional trade brings together people who may be expected to have quite different behavioural norms and expectations. Managers, if they are to conduct such trade successfully, need to consciously be aware of, and respond to, such differences. The example of Lonrho, under the leadership of the late Tiny Rowland, provides a good illustration of the importance of this. Mr Rowland is credited with transforming Lonrho from an African mining company into a multi-national conglomerate at least in part as a result of his good relations with the leaders of the different African states.

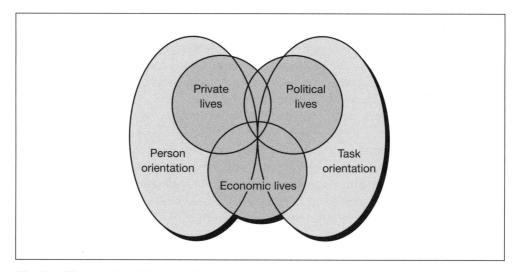

Fig. 9.1 The modernist view of society

The nature of ethics and social responsibility

Ethics is the philosophical exploration of moral questions to do with human actions (White, 1993). Ethical decision making, then, is about making decisions in a morally sensitive or defensible manner. Acting in a socially responsible manner may be defined, in general terms, as doing things that at least safeguard the interests of society and that, if possible, improve them.

Two points may immediately be made:

1 The two basic concepts are not synonymous. Individuals or subgroups may choose to act ethically, as they see it, despite the apparent wishes of society and, indeed, may suffer persecution for doing so because they are seen to be acting in a socially *irresponsible* manner.

2 The two concepts may have differing scope of meaning. Ethical behaviour clearly encompasses both action and motive, which is the moral welfare of the individual. Ethical evaluation of an action is essentially an internal process, involving doing what you think is right.

By definition, it is not possible to regard oneself as ethical if one is merely responding to the ethical expectations of others since this would be a social response. Social responsibility is, in itself, ambiguous regarding means and ends. On the one hand, some organisations, for example the UK Cooperative Movement, may have social well-being as part of their core purpose. Clearly for such organisations social responsibility constitutes a prime goal. On the other hand, a different interpretation might be that social responsibility is closely related to marketing because it is about giving the customers what they want regardless of personal belief. If the customer is currently demanding environmentally friendly products, then it is good business to supply them.

With the contemporary media coverage of ecological issues such as global warming and acceptable methods of food production, it is easy to make the assumption that ethical and responsible decision making is a modern concept, when in fact it is not. The concept of ethics is ancient. It is generally accepted to originate with the ideas of Socrates (469–399 BC) who saw moral behaviour in terms of clarity of thinking. He argued that vice resulted from ignorance and therefore that moral behaviour could be enhanced by education. Plato (428–348 BC) extended the ethics concept towards individual ability. He saw the soul as including the three elements of reason, emotion and physical appetites. Genuine virtue is difficult to achieve because of the considerable intellect required to understand and organise these elements. Aristotle (384–322 BC) went further and saw virtue as more of a function of our personality and character, involving both our hearts and our heads.

Deontological and teleological ethics

Deontological ethics

Deontological ethics stems from the writings of John Locke (1632–1704), who discussed personal rights, such as freedom of speech and enjoyment of private property, and those of Immanual Kant (1724–1804), who focused on the rational aspect of conduct.

Deontology takes the view that actions have intrinsic moral value, in other words that they are either inherently good or bad. Kant saw ethics as logical and consistent, like mathematics, and universally valid. From this approach one may develop the idea of fundamentally inalienable rights that are not bestowed by any government but rooted in our very being. This approach rather precludes change.

There are a number of practical problems here, of which the rejection of cultural input, the preclusion of compromise, and the absence of obvious ethical hierarchy are probably the most serious. However, the approach is to be commended because it provides a reference point for appropriate behaviour in these times of rapid change. It may be right to argue that ethical standards need not move because, although the trappings of life, such as the means of transport or communication, change, the fundamental needs, such as to coexist with others and to perpetuate the species, remain constant.

Although the approach may have some conceptual validity, it is clear that the practical difficulties already outlined make it extremely difficult to identify any ethical stance that is accepted equally by all nations and cultures across the world. At a more micro level of application, however, the approach is clearly useful – for example, regarding behaviour of staff towards customers, both actual and potential. For an organisation may decide that staff, in order to present an appropriate image of their company when performing certain tasks (for example, serving a customer or answering the telephone) must behave according to certain standards (such as greeting the customer with a smile within a certain timescale and, perhaps, a spoken greeting). Measures such as these are designed to improve the extent to which the company meets its customers' expectations of issues like professionalism, helpfulness, fairness and other aspects of ethical behaviour.

Teleological ethics

Teleological ethics deals with the moral character of an action and whether it helps or hurts anyone. The approach is founded in the idea of utilitarianism, a school of thought stemming from the writings of Jeremy Bentham (1748–1832).

Utilitarianism contends that something is morally good if pleasure outweighs pain, if enough people are likely to derive use or enjoyment from it. Other writers, such as John Stuart Mill (1806–73), refined the approach by exploring the dimension of the quality of pain or pleasure. Quality is assessed according to the basis of the enjoyment, rather than the intensity of it. High-quality feelings are associated with education, intelligence, and sensitivity to others.

Again, there are practical problems. For example, how does one measure the usefulness or enjoyment of a particular action? Clearly such measurement is essential if a ranking assessment of teleological ethics is to be achieved. Furthermore, is it implied that giving pleasure makes all actions morally defensible? The answer to this last question has to be 'no', at least within any particular culture. Within the UK, for example, it is hoped that activities like theft and murder would never become regarded as ethically good even if a large proportion of the population seemed to want this.

The important advantage of this approach is that it recognises change. Although ethical standards may be regarded as reasonably permanent, they clearly are not fixed and utilitarianism permits appropriate development according to society's changing tastes and preferences.

Common ground

It must be emphasised that all of these ideas have practical relevance for decision makers. They are embodied in effective human resource management, as distinct from personnel management. Human resource management is a more diverse and comprehensive concept of staff management. It embraces more imaginative ideas, such as the importance of offering staff appropriate opportunity for personal development, as well as the more obvious pointers such as the need to select staff carefully. Also, good communications throughout the organisation will ensure that staff understand, and are committed to, what the organisation is trying to achieve.

The concept of socially responsible thinking by organisations is certainly not new either. Heald (1970) cites the example of a group of New England business people, known as the Boston Associates, involved in textile manufacture around 1812 and after. As well being pioneers in the application of the corporate structure to manufacturing organisations, the group displayed an active interest in the lives of their employees, by providing good living and working conditions as well as ensuring that they had religious, social and intellectual resources appropriate to their background and expectations. As Heald points out, these ideas were probably brought from Scotland by the then leader of the group, Francis Dowell, who had visited the works owned by Robert Owen at New Lanark in Scotland and observed Owen's demonstration of good wages and conditions benefiting both employer and employee. Many Victorian entrepreneurs were also Quakers who saw their social responsibilities inevitably following from their wealth and success.

Although it can be accepted that throughout the industrial age some industrialists made decisions in an ethical and responsible manner, it cannot be ignored that throughout the nineteenth century and prior to 1948 and the creation of the welfare state, the living and working conditions of the factory worker were often terrible. Taking the UK as an example, institutions such as workhouses, widespread malnutrition, disease, alcohol abuse and heavy industrial pollution all ensured a low life expectancy for the typical worker. So what can be concluded at this point? The obvious points are that either the ethical standards of the time were extremely low or there were few industrialists thinking responsibly. The discussion becomes more interesting if one goes on to explore these two points.

In essence it is suggested that the explanation lies in the class differences that existed within society, which engendered a feeling of arrogance amongst members of the upper stratum and obsequiousness among those in the lower. It was low expectations of the employees rather than low ethical standards of the employers that were substantially to blame for the prevailing conditions. Presumably those few factory and mill owners who did attempt to provide good conditions, as we would view them today, were then regarded at best as amusing eccentrics and at worst as dangerous subversives.

The early middle part of the nineteenth century saw the beginning of major social change within the UK. Servicemen returning from the wars wanted to feel that they had fought, amongst other things, for a better life, and women who had gone out to work as part of the war effort often did not want to go back to their old life that was based in the home. Developments such as these led to a more equitable distribution of goods and services across society and, combined with improved educational standards, significantly contributed to the trend towards increased social mobility and a challenging of the social status quo, which has continued to the present day.

Nowadays, probably more than ever before, people can be what they want to be. Predeterminators, such as social class and upbringing, have become less significant. Clearly other factors have also played a part in this change. Modern technological inventions such as television and computers have provided the information to make people aware of the world around them. These devices can be seen to have accelerated the mobility trend and expanded the scope of change. Customers have become more assertive and challenging.

This emergence of the assertive customer may be analysed in marketing terms. Industrial capacity, in the economically developed countries at least, has reached and passed the point of being able to satisfy the core needs of customers. For example, most people in the UK have a video cassette player, one or two cars, a regular holiday abroad, etc. (depending on their priorities). This means that, for the industrialist, mass production, possibly with low selling price, is no longer the answer to market success. Differentiation between one product and another is only possible on the basis of augmentation (Kotler *et al.*, 1996). Customers are now looking beyond the core benefit towards customisation and individualism; they want what they want, and this is beginning to include how a product is made and sold.

This discussion brings us up to date and explains why current events seem to indicate that social responsibility is a new requirement. It is new in terms of scope and influence. People generally are concerned more than ever about different aspects of their lives. Furthermore, they now have the determination and confidence to question what they don't like, take action, and to bring about change in order to get what they want. Pressure groups abound and are well organised and influential, particularly within the media, so they should be heeded by organisations when making decisions that may affect, for example, the environment.

Social responsibility should be comprehensively considered for all decisions because it is an issue that has become very important, if not critical, to the future prosperity of most business organisations.

The role of business in society

The fundamental strategic role of business may be defined as solving 'the economic problem', that is, the way in which to provide and distribute goods and services across society in the best possible way. As the point was summed up by Henry Ford: 'For a long time people believed that the only purpose of industry is to make a profit. They were wrong. Its purpose is to serve the general welfare.' (David Ewing, 1977).

The role of business – and hence of management, through the way in which decisions are made – is essentially about welfare and value provision. There can surely be little doubt that were business to ignore this basic mandate, the rights and privileges granted to it by society would be reduced or withdrawn. These rights may be implicit, such as a stable operating environment that is both ordered and defended, or explicit, such as immortality, limited liability and ownership of property.

Moving the discussion to a more detailed, tactical perspective, corporations both collectively and individually wield enormous power within society. Although they may be said to operate largely without democratic mandate, they are not, as discussed earlier in this chapter, free from public control, and they seek to minimise negative public attention and interference. Furthermore, as social entities themselves, corporations may find that such forces may come from within.

By fostering understanding and agreement concerning its role, any organisation may be expected to significantly ensure that conflict, both external and internal, is minimised. Such conflict is to be avoided because of three main outcomes. Conflict and tensions within an organisation are:

- undesirable because it is wasteful of resources;
- expensive in terms of opportunity cost; and
- personally harmful in that generally people like to 'feel good' about themselves and be proud of where they work.

The role of business centres on the economic requirement to produce goods and services that society wants, both now and in the foreseeable future. The economic purpose is the root of corporate being and the basis for their development of specific competencies. As well as this, there are activities that, although they may be described as peripheral because they extend outside the economic core, are nonetheless important, both for the individual company and for society at large. As Donaldson (1982) stated to the Harvard Business School:

> The terms of the contract between industry and society are changing ... Now we are being asked to serve a wider range of human values and to accept an obligation to members of the public with whom we have no commercial transactions.

Such activities may be both social and political. Political activity may include aspects as diverse as lobbying government ministers, waging wars, conquering foreign lands and perhaps, in the future, exploring space. Social activity may include sponsorship of sporting events and provision of infrastructure such as roads, hospitals and universities. The nature of these peripheral activities changes and develops over time. They may be viewed by a corporation as additional purposes and means towards the economic role. They are often selected according to the aims, interests and prejudices of the current corporate leaders. Business tends to be encouraged to participate in such peripheral activities, perhaps because it is seen as 'putting something back' into the society from which it has derived its prosperity.

However, this must be done with care if the corporation is to avoid criticism. For example, the provision of social-type services may be criticised for a number of reasons:

- Only the most safe, prestigious or popular may be provided.
- Only the most enhancing and profitable may be provided.
- Corporate leaders lack expertise in social issues and may be unwilling to support problem investigation which goes beyond or contrary to their beliefs.
- Social activity may permit organisations to impose their values on society.

A manager probably stands the best chance of avoiding these and other similar criticisms by thorough analysis of what may be termed the company's 'stakeholder environment'. Stakeholder environment analysis by a corporation through its representatives involves three factors:

1 identifying the stakeholders;

2 assessing the nature and extent of stakeholder expectations and how the stakeholders expect the corporation to behave in various situations; and

3 assessing the level and nature of stakeholder power over the organisation for expectations to be enforced.

Stakeholders themselves can be categorised, as 'internal' (such as staff, owners or customers), or 'external' (such as government agencies, pressure groups, the media, or even ordinary citizens who live and work close to the company location). And the results of the two assessments in the numbered list above can be plotted on a matrix, as illustrated in Fig. 9.2. The numbers beside the letter prefix indicate the ranking of the ethical issue described by that code – in the example given, E_1 is the most important, followed by E_2, E_3, etc. towards E_n which would be the least,

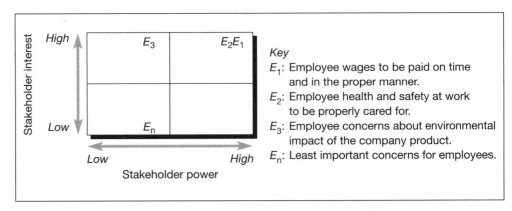

Fig. 9.2. Matrix showing an assessment of stakeholder power

important. The larger the subscript number, the lower the ranking of the ethical issue in the stakeholders' view.

A similar analysis should be followed for all the stakeholders of the corporation so that the organisation will have a meaningful representation of stakeholder concerns and be able to prioritise its actions and use of resources accordingly.

The nature of business organisations

The corporation as a moral person

Examination of the far-reaching extent of corporate power over our daily lives makes corporate morality a salient topic for discussion. Issues such as authority and obedience, liberty and human rights, allocation of benefits and burdens, the public interest and the common good, are all at stake. Separation of ownership and control, within most medium-sized or larger organisations, surely means that owners can no longer be regarded as having ultimate responsibility for what an organisation does. Is it reasonable to expect business organisations to conform to the same ethical standards as private individuals?

Although corporations may aspire to be seen as closed societies and immune from public scrutiny and accountability, such moral autonomy is of questionable acceptability and probably should not be taken as of right.

Organisations tend to be socially as well as economically useful, and that is the rationale for their very existence. As social institutions, organisations usually have some form of ideology as a basis for guidance and self-justification. This ideology may be combined with corporate language to make up the organisational culture and moral stance.

However, it should not be inferred that corporations are paradigms of moral rationality and that their culture will be a benevolent one. They often steam blindly ahead, with pre-established goals regardless of the effects of their actions, which may actually subvert the common good. The following is a discussion of a number of points, both for and against corporations taking moral responsibility for their actions.

The difficulty of allocating responsibility

The complexity of large organisations may render it impossible and/or irrelevant to allocate blame to a particular executive. Employees work interdependently, both as individuals and within teams. Their sense of personal identity and individualism is often either suppressed or lost. Furthermore, employees work in the name of their employer. All of this has the consequence that concepts of individual responsibility and accountability are irrelevant to such structures. Indeed, the organisation may seek to protect individual employees by eliminating individual accountability.

To approach the issue from the other direction, complainants – particularly those external to the company – are often not interested in allocating blame, seeking instead to have either damage made good or some form of compensation. The important thing is for the organisation to take responsibility for the actions that have been carried out in its name. Individual allocation of blame, so far as the complainant is concerned, is a secondary issue, perhaps in terms of seeing justice done.

The reciprocal-treatment argument

If we behave morally towards organisations, should they not do so towards us? The intuitively reasonable answer seems to be 'yes, they should'. However three issues arise here for consideration when one organisation appears to treat another unfairly:

- *Causality.* Is the organisation definitely and exclusively to blame for causing the unethical act? Were there no other (external) factors involved?
- *Second-order intentions of the organisation.* What were these? Was the disagreeable act merely the means to an end?
- *The business entity may have a moral relationship with others.* Are those relationships obstructing the relationship with the original organisation?

The irreducibility argument

A counter point to the above is to remember that, although corporations can act legally in their own name, in practical terms they can do little without their human agents. Thus, can there be a moral distinction between the corporation and its executives and the decisions that they make? The answer to this is somewhat complex and depends on factors such as the purpose of the business, its culture and its leaders.

The influence of organisational purpose can be discussed using a continuum of three categories:

- *An abstract organisation.* This would be one that is least reducible to its members, where it was created and defined with reference to some common objective or structure that the members may share to varying degrees.
- *Co-operative associations.* These are purpose-oriented organisations but members share the objectives of them.
- *Concrete organisations.* These are defined by membership and this carries obligations, rights and responsibilities. Goals and objectives are non-existent or loosely defined. Examples of these organisations are clubs, associations and communities.

Regarding culture, it is appropriate to consider how an organisation may develop its individual version of this. It may be something that perhaps an organisation simply has. Culture is a management tool, something to be manipulated as appropriate. It reflects the beliefs and wishes of those (probably senior) managers who have either imported the culture into the organisation from broader society or created it. This view of culture clearly supports the view that organisations are reducible to their members. The alternative is that culture is something that an organisation is, a product of the social interactions, negotiations and shared symbolism. This view sees culture as largely unaffected by changes of staff, with the consequence that organisations are moral entities in their own right.

Persons: legal, biological and moral

In Roman law two thousand years ago, the term *persona* referred to anything that could act on either side of a legal dispute. Persons are creations of the law, and existence outside the legal framework is incidental. This is fictional theory of the person (French, 1979). Alternatively, many modern thinkers and legal frameworks, for example the concept of limited liability, regard corporations as umbrellas that cover, and possibly shield, certain biological persons. This is aggregate theory.

Both of these conceptual approaches present the corporation as having rights, being the subject of rights as opposed to the administrator of rights. This is a key distinction as it is only accidentally true if the subject and administrator of rights is one and the same person. The law does not require this to be the case.

Being the subject of rights may be likened to scaffolding around a new building, it is necessary to erect the structure but it can be substantially discarded when the building is up and ongoing on a day-to-day basis. Similarly, the subject of rights is of little ongoing, and therefore, moral significance. It is in the administration of those rights that moral personhood is embedded, and clearly the corporation's executives perform this function when making decisions.

Although the debate may appear evenly balanced and it is obviously true that a corporation can only act through its staff, there are significant arguments for believing that certain organisations should be moral entities in their own right. The essential point here is that certain organisations, either by accident or design are simply not reducible to their members. Large and complex organisations tend to have their own behavioural culture which members are expected to follow. Individuals, unless they are top level managers, leaving or joining such organisations have little or no effect on such culture and, indeed, are expected to adapt their personal behavioural norms to those of the company. Most commercial organisations were formed with reference to some purpose rather than membership so their actions tend to be primarily task focused with stakeholder expectations second.

Environmentalism and waste management

It is generally accepted that mankind is now facing an ecological crisis. Perhaps the most important force that is driving this is population growth. The world's population is expected to increase from some 6bn in early 1999 (US Bureau of Census) to almost 10bn by 2025 (Cannon, 1994) with the developing world expanding from 74% to 86%.

The environmental ethic obliges us to face some economic truths.

- Growth must be managed so that it is compatible with sustainable resource consumption.

- Resources are limited and not all interests can be satisfied, so whose interests should be defended and what are we willing to sacrifice for them?

- To what extent are we prepared to adopt lifestyles within apparent limits of compatibility?

Although it is clear that ethical and responsible decision making is generally a matter of answering these and similar questions, it is less clear which sector within society should actually do this. Should it be government, business or some other group within society? The implied view of most governments is one of an autonomous representative body. Once appointed, it is not required constantly to refer to the electorate for confirmation of proposals. Thus, the government's role is to respond to public concern by developing a policy framework for environmental protection via both direct action, such as data collection and education regarding environmental issues, and indirectly by legislation, such as 'polluter pays' laws, cradle-to-grave responsibility, and market mechanisms such as taxes and licences.

Some writers, such as Bowie (1990), claim that business has no direct responsibility for two main reasons:

1 Business has no ethical obligation to protect the environment because this would make impossible and counter-profit demands on the organisation.

2 If consumers are unwilling to pay the cost of environmentally friendly products, it is not the responsibility of firms to correct this market failure.

Concerning the first point, this is essentially a restatement of Friedman's (1970) view. It may be true that people tend to see themselves differently either as consumers or citizens and behave accordingly; individuals employ a dual aspect to decision making. Consumers think of themselves and their own needs, while citizens take on a broader view of what is best for the community. While this may be an empirical truth, it may also be viewed as a regrettable expediency, a reluctance to accept responsibility.

While ethically based purchasing may not be appropriate as a dominant creed, individuals are the ultimate users and choose (rather than accept or tolerate) levels of pollution, so individuals should bear greater responsibility than as yet exercised. Hoffman (1990) provides further argument by calling for organisations to show co-operation and leadership, moral vision, commitment and courage over these issues. If they do not wish to be seen as shallow or deceptive, corporations must be prepared to pay a price in order to achieve a long-term gain.

If it is insisted that environmental welfare is the province of government, then there is surely an implied obligation not to intervene in the political arena in order to defeat or weaken legislation. Firms cannot 'have their cake and eat it', that is, they cannot claim that correction of market failure is the responsibility of government and then interfere in that process to weaken it or water it down. So, co-operation is the key and the way forward with regard to ethical and responsible decision making in relation to environmental matters.

Waste management

Turning now to the specific concept of waste management, it should be stated that the benefits of a waste-management strategy within a corporate environmental policy are numerous. They include:

- Clean technologies;
- Health and safety benefits;
- Reduced risks and liabilities;
- Savings in inputs, management and disposal;
- Marketing and stakeholder benefits;
- Identification of reuse in present form, recycling in alternative form and opportunities – these ideas are possible products in themselves.

However, it is hoped that organisations will adopt a broader approach to waste management by considering a range of issues relating to

1 *Inputs.* Are materials used efficiently, are natural resources being depleted and are toxins being left 'around' for innocent victims to encounter?

2 *Processes.* Is energy consumption efficient and sustainable, are the health and safety of both employees and nearby residents being properly protected, and are waste products being managed efficiently and effectively?

3 *Outputs.* Can any outputs harm users now or in the future, is the packaging and distribution safe and efficient, and how will the waste products be disposed of when they have been used up?

Ethical and responsible decision making is concerned with the use of an appropriate and proactive philosophy. It is about being input-oriented rather than output- and purely profit-focused. An input-oriented organisation takes a more holistic view of its activities by looking at potential costs and benefits of waste materials, resources and by-products, as well as those of its core outputs. Figure 9.3 shows the essential differences.

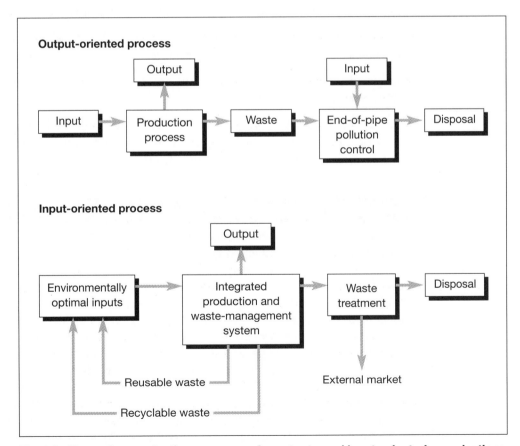

Fig. 9.3 Alternative production processes for output- and input-oriented organisations

211

Summary of the chapter

- Economic and societal developments make ethical and responsible decision making a relevant and important aspect of the management function because of the changes that have taken place within society over the last half-century.

- The precise nature and extent of appropriate ethical and responsible decision making is subject to ongoing debate.

- The dominance of economics based on the free market at national and international level, and in some cases affecting national culture, have had an impact on the extent to which organisations and individuals are prepared to act ethically when making decisions.

- A society's ethical orientation can either be based on unitarianism, separatism or modernism.

- An individual's ethical decision-making stance can be either task-oriented or person-oriented.

- Ethical decisions made by organisations can be political or social in nature, depending on the internal and external stakeholder pressures.

- In order for individuals to make ethical and responsible decisions, they need to have mental health as well as relevant information and be aware of externally set limits.

- Large and complex organisations can probably be regarded as moral entities in their own right.

- Environmental protection must be regarded as the responsibility of all sectors of society. A policy of waste management, in whatever context, can be of great benefit to organisations, individuals and society.

Case Study 18: Banford University

In late May 1997 the authorities at Banford University received a number of complaints from undergraduates. It appeared that a number of the students had suffered the theft of some of their belongings from their study-bedrooms. The subsequent investigation showed that all the incidents appeared to be the result of ground-floor windows being left open (Banford had been experiencing some exceptionally hot and humid weather), with items being removed from window sills. Although the thefts had so far been minor and included only small sums of money or other valuables, the university's authorities were concerned about the general security and safety implications for their students.

The Vice Chancellor and her senior porter decided to set a trap for the culprit(s). The senior porter, together with two of his staff, would turn on the light and open the window of a study bedroom belonging to a student who had gone home for the weekend. The three of them would then hide outside in nearby bushes and hopefully catch the thief red-handed. There were very few other windows open that evening because nearly all the students had either gone home or were out for the evening.

At about 10.30 p.m. a masked figure crept towards the open window, reached inside, and removed a rubber model of Wallace and Grommit. Seeing this, the three porters leapt forward and took hold of the arms of the thief. The thief's mask was removed, to reveal the face of Professor Richard Jessop, the university's youngest and most outstanding scientist.

Professor Jessop was 35 years old and was not married. He had been at Banford for only two years, having previously worked with the US space agency NASA at Cape Kennedy. He also currently had a key role in the liaison between NASA and scientists in the Russian Federation.

At a meeting between the Vice Chancellor, the senior porter and Professor Jessop, it was decided that if Jessop gave an undertaking never do anything of this kind again, then no further action of any kind would be taken. He readily agreed to accept such an undertaking.

The following week the Students Union issued a press release, which called for a meeting to discuss the conduct of Professor Jessop. It transpired that a student, living two rooms down from the open window that was used to trap Jessop, had seen the whole thing. The student had recognised Jessop and reported the incident to a Student Union representative. The Union had contacted the office of the Vice Chancellor to be told of the 'No further action' decision.

Questions for discussion

1 *Identify and discuss the ethical issues raised in the case.*

2 *Critically evaluate the actions of all the parties involved. Should they have acted differently and why?*

Case Study 19: Fruits of the Orchard Ltd

In 1996 Fruits of the Orchard Ltd (FO Ltd) and three of its senior executives were convicted of serious fraud. They admitted that they had knowingly sold adulterated grape juice. This was in a bottle labelled '100% pure juice of the fruit' and intended for the health-conscious consumer.

The company was fined £500 000 but estimated the total cost to be in the order of £5m when all the consequent civil actions and loss of business had been taken into account. Furthermore, the managing director William Jones, the production director John Neil and the marketing director Susan Millar were each given a six-month suspended jail sentence. The trial had revealed that the three directors had committed fraud and had tried to conceal their activities driven, apparently, by the severe financial pressures facing the company.

In 1990 FO Ltd was approached by Global Juices Corporation and offered grape-juice concentrate at a price 20 per cent lower than the cost of producing comparable juice in its own vineyards. This price translated into annual savings of £300 000 and made the company marginally profitable.

John Neil had considerable misgivings about the concentrate and arranged for laboratory testing of it. These tests failed to prove that the product was synthetic and, despite his voicing of continued concerns, the board of directors voted to buy the Global concentrate. Nevertheless, by the end of 1991 John Neil believed that there was enough circumstantial evidence to indicate that the grape concentrate was substantially synthetic. At his trial he claimed that he had informed his co-directors of his belief.

Earlier, in the spring of 1991, FO Ltd had been taken over by Eurofrute plc. The FO Ltd directors remained in post but were required to ensure that FO Ltd achieved certain performance targets, one of which demanded that profits should always be as good as or better than those of previous years. As Jones said in court, 'Under Eurofrute there was no room for performance slippage – that would have meant our losing our jobs.'

The performance targets meant that, in the immediate future at least, FO Ltd would have to continue using the Global concentrate. The company took the view that there was no proof that the concentrate was not genuine (neither did they have proof that it was); and anyway, it was demonstrably not doing harm to anyone.

In 1992 a pressure group, Action for Healthy Children (AHC) became concerned when a number of its members reported that the behaviour of their children often changed radically after they had consumed certain soft drinks. Grape juice from FO Ltd was one of the products identified and was included in the subsequent AHC investigation.

By December 1992, AHC had conclusive proof that FO Ltd's grape juice was 99.5 per cent man-made. AHC passed a copy of its information to FO Ltd, but the response of FO Ltd was to remain silent: they neither admitted any error nor withdrew any of their grape juice from sale. They did not co-operate further, either with the continuing investigation by AHC or with the vociferous band of investigative reporters who by then were pursuing both FO Ltd and Global Juices Corporation. (On some days these reporters were literally banging on the door of FO Ltd.)

Susan Millar made statements to the press supporting FO Ltd's position and emphasised the lack of hard evidence against their grape juice. Meanwhile, William Jones allowed current stocks to be distributed in the usual way. Contracted future deliveries were offered to customers in developing countries at substantial discounts. Arrangements were also made to supply customers in developed countries with juice obtained from local growers. This policy was continued for nine months until the contract with Global Juices expired.

When asked in court why the stocks of Global Concentrate had not been destroyed and replaced in December 1992, William Jones said that he might as well have destroyed the company at the same time, 'because that is what would have happened'.

Questions for discussion	1 *Identify and discuss the ethical issues raised in the case.*
	2 *Critically evaluate the actions of the three directors.*

References

Bowie, N. (1990) 'Morality, money and motor cars', in *Business, Ethics, and the Environment: The Public Policy Debate*, W. M. Hoffman *et al.* (ed.), Quorum Books, New York.

Buchholz, R. A. (1993) *Principles of Environment Management: The Greening of Business*, Prentice-Hall, Englewood Cliffs, New Jersey.

Cannon, T. (1994) *Corporate Responsibility*, Pitman Publishing, London.

Donaldson, T. (1982) *Constructing a Social Contract for Business in Corporations and Morality*, Prentice-Hall, Englewood Cliffs, New Jersey.

Drucker, P. (1973) *Management: Tasks, Responsibilities, Practices*, Heinemann, London.

Ewing, D. (1977) *Freedom Inside the Organisation*, McGraw-Hill, New York.

French, P. A. (1979) 'The corporation as a moral person', *American Philosophical Quarterly*, 3, pp. 207–15.

Friedman, M. (1970) 'The social responsibility of business is to increase profits', *New York Times*.

Friedman, M. (1971) 'Does business have social responsibility?' *Bank Administration*, April, 13–14.

Heald, M. (1970) *The Social Responsibility of Business*, The Press of Case Western Reserve University, Ohio.

Jeurissen, R. (1995) 'Business in response to the morally concerned public', in H. van Luijk and P. Ulrich, *Facing Public Interest: Ethical Challenge on Business Policy and Corporate Communications*, Kluwer Academic Publishers, Netherlands.

Kotler, P., Armstrong, G., Saunders, J., and Wong, V. (1996) *Principles of Marketing*, The European Edition, Prentice-Hall, Europe.

Pratley, P. (1995) *The Essence of Business Ethics*, Prentice-Hall International (UK) Ltd.

Ulrich, P., and Thielemann, U. (1993) 'How do managers think about market economy and morality? Empirical studies into business-ethical thinking patterns', *Journal of Business Ethics*, 12, pp. 879–98.

US Bureau of Census (1998) International Programs Center.

White, T. I. (1993) *Business Ethics: A Philosophical Reader*, Macmillan Publishing, New York.

CHAPTER 10

The implementation of a decision

At the end of this chapter you should:

- understand the importance of effective communication of a decision to those affected by it;

- apply transactional analysis to evaluate the effectiveness of communications in different contexts;

- be able to analyse why resistance to change occurs in a range of circumstances, and make recommendations as to how such resistance might be reduced or avoided;

- appreciate the importance of organisational culture and structure for effective implementation of decisions;

- recognise resource requirements for effective implementation of decisions; and

- be able to apply a model for monitoring and controlling decision effectiveness.

Introduction

While the prime focus of this book has been the processes and contexts of decision making, it would seem logical to discuss briefly the implementation of a chosen decision, if only because a decision that does not result in action of some kind represents an incomplete cycle – a job half done. It is, of course, perfectly possible that the decision will recommend constructive inaction; for example, in the face of economic recession and falling demand for its products, an organisation may decide quite rationally to 'ride out the storm', and not downsize or cut employees' working hours. But even this decision needs to be managed, in the sense that the situation is a precarious one, and must be monitored.

In this chapter, we shall be looking at the processes that follow the making of a decision. Since the implementation of most decisions involves change, it is important to consider briefly the management of change and, particularly, situations where there might be resistance to change. The conventional wisdom is that change is likely to meet with less resistance if employees can be involved in the processes of change; but we must consider what is an appropriate level of involvement in different contexts, and what form it might take.

Finally, the chapter will stress the need for monitoring the implementation of the decision, and evaluating its effectiveness. After all, it cannot be assumed that the initial decision was the right one; nor that the organisational outcomes will be as anticipated. Control and feedback are, therefore, vital managerial processes that reinforce the effectiveness of decision making.

Communicating the decision

Once a decision has been made, the process of implementation will begin with communication of the decision. In situations where the decision is straightforward, involves little change to established organisational procedures, and is likely to meet with little or no resistance, simple instructions – either written or verbal – are likely to be sufficient. However, more complex decisions in a more ambiguous context will need to be communicated with skill and tact.

As was briefly discussed in Chapter 2 in the context of group decision making, effective communication involves a four-stage cycle with (1) the sender delivering (2) the message to (3) the receiver, who provides (4) feedback. This was shown diagramatically in Fig. 2.2, and is reproduced here as Fig. 10.1.

Of paramount importance is the two-way nature of communication. Both the sender and the receiver must share the responsibility for ensuring that communication is effective. Thus, feedback from the receiver is necessary to measure the quality of communication. If the receiver's response to the sender's communication suggests confusion or rejection of the message, then some elaboration on the message will be necessary. Take, for example, the following communication, referring to the implementation of new stock control procedures in a factory:

> Foreman: *Harry, we're setting up a new system for stock control on Monday. You and the other charge hands will have to get yourselves familiar with it right away. It's all written down on this sheet of paper, so you'd better take it home with you at the weekend so that you and your team will be ready for the off next week.*
>
> Harry: *Hold on, Bob? What is this? What sort of new system? What's wrong with the old one?*
>
> Foreman: *Just read it, Harry, it's not difficult.*

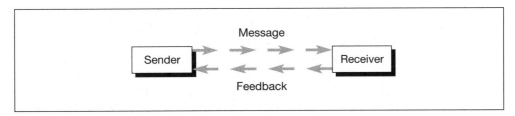

Fig. 10.1 The four-stage communication cycle

Harry: *I can't be expected to use a new system on Monday morning. Besides, we've never had any problems keeping track of stock. I can't see the need for it.*

Foreman: *It's nothing to do with me, Harry, I don't make the rules round here. They all come from upstairs, you know that.*

Harry: *Nothing's ever your fault, is it, Bob. Well I'm too busy to read this over the weekend, and anyway, why should I use my own time for company work. You can keep your new system. My team will be using the old one next week – and for a lot longer if I have my way.*

Foreman: *That's you all over! You just can't handle anything new, can you. Well, you'll be using the new system on Monday, like it or lump it, so if you don't want to look a fool, take that sheet home and read it.* (Walks away.)

The foreman's message was resisted, and ultimately rejected by the charge hand. The information about the new system was inadequate, leading to confusion on the part of the receiver who, having received no further clarification, eventually rejected the message. The sender, sensing that the message was not received clearly, failed to elaborate or improve the message in response to the receiver's feedback. Eventually, the sender distanced himself from the original message, and compounded the confusion by generating 'interference' in the message (in the form of insults to the receiver).

Unfortunately, this is not an uncommon pattern of failed communication; but we can at least draw lessons from it. The foreman had a message to convey – one containing an instruction. The content of the message, however, was confusing to the charge hand; his initial response begged further information, but was not *entirely* negative. The foreman, failing to pick up Harry's request for further elaboration, merely reiterated the original message, but this time it was obscured by added 'noise' (in the form of a terse, irritable response). From this point on, effective communication had become almost impossible. But what went wrong, and how could the communication have been improved?

If two parties are to communicate effectively, they have to know something about each other's values, attitudes, needs and expectations. The sender of the message should try to anticipate the reaction of the receiver. The receiver, meanwhile, must try to empathise, though not necessarily agree with the position of the person sending the message. In the example outlined above, there was no evidence that either the foreman or the charge hand was able to adopt the psychological position of the other. The foreman failed to anticipate the range of feelings the charge hand might feel: unease at having to implement a new stock control system at short notice; concern that he might not understand the new system; irritation that he was being asked to use part of the weekend to get to know the new procedures; perhaps fear that he might appear foolish if he could not master the system sufficiently to lead his team on Monday. The charge hand, however, failed to recognise that there could be a legitimate organisational reason for introducing the new procedures; or that the foreman had had the new system imposed upon him by more senior managers.

A more constructive approach to implementing the decision would begin by recognising why effective communication of the decision is necessary. If one party with a legitimate interest in the decision is not fully informed of the decision, or does not feel he/she has been a part, either of the decision-making process, or of its implementation, there is likely to be resistance. The diagram shown in Fig. 10.2 summarises the different elements of this communication process:

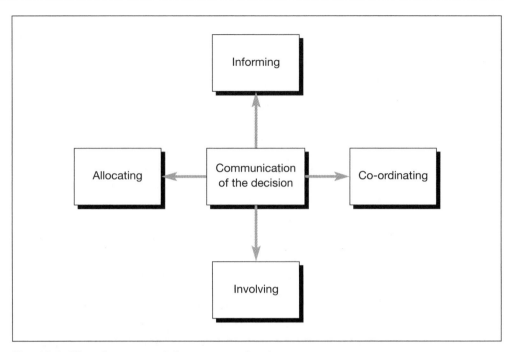

Fig. 10.2 The elements of the communication process

- *Informing people* of changes to take place and – equally important – *why* they must take place.
- *Involving people* in the change processes, with the intention of avoiding alienation and resistance to the changes. At this stage, communication is essentially educative.
- *Allocating tasks*, firstly to ensure that the decisions that have been made are put into practice, and secondly to promote participation amongst those affected by the decision.
- *Co-ordinating and monitoring* the implementation of the decision, particularly when the decision involves complex changes with many different individuals or groups affected.

Adopting this approach, the communication of the new stock-control system in our earlier example might follow the following lines:

Foreman: *How are you doing, Harry? If you've got a moment I'd appreciate your views on some new proposals the bosses have made. It seems they want to make a few changes to the stock control system. I think it's pretty important we should get an opinion from the guys at the sharp end.*

Harry: *What is it they want, then? If it ain't broke, then don't fix it – that's what I always say.*

Foreman: *I'm with you there, Harry, though it does seem we carry a lot of stock. The thinking upstairs is that we could get our costs down quite a bit if we could work on lower stock levels.*

Harry: *That's all very well, Bob, but what happens when we run out? I can't see a lot wrong with the system we use now.*

Foreman: *Well, we might gain something from it, but I think a lot is going to depend on experienced men like you keeping an eye on things, especially until we all get used to the new system.*

Harry: *What's the plan, then, Bob?*

Foreman: *It's all down here on this sheet of paper. It doesn't seem too bad really. Take a look …
they want us to make a start with the new system next week, but of course, nobody's going
to have much idea to start with. You can keep this sheet and get to know the system a bit
before we run it. You'll probably be an expert by monday! I'll be around to help, too. If we
muck in together I'm sure we'll be ok.*

Harry: *All right, Bob. I'm not sure my team will like it a lot, but we'll give it a go.*

This time we see that the reason for the change is made clear to Harry, reducing
the likelihood of outright rejection of the proposal. He has been *informed*. The
approach is participative, rather than directive. Harry is persuaded to work *with*
the foreman rather than against him to implement the new stock control system,
and *he will feel involved*. Any fears he might have had about the changes are likely
to have been allayed. Indeed, this approach has ensured that there is little or no
'interference' in the communication, and the feedback to the sender of the message
indicates that, so far, the message has been received as intended. The third stage,
that of *allocating tasks*, has begun with the foreman gently urging Harry to familiarise himself with the new stock control procedures. This stage should continue
with further tasks being allocated to the production team as the changes are first
communicated and then implemented. Finally, there is the question of *monitoring
the effectiveness* of the communication of the impending changes. In the second dialogue, there was a strong indication that communication would continue, and that
there would be support from the foreman. Monitoring and evaluation, therefore, is
non-judgemental, and conducted in a spirit of co-operation. By contrast, the earlier
dialogue was concluded with the threat that a judgement would soon be made as
to whether the new system had been properly implemented, and that blame would
be placed on Harry if the changes were not implemented effectively.

This is, of course, only the first aspect of implementing the decision to adopt a new
stock-control system. So far, the foreman has managed to avoid resistance to the new
system from the charge hand, Harry; but there is, as yet, no certainty that the team led
by Harry will accept the changes. However, before we look at ways of minimising
resistance in implementing the changes at shop-floor level, it is worth examining a
little more closely the psychological dimension of communicating the decision.

Transactional analysis

One approach to analysing, and ultimately improving, communication is known
as 'transactional analysis'. This approach, developed by behavioural scientists in
the United States in the late 1960s, identifies three communication roles – the
parent, the adult and the child. These roles do not necessarily correspond to a
person's age or status; indeed, one individual might, at different times, adopt all
three roles, though certain personality types may be more inclined to adopt one
particular role most of the time.

The parental role refers to behaviour that tends to be judgemental and often
assumes authority over others. The adult role is based on reaction to information,
and involves exploration and testing of a given situation; it demands bilateral or

multilateral communication in a way that the parental role does not. The role of child is governed by emotional response, reacting to events as a result of internal feelings; often underlying this role, however, is the sense that the individual is powerless to influence a situation other than by refusing to co-operate.

The three roles can be illustrated in a variety of situations:

Manager [parent] (to typist): *Leave what you're doing for now. This report needs to be typed right away – it's important. I need it for a meeting with the MD this afternoon.*

Typist [child]: *You can't monopolise my time. I work for three managers, and you're not the boss around here.*

Son [adult]: *I'll be going to the library this evening. I have some research to do for that essay that's due in tomorrow.*

Father [parent]: *It's typical of you to leave everything to the last minute. Why can't you organise you life a bit better?*

Young daughter [child]: *I'm not wearing that dress. I hate it.*

Mother [child]: *I'm not going to buy you any more clothes if you can't be sensible.*

It is argued by proponents of transactional analysis that the most effective communication comes from the adoption of adult-to-adult relationships. Indeed, it is easy to see how the absence of logic in the parent and child roles could stifle the effectiveness of group decision making. In our earlier example in which a new stock-control system was to be introduced within a manufacturing organisation, the foreman initially adopted the role of parent, instructing the charge hand to familiarise himself with the new system; the latter's petulant reaction was as much a psychological response to the manner in which the communication was delivered as it was to an objection to the new stock control system. In short, inappropriate communication may invite resistance.

While transactional analysis may present a logical case for adult-to-adult communications, there are still circumstances in which the parent role is adopted within organisations, usually by proponents of 'Theory X' management (McGregor, 1960), and often in organisations with notably hierarchical structures. Nevertheless, it is worth noting that, even within organisations with a clearly delineated hierarchical structure, adult-to-adult communications are likely to prove most effective. This is a fact not lost on the British Army, which has, in recent years, encouraged its NCOs not to behave towards their subordinates in the judgemental and sometimes aggressive manner of the parental role.

Implementing change through participation and involvement

Most decisions, as illustrated earlier in this chapter, involve changes to existing practices, and sometimes to personnel, organisational structures and technologies too. Indeed, it is highly likely that a change to any one of these will lead to further changes within an organisation. For example, the introduction of new technologies may result in fewer workers, or a different type of working group, being employed; this may, in turn, affect the structure of the organisation. This is the pattern of progress, and an organisation that never changes is unlikely to remain competitive in the long term.

However, it is equally understandable that the imposition of changes will sometimes meet with opposition. Such resistance can be categorised as either 'systemic' or 'behavioural'. 'Systemic' resistance to change refers to failures of the organisation's systems. Employees may be ill informed of changes taking place, or lack knowledge or skills (including managerial capabilities) in new working practices. 'Behavioural' resistance to change is based on individuals' or groups' reactions, perceptions or assumptions.

Kotter, Schlesinger and Sathe (1986) summarised a number of reasons for behavioural resistance to change, including the following:

- *Self-interest.* This may, for example, be concerned with the potential loss of a power base, and will be particularly relevant if the changes either alter the structure of an organisation or result in new technologies, reducing reliance on the specialist skills of key individuals.
- *Lack of trust in the decision makers.* The absence of trust may, in fact, have structural origins. Hierarchical structures, which often discourage participative decision making, can often result in a lack of information or poor communication.
- *Different view of the benefits.* It may simply be that no benefit is perceived from the potential changes. To some extent this is a problem of organisational culture. If organisational objectives are communicated and shared, the likelihood of individuals or groups failing to perceive the potential benefits of change will be significantly reduced.
- *Low tolerance for change.* This may be because the organisation is custom-bound, or because there may be particularly strong peer-group norms.

Clearly, for decisions to be implemented effectively, the processes of change must be carefully managed so as to avoid or overcome resistance. Much research has been conducted into overcoming resistance to change, emphasising its importance to organisational effectiveness. In the context of this book, it is not possible to do more than pick out a few of the major themes. Plant (1987) is typical of many who have researched into change management in emphasising the importance of good communications and employee involvement in the change process. Some of the key measures that may be of practical use in avoiding or reducing resistance to change are:

1 *Involvement.* Many researchers have stressed the need for the broadest involvement and participation in the change processes at all levels of the organisation. To exclude people from these processes, whether deliberately or not, is to alienate them; and to alienate them is to invite resistance to the changes.

2 *Support from senior management.* This support is required on the basis that much resistance emanates from a fear of failure. Senior managers can, therefore, facilitate change by understanding and supporting employees' needs so as to remove that fear.

3 *Change should reduce current workload.* In the competitive environment in which most organisations operate, decisions are often made with a view to increasing

operating efficiency. It may not always be possible to reduce the current work-load of employees and, indeed, efficiency gains are often made at the expense of an increase in individuals' workloads. A pragmatic approach would be for senior managers to ensure that there is an equitable distribution of work, and that there is appropriate support.

4 *Change should accord with current values.* Authors such as Peters and Waterman (1982) have stressed the significance of organisational culture to the achievement of success. If shared values are seen as a critical success factor, it is important that managerial decisions should accord with established beliefs within the organisation in order to maximise acceptance of the decision.

5 *Change should interest participants.* Naturally, it is preferable that any change should interest those affected. In practice, of course, this may not always be possible. For example, technological changes have in many industries had the effect of de-skilling the workforce. As new roles are established, with the inevitable consequence that some individuals will feel that their importance to the organisation has diminished, it is important that managers address the motivation of their staff.

6 *Change should not threaten autonomy or security.* Once again, it is not possible in most modern organisations to guarantee that changes can be implemented without jeopardising job security. Perhaps the most effective way for organisations to ensure, first, that their employees have the flexibility to respond to the changing demands placed upon them and, second, that the employees have the capability of sustaining gainful employment is through training policies. It can be seen, therefore, that decisions in organisations can rarely be taken or implemented in isolation. All organisations operate in changing environments; changing environments necessitate organisational changes at both a strategic and an operational level. The successful implementation of change will require, not only the moral support of senior managers but also support in terms of training and resources.

7 *Consensus on the adoption of changes.* While few would argue that organisational decision making should be a wholly democratic process, it must be recognised that implementation of a decision is likely to be more straightforward if there is broad support for the decision in the first place. Therefore, recognition of, and attention to, the potential causes of resistance to change are of critical importance to managers. The process of implementing change will require education, and possibly negotiation, if consensus is to be achieved.

8 *Feedback.* Although it may seem obvious to many that feedback to individuals and groups will be a necessary part of the process of evaluating changes, it is useful to formalise the monitoring of performance when changes have been made. This is partly for confidence building, but also so that adjustments can be made if targets or expectations are not being met. It should be stressed that feedback should be a two-way, or even multidirectional process.

9 *Changes should be open to revision.* It cannot be assumed that the original decision made was the right one. It is not uncommon for individuals or organisations to focus more on justification of their decision, rather than evaluating its effectiveness.

10 *Mutual support, trust and confidence.* A common sense of direction is required if an organisation is to implement change effectively. It is unlikely that this can be achieved without mutual confidence.

The level of employee involvement

While there is much agreement on the benefits of employee involvement in processes of change management, rather less has been written on the *level* of involvement that is most likely to yield the desired results. In truth, this is primarily because it is not possible to be prescriptive in this respect.

The appropriate degree of employee participation in both decision making and the subsequent implementation of a decision will almost certainly depend on the context, measured in terms of the extent to which employees will be affected by the changes and the likelihood that there will be resistance to change.

It may be worth returning here to Fiedler's (1967) contingency approach to leadership (previously referred to in Chapter 2). Change is least likely to meet with resistance in circumstances where (a) there is trust and confidence in the change leader, (b) the change does not result in task complexity, and (c) the leader has strong position power. According to Fiedler, this would result in a favourable context, which would not require a high level of employee involvement for change to be implemented successfully. Similarly, if the context is very unfavourable, strong direction may be needed, and low levels of involvement may be necessary. Most change situations, however, may require higher levels of employee involvement, since the context will be neither wholly favourable nor unfavourable.

The importance of structure and culture

If good communications and employee involvement are seen as the key requirements for the successful implementation of change, one potential barrier to its effective implementation may be an inappropriate structure or culture. Structure and culture are, in fact, often thought to be inextricably linked.

The effectiveness of the change process will, to a great extent, depend on people's commitment to the changes; and in turn, their commitment will be dependent on the organisational culture – the commonly held values, attitudes, beliefs and assumptions within the organisation. However, the measurement or identification of organisational culture is notoriously difficult, since it is inconceivable that all members of an organisation have the same values and beliefs, or that they will behave in the same way in given circumstances. Nevertheless, many authors have identified significant benefits to be gained from 'strong' organisational cultures, particularly (as in the case of Peters and Waterman's research, 1982) where the culture involves a common desire to achieve competitive advantage.

If we are to establish a useful link between organisational culture and the ability to implement change successfully, then we will have to identify broad types of culture for which we can predict the likely effectiveness of change. Such approaches to culture are essentially structural, in that culture is defined in terms of the design of the organisation. Handy (1976), for example, identifies four generic categories of organisational culture, describing the roles, the division of labour and the patterns of communication for each culture type. (Their principal features are summarised in Table 10.1.)

The four typologies of organisational culture are described primarily in terms of organisational structures. The 'power' culture, represented as a spider's web, is controlled centrally by an individual or small group (the powerful spider), from whom all major decisions emanate. The power culture typically exists within small organisations or small divisions within larger organisations. Bureaucratic structures are allied to 'role' cultures, with rules, regulations and processes dominating. Such organisations are often wary of those who step beyond the boundaries of their role, and power comes from formal position rather than expertise. Communications in these organisations tend to be vertical (from one level of the hierarchy to the next) and can be slow. Matrix structures are linked to the 'task' culture, with position power being less important than the overriding need for teams to focus on achieving their common task. Finally, the 'person' culture – a cluster of individuals, loosely bound by a common professional purpose – scarcely has a structure at all, allowing independence for the associated individuals.

Handy argued that the flexibility of the task culture, and the simple lines of communication of the power culture tend to facilitate change, whereas the rules and procedures and hierarchical structures of the role culture often create inertia, resulting in resistance to change.

The links made by Handy between organisational design and the effectiveness of change management appear to echo the views of Burns and Stalker (1961), who identified organisations with 'mechanistic' structures, and others with 'organic' structures. 'Mechanistic' structures are in their view characterised by a high degree of functional specialisation and formal authority, are based on position, and provide a clear definition of duties and responsibilities. In such organisations, established rules and procedures would tend to outlast individuals; the organisation would be suited to a stable environment, and would not, or could not change easily. Thus, the mechanistic structure is analogous to Handy's 'role' culture. The 'organic' structure, by contrast, was seen as adaptable, depending for survival on development and innovation. In such organisations, duties were more flexible, as was the pattern of communication, responding to external changes, and adapting accordingly. In short, organisations with organic structures were seen as more appropriate for situations involving change.

Table 10.1 Organisational culture according to Handy (1976)

Culture type	Initiative	Structure	Obedience	Time/task emphasis	Task set by	Supervision	Decisions	Rules
Power	high	organic	high	either	centre	limited	central	few formal
Role	low	mechanistic	high	time	supervisor	close	committee	many
Task	high	organic	low	task	team	little	team	very few
Person	high	organic	low	task	self	self	joint	flexible

There is, however, some considerable debate as to whether it is possible to design an organisational structure so as to achieve a culture of commitment to change. A sociological, rather than structural, approach to culture would suggest that achieving this commitment has more to do with a broad range personal experiences within the workplace, which may sometimes be influenced by key personnel within an organisation – often, as in the case of Anita Roddick, Richard Branson, the late Laura Ashley and others, the organisation's founder and figurehead.

Whether or not one accepts that an organisation can develop the desired culture through structure and design, there can be little dispute that the effectiveness of change initiatives will be very much affected by culture. The lesson for managers, therefore, is that, since all organisations deal with change, culture should be monitored and evaluated to ensure that it does not act as an impediment to the processes of change.

Resource requirements for implementing a decision

If a decision is to be of any benefit to an organisation, or subsection of an organisation, it has to be translated into firm actions. In order for this to take place, it should be tested for its feasibility. Feasibility is primarily to do with the resources available to the individuals or groups who will be implementing the decision. Although the specific resource requirements will depend on the nature and context of the decision, it is possible to make some general comments about the types of resources that may be needed for effective changes to be implemented. Suffice it to say that many of the less tangible resource requirements are frequently overlooked.

Logically, it ought to be the responsibility of the decision makers to identify what resources will be needed and how they will be acquired. Hamel and Prahalad (1994) warn that the appropriate way to approach resourcing change is not simply to divide up existing resources amongst competing users but to identify resource needs and acquire the best available to complete the task. This, they argue is the route to competitive advantage rather than mediocrity.

The most obvious resource requirement will, in most cases, be finance. While it is unlikely that such a requirement will be overlooked completely, it is not at all uncommon for the cost of a project to be grossly underestimated. Though it is conceivable that there may be unforeseen changes in the external environment that result in rising costs, the principal reason for this underestimate is likely to be poor budgeting. While finance may be the first requirement to launch a new initiative, the budget must take account of all other resource costs and so would be better prepared after all other resource requirements have been considered.

Implementation of the decision may alter human resource requirements, either in terms of the quantity or type of labour usage. Consideration must be given as to whether the new requirements can be met from within the organisation, and whether training is required for the development of new skills.

Increasingly, organisations are recognising the value of information as a resource. Information is a source of competitive advantage, and may have to be developed or bought in, particularly if the changes to be implemented involve serving new customers and markets. The foundation of marketing capability is, after all, customer data.

Monitoring and evaluating a decision

When a decision is made that involves organisational change, there will be some expectation on the part of the management for a particular outcome. For example, if a company decides to discontinue production of product X, and to replace it with product Y, the results of this change must be monitored and controlled. The same will be true even if the decision is likely to bring less tangible results, such as introducing a new staff appraisal scheme. Feedback will be required so that an evaluation can be made of the effectiveness of the changes. The basis of this evaluation will be managerial information in relation to the objectives of the decision. Managers will then use this information to take remedial action where necessary.

However, it would be worthwhile, at the very outset, to sound a note of caution with respect to monitoring and controlling performance; it is possible to control too much, and too closely! It is important to establish what is *relevant* control data so that useful feedback on performance is not lost amongst a mass of trivia. In fact, it is quite easy to cloud the monitoring and evaluation process by providing information that is either superfluous or irrelevant. Controls should, therefore, be restricted to factors that can be influenced by those responsible for making decisions.

Effective monitoring and evaluation of changes will require us to set up appropriate control standards. In other words, we need to know precisely what we are expecting to achieve. Bearing in mind the need for relevant control data, the first task in setting these standards is to establish what is to be measured and how the measurement is to be taken. For example, if an objective is to sell 5000 items of a new product line in the first three months after its launch, it is pointless measuring achievement in terms of profitability or efficiency. Whilst the latter may form the basis of appropriate goals for the future, control measurements should be confined to current objectives.

Generally, establishing control standards is more straightforward if the expected outcome of change is easily measurable. Sales data, for example, are easily quantifiable, but the results of a training programme for receptionists may be more difficult to assess. While most changes may be evaluated in both quantitative and qualitative terms, the former, where possible, will undoubtedly be more straightforward. The receptionists' training programme may for instance be monitored primarily in terms of the way that the receptionists welcome clients (qualitative control), though a small quantitative element may be brought in if, for example, there is measurement of how long it takes for a receptionist to respond to a telephone call.

Furthermore, control information needs to be fed back to decision makers in time for corrective action to be taken where necessary. Failure to meet this condition negates most of the benefit of any control system, since managers need early warning of impending problems, not information for a post mortem examination.

Therefore, we will need to set a timescale for the information to reach both those managing the change and the individuals or teams at the operating level.

Some organisations may take a systems view of control, arguing that, since they operate within changing environments, control systems should encompass *all* the organisation's operations, ensuring rapid and appropriate response to external changes. In this way, controls can be used not only as a means of monitoring any operational problems that may arise as a result of change but also to provide continuous guidance for the improvement of organisational performance. This approach was popular with certain large organisations in the 1970s, with control being centralised and located fairly close to the corporate planning function. Over the subsequent two decades, the trend has been for decentralised control of operations, on the basis that this is more flexible and permits greater involvement of those at the operating level. Decentralised, or 'local' control has been an integral part of major quality initiatives such as Total Quality Management (TQM).

Control techniques

There are, of course, many techniques available for analysing control data, both quantitative and qualitative. The specific techniques used will depend on the context of their operation. However, it is still worth our considering two generic control techniques, one that uses primarily quantitative analysis, and the other that uses a qualitative analysis of the effect of change on the organisation's 'soft' systems.

Quantitative control

The first approach involves categorising any deviation from the defined objectives as either 'positive' (meaning performance has been better than expected) or 'negative' (representing underperformance). The information generated by the control process can then indicate one of three outcomes: positive deviation from the stated objectives, no significant deviation, or a negative deviation. It is tempting to assume that only the last of these three possible outcomes requires remedial attention; certainly, the causes of underperformance will need to be examined immediately. But even when targets are met, or exceeded, the results bear further examination, for a positive deviation may mean that the objectives established can be achieved too easily. And even an outcome of no significant deviation from our target may mean that we are 'satisficing' – achieving our goals with something to spare.

The objectives themselves should be kept under review, and may themselves require revision. Suppose we pursue the example outlined at the beginning of this section, wherein a company replaces one product line with another and sets a target of selling 5000 items of the new product in the first three months after its launch. The company then sells 6000 items in the first three months: 20 per cent more than its target. We may feel very pleased with this success, but there is a clear indication that demand for the product may be greater than anticipated. This may not be regarded as a problem, but it is certainly a situation that requires some attention. First, we may be missing an opportunity if we fail to explore the market potential of the new product; second, it is likely that production schedules will need to be adjusted to cope with the higher-than-anticipated demand; and third, the success of the new product launch may mean that additional resources will have to be found to support this product line.

'Monitoring' does not, of course, merely mean checking results and overseeing progress, even though such actions are valid and worthwhile parts of the monitoring process. Monitoring is very much to do with ongoing testing of the organisation's (or the team's) confidence in the changes that have been made. In this way, the organisation can control, rather than simply observe, the progress being made. The control process, then, will usually involve quantitative measures of performance, but it should also include qualitative assessments of whether the changes accord with the broader organisational purpose reflected in the organisation's mission statement and in the organisation's defined and agreed social responsibilities.

Qualitative control

Many organisations might use formal, often financial, control techniques, such as budgeting, ratio analysis, measures of profitability and efficiency as the backbone of their control systems; but it is often thought that the most successful companies place equal emphasis on monitoring the less tangible, human factors. The second control technique we shall examine involves the application of the McKinsey Corporation's '7 S' framework, as described by Pascall and Athos (1982) and by Peters and Waterman (1982). The framework distinguishes between three 'hard' Ss – strategy, structure, and systems – and four 'soft' S's – staff, style, skills, and shared values.

Those organisations that emphasise the soft S's have recognised the importance of human elements of control systems. They see the control process as something more than a mechanistic exercise in data collection; it is a process that itself requires decisions to be made on the basis of human judgement. Therefore the informal monitoring of the soft issues is seen as an important complement to the more formal control mechanisms. These informal controls are usually based on regular communications within the organisation, reinforcing an open culture of trust and mutual understanding. They will often be supported by training programmes to ensure that employees have the requisite skills to perform new roles, by a commitment on the part of senior management to teamwork, and by 'socialising' employees in the organisational culture.

Taking corrective action

Taking corrective action is not always an easy task, since many people feel that this is a judgement on their ability or competence to perform their job. It is preferable, therefore, that those affected operationally by change should themselves play a part in the control process. In other words, the control should not be implemented by an individual from outside the operating team, but should include at least an element of self-evaluation. Indeed, if the monitoring and control of change is effected both by those involved at an operational level, and others who are more distant from the changes, this should maximise the likelihood of productive dialogue, rather than relying entirely on top-down control.

A constructive evaluation of change is most likely to be achieved if there is an emphasis on appropriate accountability, rather than apportioning blame. In order to gain, or increase, acceptance of the process of monitoring change, it may also be helpful if contingency plans are drawn up before the changes are implemented. This would involve anticipating possible problems before they arise, and deciding upon the remedial action that would be necessary in different circumstances. What, for example, would we do if our example company were only able to sell 3000 items of our new product line in the first three months, rather than the projected 5000? By addressing, even before the new product's launch, the fact that this is a possible scenario, some of the criticism that the sales team might perceive if sales were to prove sluggish might be averted. This type of scenario planning can reduce the sense of failure on the part of individuals or teams if there should be a negative deviation from the anticipated outcomes of change.

It is also worth noting that scenario planning can be equally useful if there is a positive deviation from out expectations.

Summary of control standards

In the light of the foregoing, essential components of an effective control system can be set out as follows:

1 Control standards – what is to be measured.

2 Restriction of controls to those factors which can be influenced by the decision makers.

3 Statement of procedures to be used – how measurement is to be made.

4 Clearly defined objectives of the decision made and implemented.

5 Accountability without culpability.

6 Senior management's support to implement remedial action where necessary.

7 Mechanisms for implementing corrective action, which may include prepared plans, in readiness for a range of scenarios.

8 Recognition of what does, and what does not, require remedial action.

9 Reappraisal of corrective action.

The control cycle

The process of monitoring and control must be seen as a continuous cycle; it is not a one-off event occurring immediately following the implementation of change. The cycle we are suggesting here (summarised as Fig. 10.3) is based upon what have now been identified as the key elements of a system for controlling change.

The starting point for the cycle will be the objectives of change, identified by the decision makers. These objectives will have been tested for their feasibility and their consistency with broad organisational goals. So, at the start of the implementation stage, they will probably be accepted as appropriate, but anyway will be open to review later.

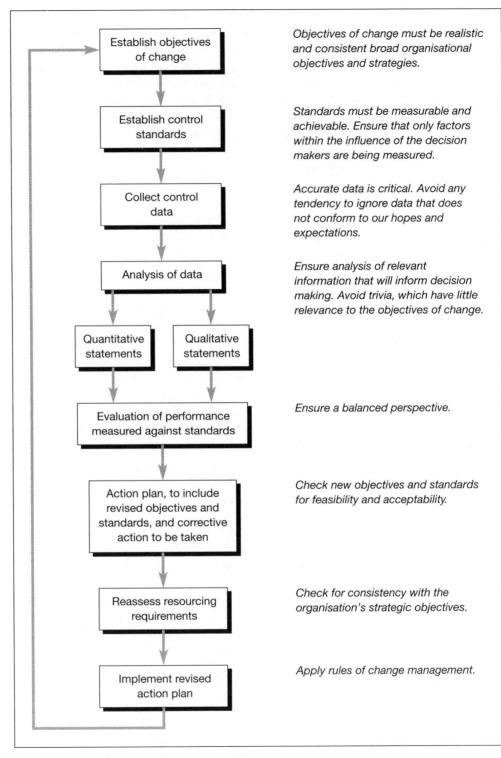

Fig. 10.3 The control cycle

The next stage of the cycle will be to establish the control standards. The formal 'hard' targets will have been set out by the decision makers in the objectives for change. Measures should be established, ensuring, as described earlier, that monitoring is only of what the organisation has set out to achieve. The 'soft' objectives must also be monitored, and ways must be found of measuring and assessing these intangible goals. For this purpose qualitative data will be required, so it will be necessary to set in place a reliable mechanism for monitoring these aspects of the changes. Normally, more than one perspective will be sought in order to reduce the subjectivity of the judgement.

Once the changes are implemented, control data must be collected. This phase is fairly mechanistic, particularly as far as quantitative data is concerned. The key requirement in this phase is accuracy. The data must then be analysed in order to produce managerial information. The analysis stage will indicate whether or not the control targets have been met. Who is responsible for this analysis will depend on the culture and structure of the organisation (or a subsection of it), but there is scope at this stage for the involvement of those implicated in the changes, and this ought to reduce resistance both to the changes and to the monitoring of performance.

The analysis of results will give an indication of whether targets are being met. Whether or not remedial action is to be taken (on account of either under- or overperformance) is normally a managerial decision. If no remedial action is deemed necessary, the first 'circuit' of the control cycle is complete, and the process should continue with further monitoring of objectives. Since objectives have so far been met, it may be tempting to think that they require no further review; but objectives must be seen in context. If the context changes (e.g. if new competitors emerge, or macro-economic conditions change), then our original objectives may have to be revised.

If remedial measures are deemed necessary, an action plan will be required. The action plan may focus on any or all of: the original objectives, the control standards that have been set, and the resources at the organisation's disposal. The control may discover that our objectives were unrealistic or inappropriate to our circumstances. In this case, the original decision was probably wrong, and may need to be refined or, at worst, reversed. (If the latter is the case, then we must call into question our decision-making processes, as discussed in earlier chapters.)

Adjustment of the control standards may, superficially, seem more straightforward although, since they are linked to objectives, the latter may also have to be revised. The whole matter of adjusting control standards then becomes more complex when the potential impact on organisational strategy is considered. Suppose, for example, that there is a significant positive deviation from an objective target for a newly launched product. No doubt, verification will be required to establish categorically that the new product is proving more successful than anticipated, but once this has been demonstrated, corporate strategy may have to be altered to account for the new opportunity that has been created.

Underperformance compared with the control standard may reveal a flaw in our resource strengths. The term 'resources', of course, covers a huge area of the organisation's or unit's capabilities, some of which can be improved more readily than others. Human resources, for example, may be underperforming because of a failure to meet training needs. (This may include the management of change.) Equally, the underperformance may be due to inadequate information or physical resources. Whatever the source of resource deficiency, this will need to be reflected in the action plan.

Finally, the revised action plan, in terms of amended objectives and new control standards will have to be communicated to the operating team. This communication is a vital part of the monitoring and evaluation process if we are to ensure appropriate accountability without blaming individuals for the fact that the original targets have not been met. Commitment must also be sought to ensure that any resource weaknesses are rectified.

One circuit of the cycle has now been completed, but the process of monitoring and control is far from finished. Changes and revisions to existing practices will be made from time to time, and these will have to be fed into the control cycle. Also, as the external environment changes, and the organisation's strategies change, so new operational decisions will have to be made. Monitoring and control will, therefore, continue to be a vital part of implementing new decisions.

Summary of the chapter

- This chapter began by returning to a communication model first encountered in Chapter 2. An example was used to illustrate how poor communication can alienate people from the processes of change following a major decision. We then included a brief discussion of transactional analysis to help identify appropriate patterns of communication so as to minimise resistance.

- We then addressed the issue of resistance to change in a little more detail, identifying some well known theories of why resistance occurs, and what measures managers might take to avoid or reduce it. The key themes running through all the theory on change management were employee involvement and participation. Since the extent of involvement and participation possible in many organisations is largely determined by their structure and culture, these two important issues were also explored.

- There was a brief discussion of the resource requirements for effective implementation of decisions, with particular warnings against the temptation to 'make do with what we have already got'.

- The chapter concluded by developing a model for monitoring and evaluating the process of decision implementation and change. The centrepiece of this model was a control cycle, which should be seen as part of an ongoing process of self-evaluation for an organisation.

Case Study 20: Rawtenstall Fine Sausages plc

For 23 years Rawtenstall Fine Sausages plc (RFS) has produced and distributed sausages to delicatessens and specialist retailers throughout the North of England. George Wagstaff, one of the three founders of the business, is still the managing director, but at the age of 62, he is beginning to think of retirement. Indeed, his nephew, Martin Wagstaff, who has also been with the company since the outset, and was appointed to the Board two years ago as Director of Marketing, would, in George's eyes, make an admirable successor. George has always been willing to give Martin a helping hand in his career, and feels the young man has done very well in the business.

George believes Martin has worked hard to get where he is, and deserves to take over the reins when the time comes for George to call a halt and stand down. It has troubled him, therefore, that a vociferous group of shareholders has been maligning Martin as indecisive and reactionary, and wants him replaced on the Board by the exceptionally youthful Mark Lyons. The group by no means represents a majority, but their influence has grown and there is certainly a groundswell of support for their views within the company, particularly amongst the younger managers. It is true that Lyons is a capable young man, and well qualified, with his degree in Statistics and his Marketing Diploma, but what substitute could there be for experience?

The business has done well too, growing steadily with many new clients coming to the company asking to be supplied with RFS's high-quality products. There is no doubt that RFS has deserved its fine reputation amongst its customers, who are now spread not just throughout Lancashire and Yorkshire but also into Cumbria, Durham and Derbyshire.

The fair value of RFS's net assets is estimated at £4.2m; the company has healthy profits and is low-geared, but the frustration of some of the shareholders has been growing for some time. Ten years ago RFS had gone in for some gentle expansion, when they acquired the net assets of a medium-sized private company making a range of high-quality dairy products. 'It is ironic,' mused George, 'that it was Martin who, as a young marketing manager, suggested we take over the Nelson dairy; and now that rowdy pressure group is calling for his head because he is not expanding the company's markets fast enough for them. Who wants to sell abroad when there are more than enough customers on our doorstep?' It is true that, although the dairy business has always made a modest profit, it has not matched the core sausage business in terms of either profits or growth. 'But is that not an argument in favour of sticking to what we know best?' thought George.

George Wagstaff has been convinced for some months that Mark Lyons is himself behind some of the protests, and that the options for expansion that he has asked the Board to consider are in effect his manifesto for his election to the Board. George also feels equally sure that if he and Martin do not support one of the proposals at next week's Board meeting, it could be curtains for both of them. He's pondering for the umpteenth time over the choice before him.

The options are thus:

- It seems likely that, at a price of £1.5m RFS could obtain a 60 per cent controlling interest in a Belgian *charcuterie*. The estimated fair value of the Belgian company's net assets is £1.8m.

- Alternatively, at an estimated cost of £3.6m, RFS could set up a subsidiary in the US.
- The third option is to take over the total net assets of an ailing producer of luxury ice cream based in Cheshire. This would cost £1m, representing the fair value of the company's net assets, and it seems that the company is badly in need of an injection of new capital.
- The final option involves a major shake-up of RFS's existing operations. Lyons has written to the Board declaring that his own research indicates that there is a very considerable UK market for high-quality sausages, and that the Board might consider a major programme of expansion, including moving into the frozen-food market. Lyons believes there are significant economies of scale to be gained if new machinery can be purchased and modern working practices introduced.

The more George thinks about the options, the less he likes any of them. But he knows that he will be forced into choosing one of them. What is more, he knows that his nephew will be charged with implementing the Board's chosen option, and this would be Martin's one opportunity to demonstrate that he is the right man to become the next Managing Director. But his other concern is for the loyal employees who have served RFS so well over many years.

<table>
<tr><td>Questions for
discussion</td><td>1</td><td>What factors do you think the Board of Directors ought to consider before a decision is made regarding the possibility of expansion?</td></tr>
<tr><td></td><td>2</td><td>If the Board of Directors decides to go ahead with plans for expansion, what strategic direction might be appropriate? (Consider the strategic fit of each of the options with RFS's current business.)</td></tr>
<tr><td></td><td>3</td><td>Assuming the directors of RFS decide to go ahead with expansion and that they accept your recommendations as to which is the best of the options outlined, what sort of control systems would be appropriate for the newly expanded business?</td></tr>
</table>

References

Burns, T. and Stalker, G. M. (1961) *The Management of Innovation*, Tavistock, London.

Fiedler, F. E. (1967) *A Theory of Leadership Effectiveness*, McGraw-Hill, New York.

Hamel, G. and Prahalad, C. K. (1994) *Competing for the Future*, Harvard Business School Press.

Handy, C. B. (1976) *Understanding Organisations*, Penguin, London.

Kotter, J., Schlesinger, L. A. and Sathe, V. (1986) *Organization: Text, Cases and Readings*, Irwin, Homewood, US.

McGregor, D. (1960) *The Human Side of Enterprise*, McGraw-Hill, New York.

Pascall, R. T. and Athos, A. K. (1982) *The Art of Japanese Management*, Allen Lane, London.

Peters, T. and Waterman, R. (1982) *In Search of Excellence*, Harper & Row, New York.

Plant, R. (1987) *Managing Change and Making It Stick*, Fontana, London.

CHAPTER 11

Delegation, negotiation and conflict

Learning objectives

At the end of this chapter you should:

- be able to define the role of delegation and negotiation within decision making;

- understand and outline the process of delegation and negotiation;

- be able to outline the benefits of delegation and negotiation;

- understand the organisational factors that determine the use of delegation and negotiation;

- appreciate the need for managers to maintain balance between delegation and control; and

- appreciate and understand the effect of conflict on the decision-making process.

Introduction

So far we have discussed the ways in which individuals' make decisions, the constraints that they face and the various decision-making tools that can be used. What, however, are the two most important aspects to effective decision making from the organisational and individual point of view? The answer is, from the individual point of view, the extent to which decisions are universally accepted and thus the extent to which individuals feel committed to the decision. From the organisation's point of view, the most important aspect of an effective decision is one that maximises the outcomes.

It is people who at the end of the decision-making process determine whether or not the decision is effectively implemented. If individuals do not feel that they own or have control over decisions that are made on their behalf, why should they feel committed or attempt to maximise the decision outcomes? The whole point of effective decision making is ideally to achieve consensual progress toward a common goal that benefits the individual, the organisation and other stakeholders. To achieve such an ideal outcome, individuals must feel committed to the decision, the decision-making process and its implementation. If this is missing, of what value is the decision in terms of its effectiveness?

Consensus is therefore important to the decision-making process. The achievement of consensus is possible through delegation and negotiation – that is, delegated decision making and negotiated decision-based outcomes. The aim of such an approach is to foster ownership, control, and commitment to decisions through the involvement of individuals in the decision-making process.

It must be borne in mind, however, that not all employees want to be involved in decision making and there is a need therefore to caution against the belief that employees always welcome the opportunities that delegation can bring. The extent to which delegated decision making can be used will be dependent on the context, but principally on the nature and motivation of the individuals involved.

The aim of this chapter is therefore to consider the role of delegation and negotiation, and the ways in which they can be used as a means of achieving delegated decision making. The chapter will also discuss the effect of conflict on decision making.

Delegation

Responsibility and the authority that should go alongside it are both complementary to decision making and can be achieved, if a democratic involvement culture is the organisational norm, through the use of delegation. Delegation can be defined as the process by which tasks and the relevant authority are passed on to individuals within an organisation. Delegation allows subordinates to become involved in decision making and actually to make decisions as opposed to participative decision-making approaches, and thus to share the responsibility for making the decisions. This is perhaps a subtle difference but the extent to which delegation does in fact involve the sharing or otherwise of authority will be dependent on the prevailing organisational cultural norms and the management style.

The actual process itself can be shown through the use of a simple flow diagram as represented by Fig. 11.1.

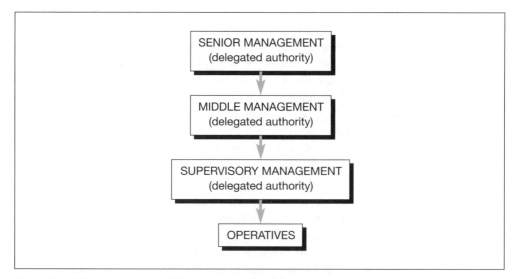

Fig. 11. 1 The process of delegated authority

The delegation process

It should be noted that delegated decision making is not a form of abdication of responsibility. Delegation still requires the involvement of managers in the decision process and also in the clarification of a range of issues that could potentially create barriers to effective delegation and hence the decision-making process.

The delegation process should involve a number of steps that must clearly define the decision-making parameters and what is expected of the decision makers. These include the following:

- Tasks must be clearly defined.
- Tasks must be clearly related to other projects and the goals of the organisation.
- Levels of performance required must be specified.
- Time factors must be specified.
- The amount of freedom that subordinates have to make and implement decisions must be specified.
- The amount of authority that the decision makers have must be clear.
- There must be trust of subordinates to complete whole projects.
- Meaningful support must be provided in the form of training, if necessary, and there must be access to information and people that are required for the successful completion of the task(s).

Barriers to delegation

The barriers to effective delegation are usually managers, subordinates, the organisation's culture, the complexity of the task and the importance of the decision to the organisation. These are expanded below in turn.

- *Managers.* Some may be resistant to giving up what they see to be their right to exercise authority by virtue of their position within the organisation. Other concerns will focus on the worry that subordinates are not up to the tasks in hand and that delegating authority is a sign of weakness. The extent to which any or all of these will influence delegation will be determined by the prevailing culture. For example, if the management style were 'macho', then it would be very unlikely that delegation will take place because to delegate would be deemed by other managers as a sign of weakness. The fact that such an approach would alienate subordinates and therefore have an effect on their commitment to decisions would not be an issue, reflecting the management style; however, it would be for managers who wish to be accepted by their colleagues.
- *Subordinates.* Some may not wish to accept delegated decision-making powers because of the responsibility that it involves. They may also lack confidence because they fear the ramifications of failure or they feel that they do not have the necessary experience fully to accept such responsibility. Such a situational factor can be addressed through management supporting subordinates in the form of training and development in order to bolster their confidence and hopefully provide a base from which they can operate and feel safe when making decisions.

- *Organisational culture.* This barrier relates to the cultural aspects and the way in which individuals have been expected to perform prior to the introduction of delegation. If the norm was one of delegation, then further delegation will on the whole be accepted; but if it is a new experience that goes counter to the previous norms, individuals may be reluctant to participate because it is counter to their perceptions.

- *Complexity of task.* This relates to the degree of complexity and the extent to which the appropriate level of expertise exists at subordinate level in order for the task to be completed satisfactorily. If the expertise does exist, then the delegation of the task must be to those individuals who have the expertise. A lack of the appropriate expertise at the subordinate level will need to be addressed if the organisation is looking to increase the amount and extent of delegation in the future. This issue also relates to subordinates' confidence in their own ability and that of the organisation to support them (see Organisational culture).

- *Importance of the decision.* This will determine the extent to which decision-making powers are actually delegated. Unless a manager and the organisation *per se* have absolute trust in subordinates, it is unlikely that very important decisions will be delegated below a certain level of authority. For example, if large sums of money are involved and if the decision carries a high risk for the organisation, it is very likely that the decision would at the very least be taken by a middle manager. There is a need therefore for managers to have a clear idea in their own minds as to the extent to which delegation will occur. And this must then be clearly communicated to subordinates in order to avoid false expectations as to the amount of power that will actually be delegated.

If we consider the following example, we can see that the process of delegation is not one that simply involves stating that delegation will take place but that it requires far more consideration of what is actually involved if it is to be successful.

Exhibit 11.1 **Webcom**

Emma and Olivia Preuss formed Webcom two years ago, and from employing one part-time employee they now employ over 120 people. Their business has been very successful and they are now at a stage in their development whereby they must, if they are to continue to be successful, run the business in a more organised fashion. The two most important issues are how to organise the business and how to get the best from their employees.

In order to address these issues, they have decided to structure themselves in a more organised way and, more importantly, they argue, to create a culture that is democratic in nature in order to harness and foster the creativity of their employees. A key aspect of the culture will be the amount of delegated decision making that will take place, which both management and subordinates will be expected to embrace fully.

If the culture that they wish to create is to be successful, they need to consider a number of things that must be in place in order for the business to operate along the lines that they envisage:

- Emma and Olivia will have to determine the extent of delegation that best suits their needs and recognise that as the business grows there will be a need for greater delegation in order to foster quick decision making and the creativity that they seek.

- As the confidence of subordinates grows, so may their desire to take on more responsibility, which will need to be met if their commitment and enthusiasm is to be maintained. This will be especially so as delegation becomes the norm.

- If the delegation-based nature of Webcom's culture is to work, then subordinates must be trusted, their mistakes should be tolerated within reason and learned from, and their ideas should be genuinely welcomed.

- Tasks must be clearly defined in order to avoid overlap, potential confusion and conflict.

- The concept of accountability alongside delegated authority must be clearly explained to all employees, in that assigned responsibilities must be met.

- Barriers to delegation on the part of managers and subordinates must be identified and addressed.

- Line authority should be given to individuals in order for them to complete tasks quickly and efficiently. For example, if someone has responsibility for purchasing materials, then they should have the authority to ensure that they can do so quickly and efficiently in terms of price, quantity and quality.

- Individuals who have delegated tasks should also be given delegated authority to ensure that any related orders that may be given are accepted and recognised as valid.

Situational aspects

The extent to which delegation can take place effectively will, in the final analysis, be mostly dependent on the extent to which individuals are prepared, and feel able, to participate in the process. Hersey and Blanchard (1993) put forward that 'As a general rule, you can select the appropriate decision-making style by using Situational Leadership to determine "who owns the decision".' They relate the appropriate delegated decision-making style to the extent to which individuals have:

- Information;
- Knowledge;
- Experience;
- Understanding.

The extent to which these are prevalent will determine which one of four decision styles should be used:

- *Authoritative*. Subordinates lack experience, information, knowledge and understanding. Under such conditions they should be directed with little or no freedom of action.

- *Consultative*. Subordinates have some knowledge but not enough to make the final decision. Consultation is used as a means of soliciting ideas only.

- *Facilitative*. Subordinates have some experience, information, knowledge and understanding. They therefore share the decision making but do not make the final decision.

- *Delegative*. Subordinates will have a sound understanding of the issues and are also prepared to take responsibility for making decisions. They should therefore be given the freedom to take ownership and to make the final decision.

The four styles can be represented in the form of a continuum and linked to information, knowledge, experience and understanding, as shown in Fig. 11. 2.

The situational approach recognises that individuals at all levels within an organisation may have something to contribute to decision making and that decision making is not the sole preserve of management. In an ideal organisation staffed with ideal employees, the delegative style of decision making would be used as a means of galvanising employee commitment and creativity. As Hersey and Blanchard state, 'If your followers have a thorough understanding of the subject and a willingness to deal with it, you should use a delegative style. Give them the ball and let them run with it.' Allowing employees to 'run with the ball' emphasises that their contributions are respected and valued, which is fundamental to individual job enrichment (Hackman and Oldham, 1980) and hence motivation and commitment to future involvement in decision making.

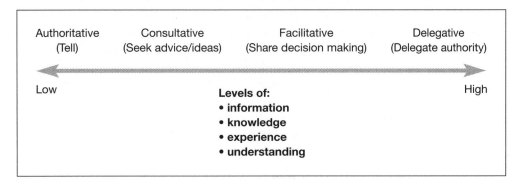

Fig. 11.2 The situational decision-making continuum

Negotiation

Negotiation can be defined as the process in which individuals bargain in order to arrive at a joint decision. Lowe and Pollard (1989) define it as '… a joint exploration of the situation in which potential adversaries find themselves, and as a joint attempt to find mutually satisfactory solutions.' The aim, therefore, of negotiation is to arrive at a consensus-based decision that all parties to the decision can accept and feel committed to.

From the organisational perspective, negotiation may be seen to be – external and internal constraints permitting – the ideal way in which to make decisions because of the consensual nature of the process, which in itself can help to reduce conflict between those involved in the decision. Conflict as a part of decision making will be discussed later in the chapter.

In everyday life as well as within the organisational setting, we make decisions that are based on negotiation. Some are important decisions while others are less so. For example, when buying a second-hand boat we would negotiate with the seller in order to obtain the best deal possible because it is important to maximise the benefits of purchase. Other decisions may be more mundane in nature such as which ice cream to buy or what clothes to wear to a party. To those faced with such decisions the achievement of a satisfactory outcome is no less important and a decision is arrived at through negotiation either with others or with oneself.

Regardless of the importance of an outcome, negotiation can be useful as a means of reaching a decision that is acceptable to those concerned – for example, a decision about which film to see when there are conflicting views held by children and parents. The resolution of the situation can either be achieved by autocratic means (that is, the parents simply decide on the children's behalf) or it can be dealt with in a more democratic way by discussion of the alternatives and then trying to achieve a consensus. If the decision is imposed, it may detract from the children's enjoyment of the film, based on their attitudes to having a good time being pre-determined by the lack of negotiation. The same can be said, for example, of individuals faced with an imposed decision that they fundamentally disagree with by a line manager but nevertheless feel compelled to go along with. Their attitudes having been affected by the imposition of the decision and this will feed into their levels of commitment and possibly negate any desire they may have had to maximise the decision outcomes.

Negotiation is therefore an important part of decision making because it allows bargaining to take place and, by definition, that is involving individuals in the decision-making process.

The negotiation process

The negotiation process involves a number of stages, as illustrated by Fig. 11. 3. The consensus is the ideal outcome, but outcomes in themselves do not have to be ideal in order to be acceptable. Stott and Walker (1992) state that when involved in negotiation there is a need to clearly define and accept three possible outcomes:

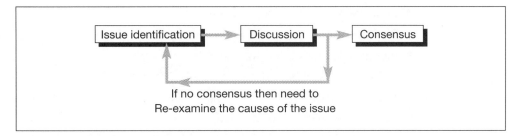

Fig. 11.3. The negotiation process

- *Target*. This is the ideal outcome, but it should be realistic in order not to preclude the other party from wanting to take part in the negotiation.

- *Acceptable area*. This represents what the individual is prepared to accept and be satisfied with.

- *Threshold limit*. This represents the very least that the individual is prepared to accept. It is the base minimum that will maintain satisfaction.

If the individuals involved in the negotiation process can accept the possibility of three forms of outcomes, then they are part-way to successful negotiation. It is the outcomes that cannot be accepted in their entirety that causes dissatisfaction and leads to a satisficing approach to decision making. If the recognition of three possible outcomes is important, then so too are negotiation skills.

Negotation skills

Negotiation skills are essential to effective negotiation. If an individual does not have such skills, then what chance is there for an outcome that even falls within the 'acceptable area' when up against someone who is well versed in negotiation and has acquired effective negotiation skills. For there to be meaningful negotiation, both parties should negotiate from positions of equal standing so that a win–win outcome can be achieved in order to avoid resentment of the outcome on the part of one of the parties. Again, negotiation with regard to decision making is concerned with the achievement of a meaningful and acceptable consensus-based outcome that does not alienate any individuals involved in the process.

Effective negotiation skills can be summarised as follows:

- Research the issue and those involved in order to set a clear and acceptable agenda.

- Make positive statements and state your case early in order to help set the agenda.

- Do not personalise the issues but use objective argument.

- Listen to the arguments presented by the other parties.

- Listen to, but do not rush to accept, initial offers.

- Make counter offers if necessary.

- If appropriate, do not be afraid to seek help and advice from others.

- Rehearse what needs to be discussed.

- Play to your strengths, and if necessary act on the other party's weaknesses.

- Present options so that they enable a win–win outcome (for a discussion on this and other outcomes, refer to the section on conflict later in this chapter).

These skills are not to be seen as a perfect list that will enable all individuals to negotiate effectively. The list itself is merely a starting point for preparing to negotiate and is no substitute in the long term for experience in negotiating.

Bias in negotiation

With the best will in the world, as discussed in Chapter 4, it is sometimes very difficult to eliminate bias in decision making, and the same can be said of negotiation. A recognition that bias can and does exist is important in ensuring that the negotiation process is objective, meaningful and produces a win–win outcome. If bias by one party is evident, it will create a climate of distrust and the other party may feel inclined to react in the same manner. The outcome of such a situation will be one of friction. Discussion will not be open and reflective, and thus the negotiation process will end in failure without agreement having been reached.

Bias in negotiating can take many forms. Some are set out hereunder:

- *Sticking to a course of action regardless of evidence* that might suggest that a different standpoint should be adopted. Such a course of action will waste time and effort and might possibly prevent an acceptable outcome being achieved, because if one party is not prepared to adjust its views then there is no possibility of discussion that will enable a negotiated outcome to be achieved.

- *The belief that gains must be made at the expense of the other party.* Such a belief is aimed at winning in the sense that the other party is defeated or has been prepared to give way on a number of key issues. This approach does not enable a win–win outcome to be achieved because one party is solely concerned with winning concessions and is not prepared to give ground in order to create a climate of give and take.

- *Judgements that are based on irrelevant information* may tend to influence individuals to the extent that they lose sight of the important issues. They become fixated on a point and are not prepared to change their view of the situation in order that progress can be made. In effect the negotiations become bogged down.

- *The availability of information and the way it is presented* can again fixate the attention of the negotiators. Some individuals will rely too readily on initial information and the way it is presented, to the exclusion of other more relevant information presented at a later date and in a different way. This will prevent meaningful discussion because one party has totally accepted the information as if it was absolute fact and thus influences the way that party negotiates.

- *Some individuals have an overinflated sense of their own judgement* and fully believe that they are always right and everyone else is wrong. Such a belief will prevent them from accepting and discussing in a serious way the views of others. Therefore there is no meaningful discussion and negotiation is not based on true two-way dialogue.

Exhibit 11.2

Bridge Engineering

William Cole had worked for Bridge Engineering for almost ten years. As foundry manager he was tasked with not only the smooth running of the foundry but also with ensuring that the processes that the company used reflected the advances that were being made with regard to foundry methods generally. He also had specific responsibility for waste recovery as a means of reducing costs and conforming to current environmental legislation.

William had acknowledged for some time that although the company was conforming to legislation, it could in fact be doing far more to minimise waste. Although he had no specific training in this aspect of foundry management, he had some ideas as to what could be done to improve things. He did, however, have one foundry supervisor that had recently completed a training programme in waste recovery and who was keen to put into effect what he had learned. He had also expressed an interest in accepting the responsibility to implement some changes, but only if it led to promotion.

After some initial discussions on the possible introduction of an improved waste management system, William asked the supervisor if he would in fact implement the new system and also train the staff involved. Unfortunately the supervisor did not see it as part of his job to train staff. William felt that he did at the very least have the responsibility to explain the new system to the staff and to spend a few hours spread over a month or so to ensure that it was implemented correctly. William was somewhat surprised at the supervisor's response as he was considered to be a hard working and committed individual who was liked and respected by his colleagues making him an ideal person to oversee the introduction of the new system.

From the supervisor's point of view, he firmly believed that if he were to 'manage' the introduction of the new system, then he would be doing William's job but would not be receiving anything in return; therefore why should he accept the responsibility? He was prepared, however, to run one briefing session on the new system in support of William actually managing the project. What should William do to get the supervisor to manage the project?

William could instruct the supervisor to do as he is told and to get on with the introduction of the new system. William was very reluctant to do this because he believed to do so would alienate the supervisor which would not make for a good working relationship; furthermore, he was worried about the qualitative aspects of the project if the supervisor's 'heart was not in it'. William decided to negotiate further with the supervisor.

William's desire to negotiate was founded on the belief that, given the right incentives, the supervisor would respond positively and not only would he ben-

▶

efit but so also would William in more of his time being freed up to get on with other things.

What was the basis for negotiation? William would be happy if the supervisor dealt with the training of the staff and also if he held briefing sessions. The benefits that William could offer the supervisor would be the prospect of promotion or the possibility of further training, which would put him in a strong position for promotion set against the other staff, especially if William gave him his support. Both parties therefore had something to gain from negotiating and from moving from what could possibly be fixed positions that would not benefit either of them – and certainly not the supervisor with regard to his future promotion prospects.

Conflict and its effects on decision making

Being able to manage and reduce conflict within decision making is essential in order to ensure that individuals feel that they have taken part in a meaningful process and that they have gained something. As referred to earlier, the ideal outcome is one that involves a win–win situation, which does not alienate individuals from participating in decision making in the future.

Some would argue, however, that an element of conflict is healthy. Robbins (1991) puts forward that '… an increasing number of practitioners now accept that the goal of effective management is not to eliminate conflict. Rather, it is to create the right intensity of conflict so as to reap its functional rewards.' Such a view is linked to the interactionist view of conflict (see below), which would be opposed by the traditional school of thought that believes that trying to achieve a balanced degree of conflict is difficult because of the prospect of the conflict becoming dysfunctional.

There are three differing schools of thought on conflict:

- *Traditional.* All conflict is dysfunctional and must be eliminated. Conflict detracts from organisational performance.

- *Human relations.* This viewpoint assumes that human nature will make conflict inevitable and that it should be accepted, but not to the detriment of the organisation.

- *Interactionist.* Here, controlled conflict at a minimum level is desirable as a means of improving organisational performance because it helps to prevent an organisation from becoming stale and static. It is seen as a way to move an organisation forward because of its competitive nature, which can spur individuals into action through having to respond to a conflict situation.

Even if the interactionist view is held, there is still a need to recognise the inherent dangers in trying to use conflict as a means of adding to organisational performance. If employees perceive that conflict is bad and they are losing in conflict situations, then they will be demotivated and thus will not add to the effectiveness of the organisation. Employees who feel alienated because of the results of conflict will begin to disengage from organisational life and certainly not want to engage in decision making.

The results of conflict linked to decision outcomes, whether they are negotiated or not, are important in determining levels of individual involvement in decision making, motivation and commitment. There are four possible outcomes to conflict situations.

- *Lose–Lose*. No one wins and the result is animosity.
- *Lose–Win*. The unassertiveness of one party lets the other win. The result is that the unassertive party has not only lost but has done so by giving in, sometimes at great personal cost.
- *Win–Lose*. One party is strong and the other is weak. The winning party has not won through reasoned debate but simply by strength – possibly talking the longest and the loudest so that the other party is beaten down. The losing party then feels demotivated.
- *Win–Win*. This is the ideal outcome in that both parties feel that they have won, and not only have they found a satisfactory solution but they are collaborating.

It is clear from the potential outcomes that the first three are not going to do much for organisational performance because of the impact they will have on attitudes toward decision making, which can result in a range of dysfunctional behaviour. In particular, participation will be reduced; motivation to participate, in a maximising-outcome sense, will be reduced; commitment to decisions will be minimal, if not non-existent; and decisions will themselves not necessarily be of a high quality because of the way in which they were made.

Coping with conflict

The range of dysfunctional behaviour will manifest itself in a number of specific ways and can be related to the conflict-resolution strategies put forward by Thomas (1975). Depending on the degree of assertiveness and co-operation amongst the decision makers, a number of coping strategies may be employed by individuals. If individuals are both assertive and co-operative, then functional behaviour will be evident; however, if there is little or no assertiveness and co-operation, then there will be little dialogue and thus no decisions will be made. Depending, therefore, on the levels of assertiveness and co-operation, the outcome can be lose–lose, lose–win, win–lose or win–win, as illustrated in Fig. 11.4.

Thomas (1975) identified five coping strategies that individuals may employ as a means of dealing with conflict.

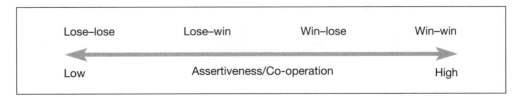

Fig. 11.4 Assertiveness and co-operation continuum linked to conflict outcomes

1 *Avoidance.* This simply involves avoiding or withdrawing from the conflict. This may be done because an individual is not confident and hence lacks assertion, or it may be used as a means of not being prepared to fixate on trivial issues. This strategy will therefore be used as a means of signalling that an individual does not wish to be confrontational about an issue or it arises because one party is lacking in confidence, possibly based on a lack of experience and negotiation skills.

2 *Accommodation.* This is used to maintain good relations by giving ground on certain issues in order to create goodwill or if the issue is not important enough to hold up the decision-making process.

3 *Forcing.* This involves the use of, for example, authority or simply being very assertive as a means of ensuring that individual needs are met at the expense of others. This strategy can alienate individuals from the decision-making process because of its potentially combative approach, but it may be useful when there is a need for a quick decision or if the support of subordinates is not essential.

4 *Compromising.* This involves the parties to the decision being prepared to give equal ground on issues. The approach does, however, require that the parties are negotiating from positions of equal strength.

5 *Collaboration.* This brings openness, honesty, respect and good communications. The parties to the decision not only seek to satisfy their interests but there is a clear recognition that the other party will wish to do the same; hence the need for respect of other people's point of view. Such an approach will therefore aim to provide an outcome that is beneficial to all concerned, and is deemed to be the ideal in that it is a win–win situation.

The approach taken by individuals to decision making and the way in which they seek to cope with conflict will have an effect on the way in which the decision is made and also its quality. Individuals who, for example, are unassertive and wish simply to avoid conflict will not contribute much to the process and in effect are not helping to maximise the decision outcomes. The same can be said of those individuals who are overly assertive and competitive in approach. The two approaches that enable individuals to play an active and meaningful part in the decision-making process involve compromise, which can then lead to collaboration and a win–win outcome that encourages the involvement of individuals and maintains their commitment.

It is worth remembering that some degree of conflict, albeit at a low and controlled level, can be beneficial. As Handy (1993) stated, '... differences are essential to change. If there were no urge to compete and no need for disagreement, the organisation would be either in a state of apathy or complacency ...'

Summary of the chapter

- Delegated decision making is not about abdication of responsibility but is concerned with the involvement of individuals in the decision-making process.

- Barriers to delegation must be identified and acted upon if the process is to be successful. Management, subordinates, the organisational culture, the nature of the task and importance of the decision can all create barriers.

- In order for effective delegation to take place, individuals must be willing and able to participate in the process. Their willingness and ability to do so will be dependent upon information, knowledge, experience and understanding.

- Willingness and ability on the part of subordinates to participate in delegation will also determine the decision-making style of management, which (depending on the degree of co-operation) can be authoritative, consultative, facilitative or delegative.

- Negotiation involves bargaining in order to achieve a joint decision.

- Bias in negotiation must be identified and eliminated in order to ensure that the process is objective, productive and a win–win outcome is achieved.

- The control of conflict is essential for the achievement of meaningful negotiation and decision making.

- There are three schools of thought on the value of conflict: traditional, human relations and interactionist.

- Conflict outcomes can be lose–lose, lose–win, win–lose or win–win.

- Individuals can adopt different strategies for coping with conflict: avoiding, accommodating, forcing, compromising and collaborating.

Case Study 21: Delegation at Standings Engineering

The personnel department at Standings Engineering is managed by Alec Robertson. He has worked for the company for four years and he now believes it is time to begin to delegate some of his responsibilities to his subordinates, all of whom he has personally hand picked and trained in what he refers to as 'the art of personnel management'.

The company's expansion plans require the recruitment of 15 machine operatives over the next five months. Although he would have done this himself in the past, he feels that it would provide an ideal opportunity for some of his staff to practise what they had learned since he has been in charge.

Alec has faith in all of his staff and has come to trust their judgement and believes that the department could most probably run itself. The problem that he faces is whom to ask to recruit the new machine operatives. He decides to base his decision on the following criteria:

- Ability to get the job done within the specified time.
- Experience.
- Willingness.
- Ability to involve others in the selection process if necessary.
- Ability to deal with non-routine issues if they arise.
- Confidence to make the final decision.

After some consideration he decides to ask Rachel, who in Alec's judgement fulfils all of the criteria and has worked in the department for over two years and knows the procedures quite well.

Alec's next step is to ensure that Rachel is fully briefed. Alec takes time to discuss with Rachel what is required and also to emphasise that if she needs any help or support she can see him at any time. Rachel, although somewhat apprehensive at first, decides to accept the task and feels comforted by the fact that Alec would provide support and not regard such a request as a sign of failure or inability to do the job well.

Questions for discussion	1 *Does the way in which Alec is handling the delegation process show good practice?*
	2. *Could he have handled the process differently?*
	3 *How important is the offer of Alec's support to Rachel, and why?*

References

Hackman, J. R., and Oldham, G.R. (1980) *Work Redesign*, Addison-Wesley, Reading, Mass.

Handy, C. (1993) *Understanding Organizations*, 4th ed., Penguin, London.

Hersey, P. and Blanchard, K. H. (1993) *Management of Organizational Behaviour: Utiliziing Human Resources*, 6th ed, Prentice-Hall International Editions.

Lowe, T. and Pollard, I. (1989) 'Negotiation skills', in Riches, C., and Morgan, C. (eds), *Human Resource Management in Education*, Open University Press, Milton Keynes.

Robbins, S. (1991) *Organizational Behaviour: Concepts, Controversies and Applications*, Prentice-Hall, Englewood Cliffs, New Jersey.

Stott, K. and Walker, A. (1992) *Making Management Work: A Practical Approach*, Prentice-Hall, Englewood Cliffs, New Jersey.

Thomas, K. (1975) 'Conflict and conflict management', in Dunnette, M. (ed.), *The Handbook of Industrial and Organisational Psychology*, Vol. 2, Rand McNally.

APPENDIX

Table of Present Value Factors

Chapter 5 gives a description of discounted cash flow analysis and the calculation of Net Present Values for various options that a decision maker may be faced with. Part of the calculation process involves establishing Present Value Factors, and these are set out overleaf in tabular form for all common rates of discount and terms of years. See Chapter 5 for further details.

Present value of 1 at compound interest $(1 + r)^{-n}$

Years (n)	Rate of discount (r)															
	1%	2%	3%	4%	5%	6%	7%	8%	9%	10%	11%	12%	13%	14%	15%	16%
1	0.990	0.980	0.971	0.962	0.952	0.943	0.935	0.926	0.917	0.909	0.901	0.893	0.885	0.877	0.870	0.862
2	0.980	0.961	0.943	0.925	0.907	0.890	0.873	0.857	0.842	0.826	0.812	0.797	0.783	0.770	0.756	0.743
3	0.971	0.942	0.915	0.889	0.864	0.840	0.816	0.794	0.772	0.751	0.731	0.712	0.693	0.675	0.658	0.641
4	0.961	0.924	0.889	0.855	0.823	0.792	0.763	0.735	0.708	0.683	0.659	0.636	0.613	0.592	0.572	0.552
5	0.952	0.906	0.863	0.822	0.784	0.747	0.713	0.681	0.650	0.621	0.594	0.567	0.543	0.519	0.497	0.476
6	0.942	0.888	0.838	0.790	0.746	0.705	0.666	0.630	0.596	0.565	0.535	0.507	0.480	0.456	0.432	0.410
7	0.933	0.871	0.813	0.760	0.711	0.665	0.623	0.584	0.547	0.513	0.482	0.452	0.425	0.400	0.376	0.354
8	0.924	0.854	0.789	0.731	0.677	0.627	0.582	0.540	0.502	0.467	0.434	0.404	0.376	0.351	0.327	0.305
9	0.914	0.837	0.766	0.703	0.645	0.592	0.544	0.500	0.460	0.424	0.391	0.361	0.333	0.308	0.284	0.263
10	0.905	0.820	0.744	0.676	0.614	0.558	0.508	0.463	0.422	0.386	0.352	0.322	0.295	0.270	0.247	0.227
11	0.896	0.804	0.722	0.650	0.585	0.527	0.475	0.429	0.388	0.350	0.317	0.288	0.261	0.237	0.215	0.195
12	0.887	0.789	0.701	0.625	0.557	0.497	0.444	0.397	0.356	0.319	0.286	0.257	0.231	0.208	0.187	0.169
13	0.879	0.773	0.681	0.601	0.530	0.469	0.415	0.368	0.326	0.286	0.258	0.229	0.204	0.182	0.163	0.145
14	0.870	0.758	0.661	0.578	0.505	0.442	0.388	0.341	0.299	0.263	0.232	0.205	0.181	0.160	0.141	0.125
15	0.861	0.743	0.642	0.555	0.481	0.417	0.362	0.315	0.275	0.239	0.209	0.183	0.160	0.140	0.123	0.108
16	0.853	0.728	0.623	0.534	0.458	0.394	0.339	0.292	0.252	0.218	0.188	0.163	0.142	0.123	0.107	0.093
17	0.844	0.714	0.605	0.513	0.436	0.371	0.317	0.270	0.231	0.198	0.170	0.146	0.125	0.108	0.093	0.080
18	0.836	0.700	0.587	0.494	0.416	0.350	0.296	0.250	0.212	0.180	0.153	0.130	0.111	0.095	0.081	0.069
19	0.828	0.686	0.570	0.475	0.396	0.331	0.277	0.232	0.195	0.164	0.138	0.116	0.098	0.083	0.070	0.060
20	0.820	0.673	0.554	0.456	0.377	0.312	0.258	0.215	0.178	0.149	0.124	0.104	0.087	0.073	0.061	0.051

							Rate of discound (r)									
Years (n)	17%	18%	19%	20%	21%	22%	23%	24%	25%	26%	28%	30%	35%	40%	45%	50%
1	0.855	0.848	0.840	0.833	0.826	0.820	0.813	0.807	0.800	0.794	0.781	0.769	0.741	0.714	0.690	0.667
2	0.731	0.718	0.706	0.694	0.683	0.672	0.661	0.650	0.640	0.630	0.610	0.592	0.549	0.510	0.476	0.444
3	0.624	0.609	0.593	0.579	0.565	0.551	0.537	0.525	0.512	0.500	0.477	0.455	0.406	0.364	0.328	0.296
4	0.534	0.516	0.499	0.482	0.467	0.451	0.437	0.423	0.410	0.397	0.373	0.350	0.301	0.260	0.226	0.198
5	0.456	0.437	0.419	0.402	0.386	0.370	0.355	0.341	0.328	0.315	0.291	0.269	0.223	0.186	0.156	0.132
6	0.390	0.370	0.352	0.335	0.319	0.303	0.289	0.275	0.262	0.250	0.227	0.207	0.165	0.133	0.108	0.088
7	0.333	0.314	0.296	0.279	0.263	0.249	0.235	0.222	0.210	0.198	0.178	0.159	0.122	0.095	0.074	0.059
8	0.285	0.266	0.249	0.233	0.218	0.204	0.191	0.179	0.168	0.157	0.139	0.123	0.091	0.068	0.051	0.039
9	0.243	0.226	0.209	0.194	0.180	0.167	0.155	0.144	0.134	0.125	0.108	0.094	0.067	0.048	0.035	0.026
10	0.208	0.191	0.176	0.162	0.149	0.137	0.126	0.116	0.107	0.099	0.085	0.073	0.050	0.035	0.024	0.017
11	0.178	0.162	0.148	0.135	0.123	0.112	0.103	0.094	0.086	0.079	0.066	0.056	0.037	0.025	0.017	0.012
12	0.152	0.137	0.124	0.112	0.102	0.092	0.083	0.076	0.069	0.063	0.052	0.043	0.027	0.018	0.012	0.008
13	0.130	0.116	0.104	0.094	0.084	0.075	0.068	0.061	0.055	0.050	0.040	0.033	0.020	0.013	0.008	0.005
14	0.111	0.099	0.088	0.078	0.069	0.062	0.055	0.049	0.044	0.039	0.032	0.025	0.015	0.009	0.006	0.003
15	0.095	0.084	0.074	0.065	0.057	0.051	0.045	0.040	0.035	0.031	0.025	0.020	0.011	0.006	0.004	0.002
16	0.081	0.071	0.062	0.054	0.047	0.042	0.036	0.032	0.028	0.025	0.019	0.015	0.008	0.005	0.003	0.002
17	0.069	0.060	0.052	0.045	0.039	0.034	0.030	0.026	0.023	0.020	0.015	0.012	0.006	0.003	0.002	0.001
18	0.059	0.051	0.044	0.038	0.032	0.028	0.024	0.021	0.018	0.016	0.012	0.009	0.005	0.002	0.001	0.001
19	0.051	0.043	0.037	0.031	0.027	0.023	0.020	0.017	0.014	0.012	0.009	0.007	0.003	0.002	0.001	0.000
20	0.043	0.037	0.031	0.026	0.022	0.019	0.016	0.014	0.012	0.010	0.007	0.005	0.002	0.001	0.001	0.000

INDEX